ALABASTER CITIES

SPACE, PLACE, AND SOCIETY
John Rennie Short, Series Editor

Alabaster
Cities

Urban U.S. since 1950

John Rennie Short

Syracuse University Press

First Edition 2006

06   07   08   09   10   11   6   5   4   3   2   1

The paper used in this publication meets the minimum requirements of American National Standard for Information Sciences—Permanence of Paper for Printed Library Materials, ANSI Z39.48-1984.∞™

Library of Congress Cataloging-in-Publication Data

Short, John R.

Alabaster cities : urban U.S. since 1950 / John Rennie Short. — 1st ed.

p. cm. — (Space, place, and society)

Includes bibliographical references and index.

ISBN 0-8156-3105-7 (cloth : alk. paper)

1. City planning—United States—History—20th century. I. Title.

HT167.S495 2006

307.1'21609730904—dc22   2006022053

Manufactured in the United States of America

Contents

Figures

Tables

An internationally recognized scholar, **John Rennie Short** is a professor of public policy and geography at the University of Maryland, Baltimore County. He is the author of twenty-eight books and numerous articles that cover a wide range of topics, including globalization, urban issues, environmental concerns, and the history of cartography. His recent books include *Urban Theory* (2006), *Making Space* (2004), *Global Metropolitan* (2004), *The World Through Maps* (2003), and *Globalization and the Margins* (coedited with Richard Grant, 2002).

Preface

ONE OF THE BEST-KNOWN American songs is the deeply patriotic "America the Beautiful." Its origins lie in the travels of its author, Katharine Lee Bates. Born in Massachusetts and daughter to a Congregationalist minister, she graduated in 1880 from Wellesley College where she subsequently taught English literature for forty years. In 1893 she went on a trip west. She visited the Columbian Exposition in Chicago, nicknamed the White City, a complex of temporary neoclassical white buildings of faux marble made of plaster and steel on the shore of Lake Michigan, designed by Daniel Burnham, brightly illuminated at night by thousands of lightbulbs. The exposition boasted two full-scale replicas of the Liberty Bell, as well as an assembly of peoples from all over the world, including Egyptian belly dancers, Native Americans from the Pacific Northwest, and villagers from Dahomey (now Benin) in Africa. Later in July of that same year, Bates rode a mule to the summit of Pikes Peak and saw the plains sweeping to the far-distant horizon. The Pikes Peak part of the journey was the basis for her first verse of "spacious skies" and "amber waves of grain" that have become part of the language and popular imagination of the United States.

Her visit to Chicago inspired the less well-known, final verse that contains the phrase: "Thine alabaster cities gleam / Undimmed by human tears." Both Chicago and Pikes Peak were part of the same journey. Yet what remains strongest in American popular consciousness is the first, not the final, verse. More people are familiar with the waves of grain than the alabaster cities. A land of sweeping grandeur is remembered more than the country of great cities. National representation, especially of the simplistic patriotic kind, has focused on the West and the wilderness rather than the East and the city. There has long been an antiurban bias that has ignored or forgotten the city. There are many reasons. The West is considered distinctively American, whereas the cities are more often seen as part of a broader international picture. Cities are not perceived as distinctively American as, say, the Grand Canyon, so they often fail to register in discourses of national identity. Yet the story of the alabaster cities needs to be sung as well as that of the fruited plain.

I concentrate on the period after 1945. All dates are arbitrary, but the ending of World War II does mark a significant turning point in the United States. It was not just the ending of hostilities and the return of millions of service personnel; it was also the beginning of a new era in which the United States would soon emerge as the largest, richest economy and by the end of the twentieth century as the world's single superpower. The urban condition of this nation is of significant interest. Cities were a focal point of important changes. The book's focus is from 1950 since the first post–World War II census was undertaken in that year. The half-century point is our starting point. After 1950 there were massive urban renewal, growing suburbanization, and increasing metropolitan fragmentation. The country became more urban, more suburban, and more divided. It is not a straight trajectory—there were deviations and fluctuations—but the overall story is of the full emergence of a metropolitan nation, a suburban society, and a series of fragmented civic communities.

The text weaves theoretical warp and narrative woof into four general themes. The first is the globalization of U.S. cities. From 1950 to around the mid-1970s the U.S. economy was more self-sustaining than any of its competitors; it had an unrivaled manufacturing base that established a mass middle class increasingly housed in suburbs sprouting up all around the central cities. From the mid-1970s onward an economic globalization accompanied a decline of manufacturing jobs, thus squeezing the employment basis for that large part of the mass middle class comprising low-skilled workers. The resulting income polarization that no longer rewards such workers with the benefits of well-paid jobs and middle-class lifestyles has its roots in the globalizing economy. The era of ongoing economic globalization has witnessed a return to more pronounced forms of social polarization as the fortunes of individual families and even of whole cities began to slide. The distance between the rich and poor widened along with the differentiation between expanding and declining urban economics. There was a global shift in manufacturing that eliminated many of the high-paying middle-class jobs in addition to a new level of economic competition that operated to stifle wage increases of the majority of workers. But globalization is not a force above national politics. It is not so much globalization but the response to globalization that shaped the urban U.S. Throughout this period, the principles and practices of the New Deal were abandoned in favor of a neoliberal agenda of privatization, a reduced commitment of government to the welfare of its ordinary citizens, and an emphasis on enhancing corporate profitability and improving business competitiveness. The global shift in manufacturing reduced the power of labor, which in turn strengthened the hand of business in shaping government policy to meets its economic agenda. A Wal-Mart economy replaced a General Motors economy, and though it means better deals for consumers it worsens conditions for many workers.

Second, despite the continual calls for small government and endorsements of the private market, the economic history and political geography of the urban U.S. are fundamentally shaped by the public sector. The single most important architect of U.S. cities is the federal government. Public subsidies have underwritten the expansion of owner-occupation, the growth of the suburbs, the urban development of the Sun Belt, and the creation of new networks of roads, airline, and telecommunications that have determined patterns of urban growth and decline across the country. The U.S. federal government played a huge role in reorganizing the metropolitan structures and shaping the suburban character. The amount of federal spending in a city is the biggest determinant of growth. On closer inspection the calls for small government were really about the size of the government commitment to providing welfare services to its citizens. The rhetorical reliance on the market overlooked the realities of the mixed public-private market economy of the U.S. where most public subsidies went to rich private interests, and there was a socialization of costs and the privatization of benefits.

Third, there is an increased segmentation of urban life in the U.S. As suburbs spread out across metropolitan boundaries the population separates into different municipalities responsible for taxing and spending as well as for such vital services as education. With few effective means to equalize resources the inequalities between communities are exacerbated. The poor central cities experience fiscal crisis as they lose their tax base, while rich suburban communities can spend more on education. School districts soon divide into wealthy ones that can afford the educational platforms for social progress and poor ones that become funnels of failure.

This political geography explains much of the rhetoric for small government, restricted government. On closer inspection it is owing also to the demand of the wealthier communities to keep their tax dollars within their own municipalities. We have become a meaner, more segregated society as commitment to welfare fades and metropolitan fragmentation balkanizes us into ever more different urban social worlds. And here we encounter a paradox. Over the same period the U.S. has become a more multicultural, multiethnic society. From 1950 to the mid-1960s immigration was small, and the foreign-born constituted an insignificant proportion of the population. Since then immigration has grown dramatically to levels not seen since the early 1900s. The notion of a multicultural society is celebrated, but behind the national rhetoric and the veneer of mutual tolerance lies a new form of segregation now by class more than by race. Though we talk about a multicultural society, we live in separate social worlds.

Fourth, although I have outlined some of the more regressive trends, there is also a wider spread of active citizenship. In 1950 blacks were second-class citizens, as racism marked the character of life in the Republic. Today civil rights in principle as well as in practice extend to those previously denied them. Blacks, women, and gays all have greater access to full citizenship. The story of the urban U.S. is one of private dreams and collective aspirations competing with stark economic and political realities. Urban social movements have changed and improved life in the U.S. The prospect of building a "city upon a hill" continues to exercise the collective imagination just as it did for the early Puritans. And the nature of the city, that place that connects the public with the private, the collective and the individual, is a good place to test both the beliefs and the realities of a society.

I have adopted the material to a more narrative flow rather than to the academic concern with constant referencing and footnoting. The book is written for a general reader rather than the narrow specialist. The Guide to Further Reading at the end of this book directs the reader to other opinions and illuminates the main sources I have used. For those readers more interested in scholarly debates, my *Urban Theory* (2006) is written explicitly as a theoretical exegesis. *Alabaster Cities* and *Urban Theory* are companion volumes, with shared material; the former tells a story with the theoretical underpinnings embedded in the text, whereas the latter develops theoretical arguments with an implicit narrative structure. My *Liquid Metropolis: Megalopolis Revisited* (2007) uses material from both *Urban Theory* and *Alabaster Cities* in a detailed analysis of one urban region, Megalopolis.

Some of the ideas were first developed in previously published and collaborative work. The ideas in Chapters 8 and 14 saw a previous life in an article in the journal *City,* and the arguments in Chapter 13 were first elucidated in contributions to two edited volumes, *The Entrepreneurial City* (1998) and *Urban Growth Machine* (1999). Chapter 7 is based entirely on work done with Bernadette Hanlon and Tom Vicino, and Chapter 13 draws heavily on work done with Yeong Kim. The maps were drawn with the assistance of Joe School. Hieu Truong helped with the Guide to Further Reading and proofread a number of the chapters. Two anonymous reviewers made a number of useful suggestions. One reviewer, in particular, helped to polish a rough text into something much more smooth and refined. Unless otherwise specified, tables and figures are compiled from U.S. Census data.

The first chapter describes the empirical trends behind the urbanization, suburbanization, and metropolitanization of U.S. society. There is an emphasis on numbers that marks this chapter as the most data-laden. Those readers requiring a softer entry point may want to skip this chapter until later.

Part One tells the story of the evisceration of the central core of most U.S. cities and the stimulation of suburbanization. The turning point away from this destruction of the inner city is embodied in the confrontation between Robert Moses and Jane Jacobs. Their struggle took place in New York City, but the outcome influenced cities all over the country. Part Two focuses on the social geographies of the metropolis. Specific chapters look at the decline and attempted rise of the downtown, the creation of a suburban society, and the increasing heterogeneity of U.S. suburbs that belies the traditional dichotomy of central city and suburbs. The final chapter in this section evaluates the costs and consequences of metropolitan fragmentation into a myriad of separate municipalities. Part Three discusses the social dynamics of the metropolis through an analysis of urban economic change, race and ethnicity, the operation of the housing market, and the nature of urban politics. Parts Two and Three are related. There is no simple division between space and society, social geographies and social processes. Societies are spatially embodied, and space is socially constructed. The intimate connections between space and society are clearly visible in the U.S. city. Part Four identifies some of the more dominant themes of this social-spatial nexus. I consider the importance of the "imagineering" of the city in response to the rise of increased competition between cities. I also review the arguments about the decline of civic engagement in U.S. cities. The final chapter examines the emergence of trends that are defining, and will continue to define, the character of the metropolitan U.S.

The U.S. is made up of states. The federal structure has influenced urban development. The Appendix provides a brief description of urban development in just one state, New York. The Appendix also serves a double duty as it provides a thicker historical description. Cities did not just appear in 1945, so the Appendix gives historical depth and specificity in one state, New York, to some of the themes discussed at a more general level in the book.

Like millions before me, I am an immigrant to this country. I came from Britain when I was almost forty years old. I had both read and written about U.S. cities before I came. Now I am a participant as well as a spectator, a citizen as well as an observer. The immigrant experience is a complicated one; the shifting sense of home, the convoluting identity, and the divided loyalties make for a complex position. I am, in the binational format that has become so popular, Scottish American. My wife was born in California, so my extended family lives on coasts that border the North Sea as well as the Pacific Ocean. This book was produced in this sometimes awkward, always complicated space. Patriotism, as Samuel Johnson reminded us long ago, is the last refuge of a scoundrel. I shy away from an easy love of country. An adult immigrant's experience is too complex to be expressed in easy slogans and trite formulas. I have been thinking about the material in this book for years, but began writing it only in the late summer of 2001. After 9/11 of that year I realized that this book was a long love letter to my adopted home. A very critical missive, but a love letter all the same.

ALABASTER CITIES

1

The Rise of Metropolitan America

THE UNITED STATES was an urban nation well before 1950, but after 1950 it became a truly metropolitan society.

In this chapter I want to provide an empirical basis for this statement and a factual context for later discussions. I will draw statistics derived from the U.S. Census. Figures of population growth and change are sometimes called *vital* statistics. The adjective is appropriate, as the population figures speak to the demographic pulse and heartbeat of the nation. A recounting of these data is an essential introduction to our discussion.[1]

In 1950, 64 percent of Americans lived in urban places, but by 2000 this number had increased to almost 80 percent. We need some care with these data. The threshold definition of *urban*, as used by the U.S. Census, is comparatively low and includes all people living in settlements with more than 2,500 persons. The term *urban* covers a wide spectrum of places, from small communities with a population of 2,501 to large cities with a population of almost 8 million. Despite the broad sweep of the category, the figures clearly reveal a general trend over the past fifty years for more people to live in urban places. There has been a relative and an absolute increase in the number of people who now live in urban areas with the steady drift of people from the rural areas toward the larger cities. There has been a steady decline in the number and vitality of small places, especially those areas farthest away from large cities. This trend is particularly marked in

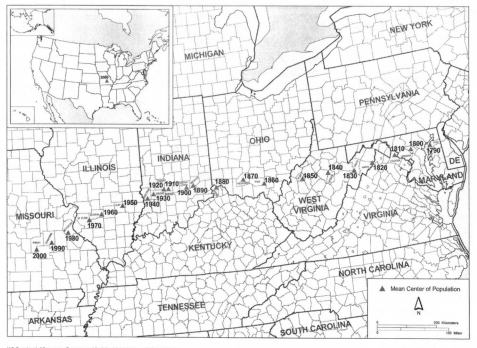

U.S. Department of Commerce   Economics and Statistics Administration   U.S. Census Bureau   Prepared by the Geography Division

1.1. Mean center of population for the United States, 1790–2000.

the interior parts of the country away from the two coastal zones. In the past fifty years the U.S. has become a more urban society.

The term *heartland* is consistently employed to refer to the agricultural areas of the Midwest. In one sense it is the center of the country. Each decade the U.S. Census calculates a mean center of population (fig. 1.1). This location is the population fulcrum of the nation. Over the years the mean center has moved steadily westward from Maryland in 1790 to the Midwest by the middle of the twentieth century. In 1950 the mean center was in Richland County in southern Illinois. Between 1970 and 1980 the mean center moved across the Mississippi River, and by 2000 it was in Phelps County, Missouri. In terms of population distribution, then, the Midwest is the heartland. But the metaphor of *heartland* also implies that it is the lifeblood of the nation. The population figures suggest otherwise. The population of Richland County was 16,889 in 1950, but by 2000 it had fallen to 16,149. In a fifty-year period the county lost population while the national picture was of a steady increase. Phelps County, the national pop-

1.2. Mean center of population for the United States, 1950–2000.

ulation center in 2000, fared much better. Its population of 21,504 had almost doubled to 39,825. But compared to the absolute increase in the U.S. population, it still remained a quiet part of the country. Taking a random sample of other nonmetropolitan counties in this region reveals an interesting pattern (fig. 1.2; table 1.1). Some counties actually lost population over the fifty-year period from 1950 to 2000, and even the population gains were minimal. Whereas the total U.S. population increased by 80 percent over the half century, the population of these six nonmetropolitan "heartland" counties increased by only 1.6 percent. Population growth passed by these nonurban "heartland" counties.

As the small, genuinely rural communities are becoming less a center for contemporary settlement, they are becoming more a symbolic space: a place of nostalgia and a site of enduring values and cultural stability in a

TABLE 1.1

Population change in six "heartland" counties, 1950–2000

	1950	2000
Fayette County, Illinois	24,582	21,802
Marion County, Illinois	41,700	41,691
Randolph County, Illinois	31,673	33,893
Shelby County, Illinois	24,434	22,893
Montgomery County, Missouri	11,555	12,136
Dent County, Missouri	10,936	14,927
Total	144,880	147,342

fast-changing world. As these communities are becoming less important in the national settlement pattern, they are looming larger in the cultural landscape of national representation. Rural areas exist more in the collective imagination of the country than they do in the population geography of the country.

Regional Trends in Urbanization

The national trend of urbanization hides some interesting regional variations (fig. 1.3). In 1950 the Northeast was already heavily urbanized, with almost 80 percent of the population living in urban areas, followed by the West and Midwest with urban percentages of 69.5 and 64.1, respectively, in 1950. The least-urbanized region was the South, where less than half of the population was considered urban in 1950. The states of Mississippi, Alabama, Kentucky, and Tennessee, for example, had less than 40 percent of their population in urban areas. By 2000 the nation had become more uniform in its percentage of urban population, with the largest increases over the period 1950 to 2000 in the South and West (fig. 1.4). By 2000 the South, in its urban population, as in so many other ways, had become more like the rest of the U.S. More than two out of every three people in the South now live in urban places, and even in the four states just mentioned, more than one out of every two live in urban places. Over the fifty-year period from 1950 to 2000, the entire country became more urban, and by 2000 the U.S. was an overwhelmingly urban nation with less regional variations.

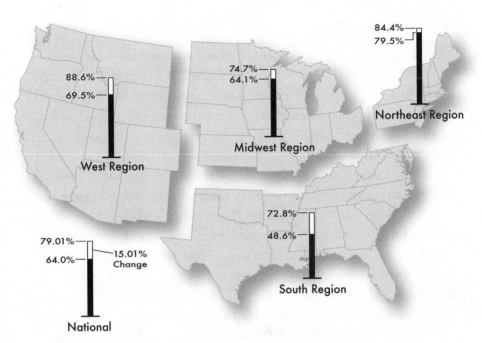

1.3. Percentage change in urban population by region, 1950–2000.

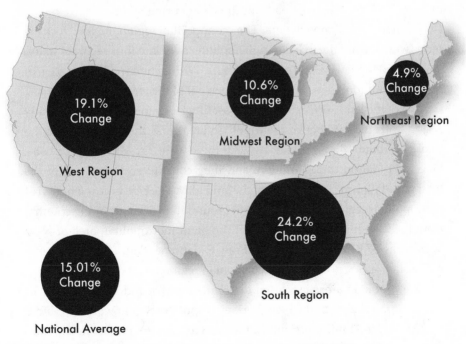

1.4. Percentage change in urban population by region, 1950–2000.

A Metropolitan Society

We can make a distinction between cities and metropolitan areas. The formal city is the legally defined limit of municipal authority. Once established, formal urban boundaries tend to remain. Annexation is governed by state law, and requirements vary; some states are more permissive than others. In the more restrictive states annexations are rare, difficult to achieve, and rarely attempted. There is inertia to the formal boundaries of cities, but although the boundaries can remain fixed, they rarely stem the movement of commuters, the flows of trade and money. Cities cast a sphere of influence beyond their formal boundaries; they are often the center of metropolitan regions that reach beyond the formal boundaries of cities.

The U.S. Census uses the term *metropolitan statistical area* (MSA) and defines it as having a core area with a population of at least 50,000 and adjacent communities with a high degree of social and economic integration with the core, including having at least 15 percent of commuters working in the central area. Take the case of New York City. Its formal boundaries encompass the five boroughs of the Bronx, Brooklyn, Manhattan, Staten Island, and Queens, yet commuters flow into the city from surrounding areas of New York State as well as from the neighboring states of New Jersey, Connecticut, and Pennsylvania. The metropolitan region of New York extends well beyond the five boroughs, spilling over into four separate states.

In 1950 there were 160 separate MSAs. With a combined population of almost 85 million, they constituted 56 percent of the total population and 7 percent of the land surface. Over the past fifty years there has been a steady rise in both the number of metropolitan areas and the proportion of the total population they contain. By 2000 there were 331 MSAs with a combined population of 226 million, and they constituted 80 percent of the total population and 20 percent of the land area. The U.S. is now a nation of metropolitan regions. These MSAs are found in every part of the country, from the 21 million people living in the giant metropolitan area of New York to the 57,813 people living in Enid, Oklahoma. Four out of every five people in the U.S. now live in metropolitan regions.

Metropolitan areas increased in population size and spatial extent. In 1950 the population of the New York metropolitan region was 9.5 million; by 2000 it was 21 million. Some of the growth rates are phenomenal, especially in the newer Sun Belt metropolitan regions: Dallas grew in the same period from 0.74 million to 5.2 million; Charlotte, North Carolina, had a population of close to 200,000 in 1950 that by 2000 had increased to 1.5 million; and Phoenix grew from a modest 330,000 to 3.2 million, a staggering 870 percent increase.

More people now live in the largest metropolitan areas. In 1950 only 29.4 percent of the population lived in metropolitan areas with a population of more than 1 million. By 2000 this figure had increased to 57.5 percent (fig. 1.5). In 1950 only 12.2 percent of the nation's population lived in metropolitan regions of more than 5 million; by 2000 this figure had increased to almost 30 percent. By 2000 almost one out of every three Americans lived in the ten largest metropolitan areas. The U.S. is now a metropolitan society.

The Suburbanization of the Population

There are two mythic journeys in the U.S. The first, a product of the nineteenth and very early twentieth centuries, was the westward trek to Cali-

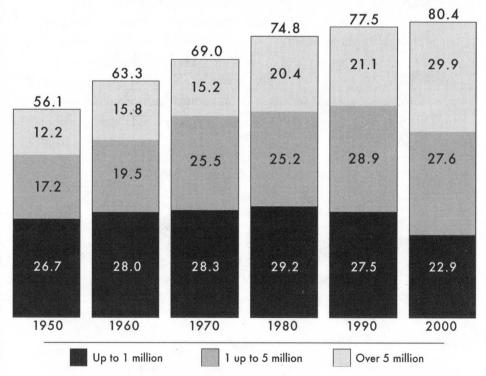

1.5. Percentage of U.S. population living in metropolitan areas, by size of metropolitan area population, 1950–2000.

fornia and the West. The second, the archetypal journey of the midtwenti-
eth century, was from the city to the suburbs. It was not only an actual journey across municipal boundaries; it was also a quest signifying
acculturation, Americanization, and success. In this second mythic American journey, the family car replaced the covered wagon and the single family home displaced the family homestead as iconic representations.

Metropolitan areas can be divided into urban cores and suburban peripheries. There has been a significant sifting of population within these
areas (fig. 1.6). In 1950 only 23 percent of the U.S. population was living in
the suburbs of metropolitan areas, but by 2000 this figure had increased to
50 percent. The suburbanization of metropolitan populations is the largest
single population change in the U.S. in the last half of the twentieth century. In 1950 fewer than one in four Americans lived in suburban areas of
metro regions, but by 2000 this figure had increased to one in two. On
closer inspection the metropolitanization of America turns out to have
been the suburbanization of America.

There are many reasons behind the suburban spread of the population.
I will discuss the forces behind this change in more detail in subsequent
chapters. For the moment, allow me to sketch the general picture. The interstate highway system laid the routes for the centrifugal sifting of population. Federally funded roads allowed people to move relatively easily
across municipal boundaries. The federal highway construction program,
especially by the late 1950s and 1960s, not only connected cities but also al-

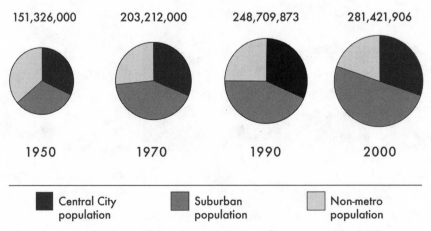

1.6. Percentage of U.S. population living in metropolitan areas, 1950–2000.

lowed commuters to travel the interstate highways into the cities from nearby and eventually not-so-nearby suburbs. The highways made it easier to live in one area and work in another. The road building created a city of endless flows and infinite mobility. Public policies also created a building boom of single-family dwellings. Developers found it relatively easy and profitable to develop peripheral developments on greenfield sites, while home owners had their mortgages guaranteed by the federal government and their interest payments tax deductible. Public policies lubricated the pull of the suburbs. There were also push reasons. For many the central city was becoming a place to leave. Urban-renewal schemes in the 1950s and early 1960s demolished many inner-city neighborhoods under slum-clearance and highway-building programs. A maelstrom of destruction in the name of progress and improvement ripped the heart out of many cities. Perceptions of rising crime, failing schools, and racial divisions all helped to push people out. White flight occurred as middle-class whites in particular made the move out to the suburbs. The move to the suburbs was not only made easy but also for many made inevitable. Once in motion, the movement had its own self-fulfilling momentum. As more families moved out, the tax base of school districts shriveled, reducing educational spending, which in turn led to declining schools, forcing even more families out.

Figure 1.7 shows the growing metropolitan range of four MSAs: Atlanta, Dallas, Detroit, and Pittsburgh. These maps show the metropolitan counties of the respective MSAs in both 1950 and 1999. Notice how all four metro areas have spread across the landscape as more counties are defined as metropolitan. In the Sun Belt cities of Atlanta and Dallas, the spread has been large and extensive. Yet even in the Frost Belt cities of Detroit and Pittsburgh, the number of metropolitan counties has increased. In the first half of the twentieth century most urban dwellers lived in heterogeneous central cities. By 2000 most of the metro population lived in homogeneous suburbs. The suburban shift was selective: it left behind the poorest and most disadvantaged. A great division emerged in the country between the affluent suburbs and the poorer central cities.

Growing and Declining Metro Areas

Although most metropolitan areas grew from 1950 to 2000, they varied in the relative central city–suburban sifting of population. Two broad types

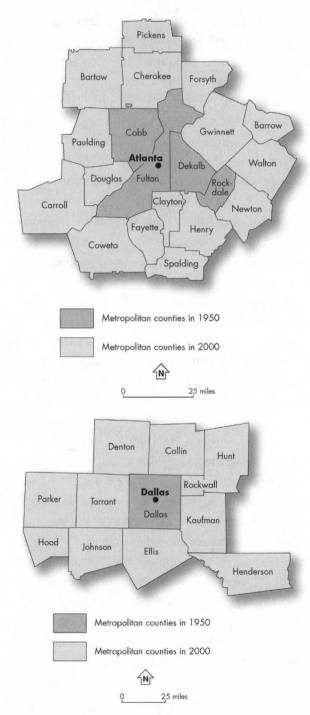

1.7. MSA counties: Atlanta, Dallas, Detroit, and Pittsburgh.

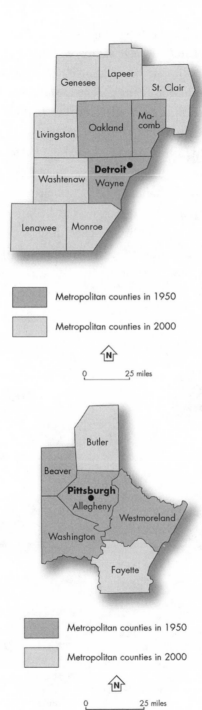

can be identified: *metro growth areas,* which saw population increases in both core and suburbs, and *declining core metros,* which experienced an increase in their overall metropolitan area but saw a marked decline in the core city.

Growth areas are predominantly located in the Sun Belt and Rain Belt of the South and West. Phoenix is a classic Sun Belt–boom MSA that saw huge population increases in both the central city and the suburbs (fig. 1.8). The MSA grew tenfold from just over 330,000 in 1950 to 3.2 million in 2000. An important factor in the growth of central Phoenix was the ability of the city to annex surrounding land. In 1950 the city encompassed only 17 square miles. By 1980 the area had increased to 325 square miles. Phoenix is the exception, even among growth cities. Seattle is a typical example of this pattern. Whereas the central core grew from around 466,000 to 563,000 from 1950 to 2000, the suburban areas grew dramatically, from 380,000 to more than 1.7 million in the same time span. The growth of the Seattle

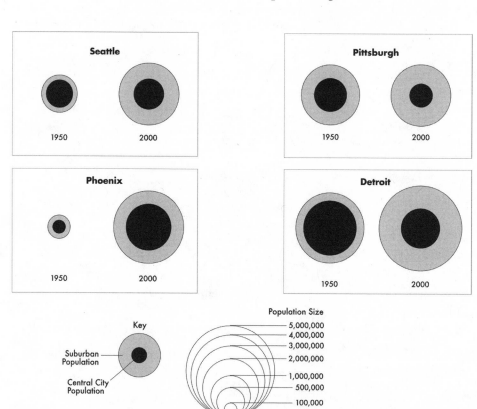

1.8. MSA population, 1950 and 2000: Seattle, Pittsburgh, Phoenix, and Detroit.

metro area took place in both the core and the suburbs, but the largest growth was in the suburbs.

Many metro areas, especially in the Frost Belt, saw overall metropolitan growth with marked decline in the urban core. Detroit shows a typical pattern of growth in the metro area, from 3 million in 1950 to more than 4.4 million in the 2000, but with a significant decline in the urban core, from almost 2 million to less than 1 million. The city of Detroit lost almost half of its population over a fifty-year period. In those metro areas with marked economic decline, even the suburban growth was limited. Pittsburgh is a good example of a reindustrializing city that witnessed a loss of manufacturing employment. The population of the metro area scarcely moved beyond 2.2 million from 1950 to 2000, while its central city saw a dramatic decline, from almost 700,000 to approximately 335,000. The metro area basically kept the same population from 1950 to 2000 but witnessed a marked redistribution of people from the central city to the suburbs. The city, unlike Phoenix, was unable to annex surrounding land; its 52 square miles in 1950 grew to only 55 square miles in 1980.

We have covered a lot of empirical material in this chapter. In summary: In the U.S. over the fifty-year period from 1950 to 2000 there was a steady urbanization that made the whole country more uniformly urban, an increasing metropolitanization, and a massive suburbanization. In a half century the U.S. became an urban nation of large metropolitan regions dominated by the suburbs.

The commonly used map of the U.S. shows the area surface of the country, not its population distribution (fig. 1.9). Western states with large surface areas but with low populations such as Montana and Utah figure more prominently than geographically smaller though much more populous states such as Connecticut and Massachusetts. The map underrepresents the large metropolitan centers and distorts the reality of the urban nature of U.S. society. To draw attention to these population realities I have constructed a special type of diagram, a cartogram, which allocates the U.S. population to the three categories of central city, suburban, and nonmetro population in line with their relative population size. The vast western states do not dominate the national picture in this national representation. The heartland of this cartogram is the central cities, not the cornfield states or the thinly populated western states. Cartograms for cen-

1.9. Map of the United States.

sus years 1950 and 2000 how a shrinkage of nonmetropolitan areas from 44 percent of the population in 1950 to just over 19 percent in 2000 (see figs. 1.10 and 1.11). From 1950 to 2000 the country has become more metropolitan as more people live in large urban regions, particularly in the suburban areas that had only 23 percent of the population in 1950 but almost 50 percent by 2000. The nation has become more metropolitan and suburban. The cartograms represent the metropolitan nature of U.S. society and the extent of increased suburbanization since 1950.

| ■ Central City | ■ Suburban | ☐ Non - Metro |

1.10. Percentage of U.S. population living in metropolitan areas in 1950.

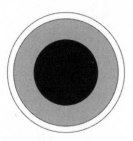

| ■ Central City | ■ Suburban | ☐ Non - Metro |

1.11. Percentage of U.S. population living in metropolitan areas in 2000.

PART ONE

The War Against the Cities

2

Urban Renewal

"We Must Start All Over Again from the Ground Up"

IN THE FIRST PART of the postwar era, from 1945 to 1970, the federal government, in alliance with municipal authorities and various business interests, declared war on the central cities. The government spent money and marshaled resources to destroy much of the urban fabric, forcibly relocating central-city inhabitants and aiding the outward movement of jobs and people.

The battle plan was unveiled at the World's Fair in 1939 in New York. An exhibit, funded by General Motors, showed a city of high-rise towers and fast, free-flowing motorways; it was a tantalizing vision presented to almost five million visitors. And in large measure, this vision brutally re-shaped central-city America.

The plan drew upon a number of foreign and domestic inspirations. Earlier in the twentieth century, futurist Filippo Marinetti preached the physical annihilation of the traditional city and said, "We must invent and rebuild *ex novo* our Modern City." In Germany Walter Gropius of the early Bauhaus School wanted to replace the shabby irregularity of the slums with giant blocks of straight lines. Other architectural modernists were equally enthusiastic for a clean, new beginning. Le Corbusier's Radiant City plans of the 1920s, for example, envisioned three million people living in giant skyscrapers surrounded by motorways. These visions of moder-nity involved the destruction of the past. They transcended political ideol-ogy and found a home in Mussolini's Rome, Hitler's Berlin, and Stalin's

Moscow. Even the liberal critic and public-housing advocate Catherine Bauer, who expounded the value of urban planning for use rather than profit, wrote in a 1934 essay, "If we are to build houses and cities adequate to the needs of the twentieth century, we must start all over again from the ground up."[1] And there were also the business interests, such as General Motors, eager to profit in the proposed transformation; their corporate success was tied to the successful incorporation of this future vision. Various downtown business interests also bought into the vision because they believed, wrongly as it turned out, that redevelopment would halt decentralization and save their investments.

The bright new future merely implicit in the interwar period was developed fully in the immediate postwar period, supported by revolutionaries and corporate executives alike, liberals as well as conservatives. The demand for a new modernist city decreed a massive transformation of the existing city, effacing its past to make room for its future. The future depended upon the destruction of the past. The construction of the modern was the annihilation of history; a forward march of progress held aloft a banner of urban renewal. Old housing, now called slums, was seen as the main problem of urban decline. A special report in *Business Week* in 1940 spoke of the "dry rot" at the core of all American cities.[2] The metaphor provided its own solution: dry rot had to be hacked away.

Urban Renewal

It began with noble aims. The major goals of the Housing Act of 1949 were to eliminate substandard housing and construct good housing. Its main goal was to provide a decent built environment. The act wended a contentious path through Congress. Senators Robert Taft, Robert Wagner, and Allen Ellender first put a housing bill before Congress in 1945. Reformers wanted provisions for low-income housing; business interests wanted urban renewal. The act passed by six votes, and it was the only part of Truman's Fair Deal legislation that was enacted by Congress.

Under Title I of the 1949 act, the federal government would pay for two-thirds of the cost of purchasing and clearing blighted houses. It remains the single largest federal urban program. By 1973, when the program officially ended, two thousand individual projects had been undertaken, covering one thousand square miles of urban land. In total six hundred thousand units were demolished, and two million people were displaced. It ranks with the removal of Native Americans as one of the largest and saddest forced migrations in the history of the nation. It involved thirteen billion dollars in federal spending (in 1973 dollars) and probably closer to almost twenty billion dollars when local-authority spending is included. In today's dollars, it amounts to almost one hundred billion dollars. The program that began with so much hope, the elimination of substandard housing, ended up destroying communities, increasing segregation, and laying the basis for subsequent central-city decline.

Assembling land for major developments in central cities is a costly and complicated process. Urban land is expensive, and landholdings are often fragmented among a variety of owners. These difficulties stymied prewar New Deal goals for major public works in central-city areas. The Housing Act overcame these difficulties by creating local public agencies (LPAs) with the power of eminent domain to acquire sites. The LPAs would acquire land, primarily through federal subsidies but with some municipal dollars, then sell or lease to private developers. Eminent domain had been used in the past to acquire land for public use, such as the construction of a transport route or a school. This new scheme involved the compulsory purchase of private land by a public agency and its transfer to a private corporation. A property owner took the Urban Renewal Agency to court, but in the 1954 ruling *Berman v. Parker,* the Supreme Court ruled in favor of the agency.[3] The legal door was now open.

The initial plan was to demolish substandard housing. The legislation stipulated that for each unit of housing torn down, one should be built. In practice, local authorities and local redevelopment agencies packed with bankers and downtown business interests implemented the plans in favor of replacing low-income housing with tax-generating commercial property. Thus the plan emanating from Washington with concern to eliminate substandard housing soon became compromised at the local level by municipalities and redevelopment agencies following their own definition of urban renewal. Under the Housing Act, agencies were not required to construct housing—the legislation required only "predominantly residential" developments, but even this vague directive was seldom followed. There was no requirement to build low-income housing, and the directive to rehouse displaced families was widely ignored. The initial housing program soon became an urban-renewal program.

The election of Dwight Eisenhower in 1952 produced a further shift away from public housing. A presidential advisory committee on housing inserted changes into the 1954 Housing Act that effectively turned the housing policy into a renewal policy. When implemented on the ground, the program involved a net loss of housing: four dwellings were demolished for every one built, and a tightened housing market emerged for low-income families as low-rent homes were demolished and replaced by more expensive housing and by commercial developments such as parking garages, hospitals, shopping centers, luxury housing, and office blocks. The 1954 Housing Act resulted in one of the largest, most regressive policies ever funded by the federal government. Housing-market conditions were worst for the poorest, whereas business interests received massive federal subsidization.

The use of Title I varied. Table 2.1 lists all those cities receiving more than one million dollars up to 1958. The geographical distribution is clearly related to big cities in the Northeast and Midwest. By 1958 New York City had received thirty-four million dollars, followed by Chicago at nearly fourteen million dollars and Baltimore at almost five million dollars. When we factor in population, Baltimore, New York, and Pittsburgh were in the lead.

Urban renewal was not restricted to Title I legislation. In many cities urban renewal was undertaken by various combinations of municipal au-

TABLE 2.1

Urban renewal grants, 1949–1958

City	Total ($ million)	Amount ($) per 1,000 of 1950 population	Rank of amount ($) per 1,000 of 1950 population
New York	34.064	4,570	2
Chicago	13.723	3,790	4
Baltimore	4.825	5,084	1
Philadelphia	3.468	1,674	9
Detroit	2.809	1,519	10
Pittsburgh	2.704	4,000	3
Cleveland	2.314	2,531	7
Cincinnati	1.895	3,767	5
Boston	1.808	2,257	8
Minneapolis	1.516	2,909	6

thorities and private developers, with very little federal assistance. In Pittsburgh, for example, federal urban-renewal funds were involved in only one out of the ten projects before 1958. By the late 1950s and 1960s, however, federal funds were being used more, as the 1954 act made it easier to use them for redevelopment rather than rehousing.

The effects were dramatic. Take the case of Detroit. The postwar master plan for the city, devised before the federal legislation, was for the destruction of low-income "blighted" housing and the construction of middle-class housing. Slum clearance, it was hoped, would revitalize the urban core and hence increase the tax-revenue base. The 1949 Housing Act gave federal assistance to these plans. The bulldozer and the wrecking ball were used to knock down densely populated black neighborhoods. In one of the six schemes, the Gratiot redevelopment site on the city's Lower East Side, 129 acres of land were condemned and almost 2,000 families were evicted. The initial plans called for 3,600 units of public housing on the site, but by 1958 no public housing was built. A twenty-two-story apartment building with expensive rents was the end result of this particular urban-renewal scheme.

The original housing in Gratiot was poor quality. It was the lowest-rent area of the city. Half of the houses did not have indoor plumbing. Slums may have been demolished, but there was no effective rehousing of the low-income residents. When the area residents began to be evicted in 1950, the most vulnerable households were displaced onto a tight housing market. Many households simply moved to nearby areas. With little assistance in getting alternative housing, displaced families simply doubled up and made marginal areas even more marginal through overcrowding. Only about one-third of the residents in Gratiot were rehoused in high-rise blocks; fully one-third could not be traced. City officials estimated that they moved less than one mile to marginal areas of the city. The end result was the "confinement of blacks to densely packed, run-down, and over priced housing."[4]

The most dramatic effect of the war on the central cities was the increasing concentration of the disadvantaged. One example is the Hough (pronounced "Huff") neighborhood, a two-square-mile tract on Cleveland's East Side. In 1900 it was a fashionable neighborhood, with large single-family dwellings housing some of the city's wealthiest residents. In 1950 it was a solid white working-class area. In 1950 only 3.9 percent of the area's population was African American, and the median family income was almost 90 percent of the county average. Hough was affected by the urban-renewal project in a neighboring area, the St. Vincent project in the Central District, which began in 1955. This neighborhood was razed to the ground, and almost 1,780 families, most of them black, were displaced. With nowhere else to go, the pressure built. In the late 1950s many white households left, and landlords subdivided dwellings. An owner of two houses and a barn converted them into thirty-three dwelling units. By 1960 the African American population had increased to 73 percent, and the median family income had fallen to 66 percent of the county average. By 2000 the total population had declined, median income had fallen, and poverty rates were very high (table 2.2).

The case of Hough is emblematic of what happened to many of the neighborhoods of central-city America since 1950. From 1950 to 1960 there was increased overcrowding of poor households, creating a time bomb. Hough was the site of a riot in 1966 that lasted for seven days. And since the 1960s there has been a further deterioration, as areas have lost both housing units and population. In many cities the residual population is now overwhelmingly poor and black.

The Federal Bulldozer

Urban-renewal programs not only demolished substandard housing but also destroyed sound housing and functioning neighborhoods. Almost 40

TABLE 2.2

Characteristics of Hough in 1950, 1960, and 1990

Census variables	1950	1960	1990
Total population	65,424	71,575	19,715
Total housing units	23,118	22,954	9,383
Median family income			
as % of county median	90.9	66.6	30.7
% of families below poverty level	—	—	50.6
% African American	3.9	73.6	97.4

Note: See Norman Krumholz, "Cleveland," 91.

percent of the dwellings that were demolished were classified as sound. As the program geared up, especially after 1954, little consideration was given to individual families or to the fate of the neighborhoods. Only one-half of 1 percent of the total budget was spent on relocation. Studies of relocated families paint a depressing picture. One study, for example, examined the fate of families relocated from Boston's West End (fig. 2.1). This thirty-eight-block, forty-one-acre neighborhood of some eighty-five hundred persons

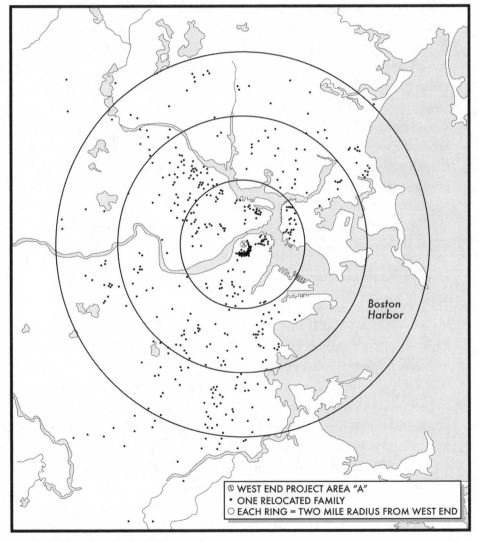

Boston Harbor

⊗ WEST END PROJECT AREA "A"
• ONE RELOCATED FAMILY
○ EACH RING = TWO MILE RADIUS FROM WEST END

2.1. Relocation of West End sample.

was demolished in 1958–1959. Luxury apartments were built on the demolished ruins of the low-rent, low-rise Italian neighborhood, and it was a similar pattern across the country as predominantly low-income housing was destroyed for predominantly upper-income and luxury housing. The study showed that for most of those individuals relocated, housing costs had increased whereas their housing quality was often only marginally improved.[5]

Urban sociologist Herbert Gans lived in the area for eight months in 1957–1958, using local services, attending meetings, and interviewing and socializing with local people. The result is a classic of urban sociology: a sympathetic yet not uncritical account of a working-class Italian neighborhood. Gans did not romanticize the place; he described it as "a run-down area of people struggling with the problems of low-income, poor education and related difficulties." But he could also see that "it was by and large a good place to live." He painted a picture of a vibrant community where life in the neighborhood revolved around family connections more than educational attainment or career aspirations. A tightly demarcated peer-group society was making a life in difficult circumstances. It was less a "slum" and more a low-rent area. But the term *slum* was the designation used to justify its destruction. Only 10 percent of the residents were re-housed in public housing.[6]

Highway Construction

The postwar highway-building program exacerbated urban clearance. At the end of World War II use of public transportation was at an all-time high: 19 billion trips were made in 1945. By 1975 the number of trips made by public transportation, despite the population doubling in size, fell to 5.6 billion. Cars became the preferred mode of transportation. It was not only a change in the mode of transportation; it was also the creation of a whole new culture as more people saw the world through the windshield of their private automobiles. Car ownership exploded from 25 million cars, or 1 car for every 5.3 people in 1945, to 134 million cars, 1 car for every 1.9 people, in 2000. It was not only that there were more cars but also more car movement as people used them to go to work, go shopping, drop off their kids at school, and go to the movies. The U.S. became a car culture, and U.S. cities transformed to accommodate the private auto. In comparison with other rich countries, public transportation received little government encouragement, and the urban structure evolved to fit the car rather than the car to fit the city.

In 1944 Congress earmarked 25 percent of all federal highway funds for road construction in urban areas. Half the cost of urban highways was to be paid by the federal government—a generous subsidy—but building new roads in urban areas was still expensive and difficult. Land-assembly and construction costs were huge. With the Federal-Aid Highway Act of 1956, however, the federal government now agreed to pay 90 percent of the costs of interstate-highway construction. The highway system eventually consisted of more than forty-one thousand miles in one of the biggest construction projects in the history of the world. The concrete motorway became so pervasive that Lewis Mumford suggested that the national flower should be the concrete cloverleaf in honor of the ubiquitous interchanges sprouting across the American landscape.

Road construction became a self-generating system. Roads and highways are still paid for by charges and taxes on automobile use. License and registration fees and federal excise taxes on gasoline go into the Highway Trust Fund that pays for road construction. Road construction generates more traffic, which in turn creates more revenue for road construction.

By 1960 the states were receiving one billion dollars a year for these expressways. Of the twenty-seven billion dollars that was spent on highways between 1956 and 1966, fifteen billion was spent on urban roadways. The construction of these motorways reshaped the city to suit the car and the commuter. The city was remade as a place of automobile flows and traffic movement, a vision of infinite mobility. But at a tremendous cost. Almost fifty-three hundred miles of urban expressways were blasted through cities. Neighborhoods were torn down and people evicted in order to make room for the expressways. Slum housing, substandard housing, and even adequate housing were pulled down to remake the city as a place of endless automotive movement. Between 1957 and 1968 alone, approximately 330,000 housing units were demolished in the federal highway program.

In Detroit the Oakland-Hastings Freeway (later the Chrysler Freeway) went right through the heart of the black Lower West Side, and the Edsel Ford Freeway bisected the black West Side. Neighborhoods were destroyed, and in their wake abandoned, depressing wastelands remained.

To make way for the Lodge Freeway in Detroit, 109 businesses, 22 manu-facturing plants, and 423 residences were condemned for a three-mile stretch, and for its total seven-mile stretch 2,800 buildings were removed. Families received thirty days' notice and no help in relocation. Throughout the 1950s and 1960s the heart of much of metropolitan America received such treatment. The worst hit were the inner-city, low-income, minority neighborhoods where housing stock was torn down and communities were riven by noisy, polluting motorways that created destruction in order to provide suburbanites with easy and quick journeys to work. The inner city became less a living neighborhood and more a deadened setting for concrete expressways. The highway program benefited the middle- and upper-income commuters; its negative costs were most severely visited upon the inner-city poor.

Housing demolition was not an incidental, unintended consequence of urban highway construction; it was planned. The director of the Bureau of Public Roads, Thomas McDonald, explicitly saw inner-city expressways as eliminating "blighted" districts. The Urban Land Institute, a think tank for downtown property owners and developers founded in 1936, pro-duced a series of pamphlets in the 1950s that promoted expressways as so-lutions to "blighted" neighborhoods and central-city decline. Expressways cut through the blighted neighborhoods to increase the accessibility of the downtown. Highway construction was explicitly promoted and used to demolish low-income neighborhoods. Expressways were used as blight busters to remove "slums" surgically and to remove from the central city the "dry rot of low-income neighborhoods."[7]

Urban expressways were routed through low-income minority com-munities: Interstate 95 in Miami plowed through the black community of Overtown; in Nashville Interstate 40 kinked so that it went through the black community of North Nashville; Interstate 81 in Syracuse cut a swath through the city's black inner-city community. Across the country urban highways smashed through low-income, and especially low-income mi-nority, communities: Interstate 10 in New Orleans; Interstate 85 in Mont-gomery and Interstate 59 in Birmingham, Alabama; Interstate 95 in Camden, New Jersey; and Interstate 77 in Charlotte, North Carolina. In most cities of the country urban highway construction blighted low-income neighborhoods and reduced housing opportunities for the poorest.

Highways did not even have the desired effect of bringing people back to the city. Rather than bringing middle-class people back, the new roads made it easier for them to escape. An unmitigated disaster, they blighted much of the central areas of U.S. cities, destroyed communities, and were completely regressive in their distribution of costs and benefits.

The urban-renewal programs and associated highway-construction programs constituted a form of high-intensity warfare against the inner city. Sound housing was demolished, neighborhoods were destroyed, and communities were broken by the bulldozer and the wrecking ball in a concentrated federal program that recast the city in the image of the futurist city first outlined in the 1939 World's Fair in New York. The future had arrived on the broken back of the historic inner city.

3

Stimulating Suburbs,
Starving Cities

"I Should Prefer to See the Ash Heaps"

THE SUBURBS are an important element of urban America as a built form, as a destination, and as a state of mind. The postwar suburbs did not just happen. They were created in large part by conscious government intervention. The federal government stimulated suburban growth through promoting suburban home ownership and highway construction. It began with the New Deal when the Roosevelt administration was eager to stimulate employment. The Federal Housing Administration (FHA) was established in 1934 as part of the National Housing Act, crafted to stimulate the employment of construction workers. The FHA insured mortgages to encourage banks to lend to potential home owners. The FHA did not build houses or give mortgages, but by guaranteeing mortgages it played an important role. The FHA, in effect, reduced interest payments, lessened down payments, and lengthened repayment periods. In some cases the FHA made it cheaper to buy than to rent. FHA lending guidelines aided the building of single-family homes in suburban areas, while their lending criteria worked against repairing existing houses, building multifamily dwellings, and providing mortgages in heterogeneous, older, inner-city areas.

From 1944 federal promotion of owner-occupation was reinforced by the G.I. Bill that enabled veterans to buy their own homes. Although administered by the Veterans Administration (VA), it was identical to the FHA program. Five million households bought homes under the G.I. Bill. In the late 1940s almost 50 percent of all new houses, approximately one million per year, were bought on VA mortgages.

FHA mortgages, especially from 1934 to 1965, and VA mortgages from 1944 were racially biased. The FHA and VA made few loans for minority neighborhoods. While the FHA and VA made suburbs less the preserve of the affluent and extended the suburban experience to middle- and lower-income households, it supported the white flight to the suburbs and the racial segregation of suburbia. The racial divide between the central city and suburbia is, in part, the result of more than fifty years of government policy.

The allocation of federally backed mortgages was biased against the central cities in favor of the suburbs. It was an explicit policy. The Home Owners Loan Corporation was established in 1933 to provide federal guarantees for home mortgages. A national inventory was undertaken to establish the creditworthiness of different neighborhoods. Local real estate professionals were involved in the survey, which began in 1936. Neighborhoods were rated A through D with corresponding colors on a map of green, blue, yellow, and red. Grade A neighborhoods were considered up-and-coming, in demand; grade B was good; grade C was full of older buildings and infiltrated by "lower-grade populations"—code for blacks, Jews, and foreign immigrants; and grade D was evaluated as poor-quality housing with an "undesirable population." The maps and accompanying texts were sent to banks and mortgage lenders. Loans were not forthcoming for people seeking housing in areas graded D and rarely in C. The red areas were starved of federally protected mortgage funds. This mapping exercise was a federal codification of the biases and prejudices of the overwhelmingly white, Anglo, middle-class real estate industry. This bias was replicated in postwar mortgage lending until "redlining," the explicit policy of denying mortgage funds to certain neighborhoods, was officially ended in 1965. But by that time the central cities already had much of their middle-class population siphoned off. The racial segregation and poor housing stock of the inner-city U.S. have many causes, but federal policies have played a major role. Denied the lifeblood of mortgage finance, many inner-city neighborhoods experienced a downward spiral. Only very high-interest financing was available, which put home loans beyond the reach of many. Landlords were forced to cut back on maintenance and to over-crowd as many people as possible to meet their loans. The more the neighborhood deteriorated, the more the mortgage-allocation decision became a self-fulfilling prophecy. The areas in cities that were colored red invariably saw a downward spiral of population outmovement, deterioration, and decline.

Public Housing

The federal government first became involved in providing low-cost housing with the 1937 Housing Act, also known as the Wagner-Steagall Act. Under this act the U.S. Housing Authority (USHA) would provide funds to municipal authorities through loans and subsidies. In four years the USHA was responsible for 130,000 units in thirty-eight states. Public housing was never politically popular. As one spokesman said, "If I had to choose between seeing every old city in the country as an ash heap and seeing the government become a landlord to its own citizens, I should prefer to see the ash heaps."[1] Under the post-urban-renewal scheme, in some measure, he got his wish.

Few in Congress felt able to champion the cause of public housing, and many undermined its funding. The 1937 act was primarily an employment stimulus to get the construction industry back to work rather than a social program. After the economy picked up during the war, there was little support for public housing as a major solution to the housing problem. However, the 1949 Housing Act, the same act that introduced urban renewal, also made provision for public housing. The act suggested the building of between 135,000 and 200,000 public-housing units each year until 1960 to meet the demand of low-income households for decent housing. Of the projected total of 2 million units, only 650,000 were built by 1962.

The 1949 act placed emphasis on local voluntary involvement. Across the country suburban municipalities did not want public housing, so almost no public housing was built outside the central cities. Public housing was ghettoized into the central cities. Denied access to the cheaper suburban land, public housing was concentrated in the expensive city land at higher densities. The act also tied the construction of new housing to slum clearance. No housing could be built unless housing was demolished. But since it was always easier to knock down than rebuild, there was a net loss of low-income housing. Moreover, the housing that was built was confined to existing slum areas, further stigmatizing public housing. In many large cities urban renewal involved the destruction of dense neighborhoods and their replacement with public-housing projects of dense high-rise towers. Quickly, they became warehouses for the poor, housing racial minorities.

Public housing took a specific form. It was dominated by large modernist blocks, often called "the projects." Poorly maintained, shoddily constructed, they became dumping grounds for the poor. The projects were emblematic for poverty and despair. While the upper- and middle-income groups got federally insured mortgages in the suburbs, the poor got ghettoized, unpopular housing in the central cities.

Even proponents of public housing such as Catherine Bauer, who in 1934 had called for rebuilding the city from the ground up, had her optimism squashed. "After more than two decades," she wrote in a 1957 essay, public housing "still drags along in a kind of limbo. Continuously controversial, not dead but never more than half alive."[2] The reformer's twenty-three-year dream had become a nightmarish reality.

Pruitt-Igoe

In 1972 part of a public-housing project in St. Louis called Pruitt-Igoe was demolished. It is believed by some that the explosion ceremoniously marked the failure of the public-housing program and signaled the loss of belief in modernist architecture. The project began in 1950 and was completed in 1956. After only a few years it had become a place of disrepair, vandalism, and crime. Things deteriorated so much that in 1972 the St. Louis Housing Authority demolished three of the high-rise buildings. A year later, with the permission of the U.S. Department of Housing and Urban Development (HUD), the authority destroyed the remaining thirty buildings.

A brief history of the project is revealing for what it tells us about public housing in the U.S. Pruitt-Igoe was part of a broader urban-renewal strategy for the city.[3] In 1947 the business-dominated St. Louis City Plan Commission outlined a scheme to bring people back into the city. During the 1930s the city had lost population. The plan, as in so many other cities across the country, called for the destruction of older neighborhoods and an ambitious new building program. One of the neighborhoods, the low-income, racially mixed DeSoto-Carr, was designated as "extremely obsolete." The initial plan called for the demolition of the existing housing and the construction of three-story apartments. The plan was given a new spin after Joseph Darst was elected mayor in 1949. He wanted to re-create New York's high-rise buildings in St. Louis. On a visit to New York City he was favorably impressed by the high-rise public-housing projects designed and built by Robert Moses. Under a 1950 plan, high-rise towers were planned for the DeSoto-Carr neighborhood. The mayor insisted on hiring the Seattle-born architect Minou Yamasaki (1912–1986), perhaps best known for being the architect of the World Trade Center Towers, who also built the St. Louis Air Terminal. His designs are characterized by stark, concrete, high-rise, modernist structures, as much minimalist sculptures as they are buildings.

Pruitt-Igoe was part of the larger ambitious high-rise vision of the Manhattanization of St. Louis. The large-scale building of modernist blocks was intended to present a dynamic, attractive image that would lure people and dollars back to the central city. Pruitt-Igoe consisted of almost three thousand units in thirty-three eleven-story buildings. Initially, the project was two separate schemes: Pruitt for blacks and Igoe for whites. As the first whites soon moved out and other whites were reluctant to move in, the whole project essentially became a black ghetto of ten thousand people.

Life in the projects is vividly recounted in Lee Rainwater's book *Behind Ghetto Walls*. The first tenants were drawn from local clearance areas. Poor maintenance and rising crime both led to the project quickly garnering a poor reputation. Landscaping was reduced to zero. Those individuals with choices moved out. The ones who remained were the poor and marginalized. One in two households was on public assistance. Almost half of all households were female-headed families. Most people liked their own apartments, but the majority were dissatisfied with the project. Residents felt there was too much trash; public spaces such as elevators and laundry rooms were unsafe, especially for women; and there were mice and cockroaches, fights, theft, and gang violence. Pruitt-Igoe was an expensive, modernist, architect-designed slum. "This is the last resort," said one of the residents, twenty-one-year-old Thomas Coolidge.

Pruitt-Igoe deteriorated, and many residents moved out. The ones left were subject to the assaults and threat of criminals and gangs. The poor reputation of the place made it even more difficult for residents to get jobs, credit, even deliveries. In 1965 the federal government spent five million dollars to upgrade the amenities. The problems persisted. In 1967 the acting director of the housing authority requested either a federal takeover or permission to demolish. The federal government gave permission to demolish in 1972.

The demolition of Pruitt-Igoe provided an arresting visual image that became the dramatic backdrop for a variety of narratives: the ultimate failure of modernist architecture, the necessary consequence of dumping poor black people into ghettos, a design failure, an act of racism, a policy mistake. Pruitt-Igoe was all of these things. The images of the buildings imploding became a potent symbol of goals and dreams crumbling into dust.

Imagined in the 1940s, built in the 1950s, and demolished in the 1970s, Pruitt-Igoe represented, in dramatic form, the failure of traditional urban renewal. The program, rather than solving the ills of the city, had in effect waged a war against the inner city and its poorest residents and failed to halt central-city decline.

High-rise public housing, like urban motorways, has also fallen out of favor. Pruitt-Igoe was the first. More followed. In 1998 the Chicago Housing Authority demolished three towers in the twenty-eight public-housing towers of the Robert Taylor Homes. The authority plans to demolish all of them. By the end of the twentieth century the federal Department of Housing and Urban Development had razed twenty-two thousand apartments that were built in the 1950s and 1960s and plans to demolish another one hundred thousand. In 1994 a high-rise public-housing project in Newark, New Jersey, the Christopher Columbus Houses, was dynamited by municipal authority. On the day of its destruction, the mayor of Newark, Sharp James, described it as the "end of an American dream that failed." But what exactly was the dream? The dream was less about public housing and more about rebuilding the city and halting inner-city decline. There were many reasons behind the failure, but first and foremost was that the public-housing program was less about providing adequate housing for low-income people and more about protecting central-city investments and a brute exercise of political power.

4

Robert Moses
Versus Jane Jacobs

"Hack Your Way with a Meat Ax"

THE GOVERNMENT'S WAR against the central cities came to an official end when the Housing and Community Development Act of 1974 replaced the urban-renewal program. It was not a sharp break. The earlier program took years to wind down, and its effects continue to reverberate today. The new direction was the result of citizen challenges to the urban-renewal juggernaut. Nowhere was this fight more emblematic than in the struggle against the Lower Manhattan Expressway and the confrontation between Robert Moses and Jane Jacobs. Their showdown embodies an important moment in the urban geography and political history of the country.

Robert Moses and the Rational City

Robert Moses (1888–1981) was the master builder of the New York metropolis for more than forty years.[1] He came from a wealthy German Jewish family and was educated at Yale and Oxford. He started off as a civic reformer passionately committed to public service and the notion of efficient government. In 1914 a reforming mayor brought him into the New York City government system. He battled against Tammany Hall and lost. Fired in 1918, he returned six years later. From 1924 until 1968 he held immense, unelected power. During his tenure in power six New York State governors and five New York City mayors would come and go. He held a variety of nonelected positions including park commissioner, construction coordinator, member of the City Planning Board, and chair of the Slum Clearance Committee and of the Housing Committee. At one time he held twelve official posts. His power was awesome. As the main point of contact between the city and federal government he was the conduit for billions of dollars of federal and state monies. He controlled thousands of federal, state, and city projects. He had immense budgetary power without ever subjecting himself to public scrutiny. His control of the bridge and tunnel toll charges in the city gave him a never-ending supply of money and power. He had both the ability and the confidence to undertake huge public works in New York State and the New York metropolitan area. Over a forty-year period he built parkways, expressways, roads, parks, playgrounds, and housing. He was a leading force in the building of Lincoln Center, the New York Coliseum, the United Nations Headquarters, Shea Stadium, and Co-op City. His road-building projects sweep around the entire metropolitan region and include the Long Island Expressway, Staten Island Expressway, New England Throughway, and Henry Hudson Parkway. To link up the watery city he built the Triborough, Verrazano, Henry Hudson, and Throgs Neck Bridges. He constructed ninety-five blocks of public housing in eastern Manhattan that housed almost 150,000 people and was responsible for the building of apartments housing more than a half-million tenants. It has been estimated that, in 1968 dollars, he built twenty-seven billion dollars of public works.

In his earlier years Moses was on the side of the angels. He constructed parks and playgrounds. He was the leading force in the creation of numerous city and state parks, including Rockaway Park, Jones Beach State Park, Battery Park, and, of course, Robert Moses State Park. Besides the park he also had a parkway, a causeway, and a dam named after him. But by the 1950s massive road construction was the dominant Moses imprint on the city.

New York State had long been a leader in the construction of roadways. The Long Island Motor Parkway (1906–1911) was the first road to be built in the U.S. only for the motorcar. Under the influence of Robert Moses the road building continued. The Henry Hudson Parkway, which began construction in 1934, was the first inner-city freeway in the country. To reduce costs it was built along the side of the Hudson River. The cost of building expressways through existing cities was too daunting, even for the hugely ambitious Moses.

The cost equation changed in 1944 when Congress earmarked 25 percent of all federal highway funds for road construction in urban areas. Half the cost of urban highways was to be paid by the federal government. Building new roads in urban areas was still expensive and difficult. Land-assembly and construction costs were still huge, and few cities attempted urban motorways until the more generous 1956 legislation. New York City was an exception. Under the unelected, but enormously powerful influence of, Robert Moses, New York State became a site for major road construction that blasted motorways through urban neighborhoods.

Moses rammed numerous expressways through the city, including the Bruckner Expressway, Staten Island Expressway, Cross-Bronx Expressway, Long Island Expressway, Major Deegan Expressway, and Brooklyn-Queens Expressway. To make way for the fast-moving car lanes he evicted between a quarter- and a half-million people. It was a massive urban-renewal project that destroyed neighborhoods and created apartments for the wealthy and bleak sterile blocks for the poor.

One of his projects was the seven-mile-long Cross-Bronx Expressway. The first eviction letters came on December 4, 1952. Local residents were told to move to make way for a new expressway that lay across the path of 113 streets, one subway line, three railroads, and five elevated rapid-transit lines. They were given ninety days to leave. Local groups tried to stop the project, but their opposition was unsuccessful. Construction began in the summer of 1955. It took twelve years, and it cost ten million dollars per mile. The human costs were even more staggering. The Bronx, once a vibrant neighborhood, was blasted into dilapidation and decline. Moses said in a television interview at the time that when building in a metropolis, "you have to hack your way with a meat ax." As a young boy, the social critic Marshall Berman witnessed the ax. "I can remember," he recalls, "standing above the construction site for the Cross-Bronx Expressway, weeping for my neighborhood." For Berman it was an early experience of modernity. In his 1982 book, *All That Is Solid Melts into Air,* he extends the experience into a very sophisticated analysis that draws upon Dickens, Baudelaire, and Dostoyevsky as well as Walter Benjamin and Goethe to describe the creative destructiveness at the heart of modernity. The book draws widely across the world, but its origins lie with a young boy looking at the destruction of his community. The title of his book is a quote from Marx's *Communist Manifesto* that tries to capture the restless, ceaseless destruction of the past to create the future. Urban renewal and highway construction were the axes of modernity. "As I saw one of the loveliest of these buildings being wrecked for the road," Berman noted, "I felt a grief that, I can now see, is endemic to modern life."[2]

The construction of the urban expressways reshaped the city to suit the car and the commuter. Moses blasted almost 130 miles of urban expressways through twenty neighborhoods, and almost a half-million people were forcibly relocated. The city was remade as a place of ceaseless mobility. Neighborhoods were torn down and people evicted in order to make room for the expressways. Underlying the vision was a basic contempt for the city—its crowded neighborhoods, its slow-moving traffic routes. The density and depth of urban living were to be replaced by sharp, clean lines and straight, fast transportation routes; a world of organic neighborhoods was to be replaced by a cold, modern aesthetic, a promise of something new writ large on the blank page of obliterated neighborhoods, whose destruction was justified by their designation as "blighted" or "slums" or "transitional." The city was reimagined as a modern space to replace outdated places, a city of easy flows to replace the city of living communities. There were fear and contempt for the existing city in all its messiness and heterogeneity and a burning desire for a remade city. Beneath the vision there was a hard core of material interests. Land conversion, development, and renewal were all sources of business and profit for builders, developers, and real estate people. The visionaries looked to Le Corbusier; the developers were influenced by mammon.

In a television interview at the height of his power, Moses said, "We wouldn't have any American economy without the automobile business. . . . [T]his is a great industry that has to go on and has to keep turning out cars and trucks and buses and there has to be a place for them to run, there have to be modern roads, modern arteries. Somebody's got to build it. . . . [P]eople must be inconvenienced who are in the way." Moses had plans for more urban expressways. He long held a vision of three expressways that would carry traffic east to west across Manhattan: a Lower Manhattan Expressway that would have swept through Greenwich Village, an elevated Midtown Expressway at 30th Street, and an Upper Manhattan Expressway at 125th Street. When his plans surfaced for the Lower Manhattan Expressway in the mid-1950s, Moses collided with Jane Jacobs.

Jane Jacobs and the Humane City

Jane Jacobs was born in 1916 in Scranton, a town on the anthracite coalfield of northeastern Pennsylvania. She had an early interest in journalism and after high school worked unpaid on the local newspaper. In the middle of the Depression she went to New York City where she found occasional writing work. She lived at 555 Hudson Street in Greenwich Village until she moved to Toronto in 1968 so that her sons would not be drafted. She wrote for a metals trade paper and freelanced for the *New York Herald-Tribune* and *Vogue*. After World War II she wrote for *Architectural Forum*.

Jane Jacobs had no formal training in architecture or urban planning. Her most famous book, *The Death and Life of Great American Cities*, owes less to academic theories or architectural visions than to her everyday life on the streets of Lower Manhattan in Greenwich Village. It combined her now honed writing skills with her experience of city living. "This book," begins the first line of the opening chapter, "is an attack on current city planning and rebuilding." Writing at the height of the war against the cities and in a New York lacerated by Moses expressways, Jacobs enunciates a new vision. She revels in the density, heterogeneity, diversity, complexity, and messiness of city life. She sees the regular use of sidewalks as essential to the safety of a city, social interaction, and the socialization of children. She extols the importance of small blocks and aged buildings. She encourages diversity of land uses, the recycling of older buildings, and the nurturing of communities rather than their destruction.

Moses and Jacobs embodied two opposing visions of the city. Where Moses saw routes, Jacobs saw neighborhoods. When he reached for the ax, she suggested holistic care. Where he saw giant new projects that prioritized the car and the journey, she saw small-scale places for congenial social interaction.

Moses makes a number of appearances in Jacobs's book. At one point he is quoted as accepting of ugly, regimented institutional public housing. At another he is described as the controller of such vast amounts of public money that he can override local opinion. In the longest appearance he is described as the architect of a plan hatched in the mid-1950s to construct a highway through Washington Square Park. Jacobs spends several pages telling the story of how two local women came up with a counterplan for the closure of the existing road. With evident delight Jacobs tells us how, despite Moses's efforts, the counterplan won out. She criticizes his plan for a downtown expressway in Manhattan. In a tart summary she notes:

> It is understandable that men who were young in the 1920s were capti-
> vated by the vision of the freeway Radiant City, with the specious promise
> that it would be appropriate to an automobile age. At least it was then a
> new idea; to men of the generation of New York's Robert Moses, for ex-
> ample, it is as radical and exciting in the days when their minds were
> growing and their ideas forming. Some men tend to cling to old intellec-
> tual excitements, just as some belles, when they are old ladies, still cling to
> the fashions and coiffures of their exciting youth. But it is harder to under-
> stand why this form of arrested mental development should be passed on
> intact to succeeding generations of planners and designers.[3]

Jacobs's book can be understood only as a riposte to Moses, his vision and his methods. It was written at a time when and in a city where Moses was rebuilding in a bankrupt, modernist fashion. When she criticizes "prome-nades that go from noplace to nowhere" and "expressways that eviscerate great cities," she is criticizing Moses. And when she writes of urban re-newal as "the sacking of cities," she is lambasting Moses. The book offers the counterpoint to the Moses city. It is the product of a particular context, but like all great books it transcends the specific. To read Jacobs today is to see the emergence of an alternative conception of the city that speaks to re-cycling, community, human scale, and public participation. The book rev-els in the role of the corner, the importance of the block, and the necessity of neighborhood. The sense of community, the feeling of urban congeniality, runs through her book. It is the city as being, lived memory, the setting for social interaction. The Moses city, on the other hand, is the city of grand vi-sions, the city as becoming, the blank page for sweeping motorways and grand ensembles. Jacobs and Moses represent two contrasting visions of the city. One is a close connection to lived experience with a profound sense of community and a palpable feeling of history. The other is the city as a centrally planned vision, a concern with mobility, and the destruction of history. The Jacobs city is diverse, organic, spontaneous. The Moses city is uniform, imposed, planned.

Robert Moses Meets Jane Jacobs . . . and Loses

Jane Jacobs did not just write against Moses. She became actively involved in the public debates and community activism over the Lower Manhattan Expressway. Moses planned an eight-lane elevated highway from the East River to the Hudson River that would have cut a 225-foot swath though Soho, Greenwich Village, and parts of Little Italy and Chinatown. It would have involved the forcible relocation of ten thousand workers and residents.

The plan surfaced in 1961. Jacobs led the community opposition to the project. There were rallies and demonstrations. She was arrested and charged with rioting and public mischief. People wore badges and carried signs that read "Moses Madness" and "Kill the Expressway." A coalition of Jews, Chinese, Italians, and Anglos resisted the Moses wrecking ball. Alternative plans were suggested that proposed rehabilitation rather than renewal. Political alliances were formed that revolved around resistance to Moses and renewal. Greenwich Village had long been an important center of dissent. The tradition of activism and organized resistance now marshaled to a defense of the neighborhood itself. At a Board of Estimates meeting in December 1962 the Moses plan was rejected. The expressway was cancelled. Jacobs had won, and Moses had lost. He would continue in power for another six years, but his influence was on the wane. The defeat of the Lower Manhattan Expressway was the beginning of the end for Moses's restructuring of New York City.

Jacobs and Moses are remembered in very different ways. Moses is now seen as an idealist turned to addled old man unable to learn from his mistakes, arrogant, undemocratic, and deeply flawed in his vision of the city. Since his death his name has become synonymous with everything wrong about urban planning and urban renewal. Robert Caro's majestic biography, *The Power Broker* (1974), did not paint a flattering picture, and subsequent writers have carried on the remorseless criticism of what and how Moses built. Jane Jacobs, in contrast, is seen as the patron saint of a humane urban vision. Her words and ideas, written from the margins of power and influence, have now become the standard orthodoxy. Her ideas of small-scale recycling buildings and congenial places have become the mantra of the New Urbanism.

Moses and Jacobs have become archetypes: Apollo and Earth Mother; power-crazed old man and the wise, kindly woman. They have become opposite poles: the bloodless, rational modernist versus the feeling, sensitive nurturer. Moses left a legacy of bitterness and regret, whereas Jacobs was midwife to a more sensitive postmodern urbanism.

And after the Turn?

Urban expressways are now no longer seen as a solution. Many urban communities resisted their encroachment, and now they no longer hold the sway they did in the time of Moses. A revolt against a freeway in San Francisco in 1959 marked the beginning of widespread resistance. As the motorway construction began to be planned for more affluent middle-class neighborhoods, resistance stiffened. People in the Greenwich Villages of the urban U.S. were not so compliant as in the Bronxes. People were becoming better organized and better connected for successful resistance. As the motorway-construction and renewal plans moved from the very low-income areas in the early 1950s to the more middle-income areas of the late 1950s and early 1960s, opposition groups were prepared. They had learned of the devastating effects from the previous schemes. The successful revolt against big-city expressways eventually led to congressional legislation in 1965 mandating the provision of housing in advance for the relocated. By that time the program was all but over.

Although the car culture is still dominant, and huge permanent damage has been done to the central cities, there have been some small-scale reversals. In 2002 the New York State Department of Transportation announced a plan to make around 250 changes to the Cross-Bronx Expressway. The director of the project noted that the expressway divided communities. Pathways for pedestrians and bicyclists are to be constructed across the road; parts of the road are to be covered to provide green space. To build the Cross-Bronx Expressway, Moses took the ax to the community. Now the road is to be refashioned to reconnect the Bronx. Jane Jacobs would be happy. Around the country people are reassessing the viability of replacing urban expressways that cut through the heart of the city. One of the most ambitious schemes was in Boston where a six-lane central artery ran through the center of downtown. Opened in 1959 the road carried almost two hundred thousand cars a day. The Big Dig, as the project was locally called, involved replacing the elevated motorway with a ten-lane underground expressway. Begun in 1991 it was finished in 2004. The elevated expressway was demolished, the site now a green space.

Traditional urban renewal, urban motorway construction, and public housing are now roundly condemned as failures. Proposed to halt central-city decline and prop up municipal coffers, supported by downtown business interests and political elites, and bankrolled by the federal government, the programs envisaged a bright new future. Slums were to be demolished, replaced by high gleaming towers, speeding motorways, and an affluent population. Instead, the programs blasted communities, destroyed the urban fabric, and helped further the continued suburbanization of people and jobs.

It is a well-known axiom that we need to learn from history. But it is more important that we learn the right lessons. For those on the political Right, the lessons of Moses and federal building programs were to distrust not unelected power and misconceived visions but federal programs in general: the federal government always gets it wrong; we cannot trust the federal government, especially when it gets involved in redistributional policies. The criticisms of urban renewal morph into a more general assault on the very principle of federal social policy. The feds spend a lot of money, and they screw it up. Therefore, goes the argument, we need to jettison all federal social policy and drastically reduce nondefense spending.

We can learn much from the failure of urban renewal and high-rise public housing. Pruitt-Igoe showed what happens when you warehouse a lot of poor people in an inadequately policed neighborhood and in poorly maintained housing. But it would be a willful misread to infer that we need to reduce the role of the federal government and abolish public housing. The case could be made for these positions, but the historical record will show that urban renewal was dominated by business interests and big-city mayors who fashioned it to attract people and investment back to the central city. They failed and failed miserably. But their failure speaks to inappropriate, deeply flawed visions; it does not invalidate government spending on cities, public housing, or policies of income redistribution and the collective pursuit of social justice. The government learned the wrong lessons because the fall of traditional urban renewal led not to a revision of federal policy for cities, but to their effective abandonment. The crumbling walls of Pruitt-Igoe symbolized many things, but none more so than the end of a sustained government commitment to the central city. When the dynamited walls of the project fell to the ground, the political weight and economic muscle of the nation shifted to the suburbs.

PART TWO

The Social Geographies
of the Metropolis

5

Downtown

"The Heart That Pumps the Blood of Commerce"

AS THE NINETEENTH CENTURY turned into the twentieth, downtowns with high concentrations of retail and commercial business emerged in both large and small cities. By the early twentieth century the downtown was the main retail and commercial center, attracting shoppers and workers from an ever expanding urban region.

The downtown also stood for a constellation of business interests that included department stores, banks, utilities, insurance companies, major newspapers, and central-city property owners. Downtown interests of landowners, shopkeepers, and commercial business leaders all sought to promote and secure the continued pivotal position of the downtown.[1] The strategies of this group may have varied over the years, but the goal was always the same: to resist the devaluation of the downtown. They initially supported mass-transit schemes because they believed that the systems would draw the dispersing population to the downtown. Beginning as early as the 1860s in cities in the Northeast, there was a campaign by downtown business interests to get cities to build mass-transit systems to connect suburban residential areas with the downtown. However, because they were expensive and unprofitable in all but the very largest cities, there was opposition from property owners and local streetcar companies. Later, subways were proposed by the downtown business community, but by the late 1920s only about 350 miles of rapid transit had been built compared to the 31,000 miles of street railways. Home owners resisted the tax increases necessary to pay for the subways.

By the early 1920s the greater use of automobiles gave residents and businesses an opportunity to move farther away from the downtown. There was a gradual erosion of downtown dominance, as only a few offices and stores set up in outlying districts and suburbanization was still limited in scope. There was enough, however, that the term *central business district* began to be used in the 1920s, a recognition that there were other business districts. The downtown remained the central, and far and away the most important, business district in metropolitan areas. There was still so much pressure on land in the bigger cities that the downtown expanded upward to justify the high land costs.

By the 1930s the first fears of decentralization were being voiced. During the Depression business demand plummeted, rents fell, and some desperate developers tore down buildings and put up parking lots to reduce their tax bills and provide some income. The growing use of the automobile also compromised the continued vitality of the downtown. Auto users, if they came downtown, caused congestion, and parking emerged as a major problem. It was easier for some potential customers to drive to less congested business areas closer to home. The response of the political elites and business community was to try to capture the auto users. Unable in most cities to persuade municipalities to underwrite mass-transit schemes, the elites now sought to make the downtown more suitable for automobiles. From the late 1930s onward this goal involved clearing space for parking and trying to get roads built.

In 1950 there were almost fifty million people living in the central-city areas of metropolitan regions. They constituted almost one-third of the total population of the country. The downtown was the commercial heart of the nation; the prime center for commerce, retail, and entertainment; and the setting for a shared urban experience. Office occupancy rates were at 95 percent, and department stores, the flagships of the retail industry, were downtown, and in 1950 they had received a major round of investment. In cities across the country, including the large cities of New York, Boston, Cleveland, Dallas, Chicago, and Philadelphia, the downtown retail chains were expanding. At midcentury, then, the downtown was still a dense agglomeration of shops, offices, and businesses attracting people from all over the metropolitan region. An article in the *St. Louis Post-Dispatch* on April 23, 1950, noted that the "downtown is not dying. Despite the low values, congestion, it is still the center, the core, the heart that pumps the blood of commerce through the area's arteries. . . . Without a vigorous Downtown," reporter Richard Baumoff continued, "St. Louis loses its chief economic reasons for existence; without a vigorous St. Louis, the whole metropolitan district falters and fails—economically, culturally, physically."

Since 1950 there has been a steady decentralization caused by a dispersal of downtown functions to a variety of suburban locations. As more freeways were built, the rate of decentralization increased. In their paper "All Centers Are Not Equal: An Exploration of the Polycentric Metropolis," L. Sarzynski and R. Hanson have measured the degree of dispersal across fifty metropolitan areas in the U.S. They found that there were still instances of strong monocentrism in selected U.S. cities, as identified by the amount of employment concentration in 1990. Their results reveal that Las Vegas, Miami, and San Jose are still strongly monocentric (table 5.1). However, even in these cities, the percentage of jobs in the core was not greater than 57.6 percent. In other words, even monocentric cities have a substantial number of jobs located outside the center.

Downtown business interests responded to the decline in two main

TABLE 5.1

Metropolitan areas by type of polycentrism

Type	Number of areas	Examples	% of all metro jobs in center
Dispersed	3	Baton Rouge	10.4
Strong polycentric	4	Los Angeles	15.1
Polycentric	6	Baltimore	23.1
Weak polycentric	6	Atlanta	16.2
Weak monocentric	19	Houston	27.5
Monocentric	9	Pittsburgh	23.7
Strong monocentric	3	Las Vegas	57.6

Note: See L. Sarzynski and R. Hanson, "All Centers Are Not Equal: An Exploration of the Polycentric Metropolis."

ways. First, the strategy of urban renewal was promoted and supported—not as a form of housing provision but as a way to maintain the commercial viability of the downtown. The urban-renewal program took the form that it did, essentially the destruction of low-income housing and its replacement with housing for bigger-spending, higher-income households, owing in no small measure to the power of the downtown business interests to shape it to fit their commercial needs. Urban-renewal programs, as they unfolded, were attempts to stem the tide of decentralization and preserve downtown property values. There were shared interests. Big-city mayors wanted downtown renewal to alleviate fiscal problems created by the decline of property values and economic activity, and sections of organized labor wanted the jobs in major reconstruction programs. Second, better freeway access was considered essential to downtown vitality. As more people continued to suburbanize and more people drove rather than used public mass transit, freeways were seen as linking the downtown to its dispersing customer base and workforce.

Both attempted solutions not only failed but actually exacerbated downtown decline. Urban renewal cleared away a lot of the life and density of the downtown areas, often replacing them with acres of dead space or non-tax-generating public spaces such as hospitals and universities. Buildings were also cleared for interstate connections and freeways. Downtowns became filled with unattractive, sterile, unusable spaces and a depressing collection of dead zones beneath elevated highways and busy intersections. And the more the freeways were built, the easier people found it to move around the entire metropolitan region, rather than restrict their journeys from the suburbs to the downtown. The freeways reinforced decentralization, and urban renewal weakened rather than strengthened the downtown.

Behind the decline of the downtown was the seemingly unstoppable force of suburban commercial development. In the last half of the twentieth century shops, businesses, and offices were established farther away from the city center. On greenfield sites, development projects were quick and cheap. Most suburban municipalities were also eager to foster development for the tax base they created. There were few zoning ordinances to limit greenfield developments. It made economic sense for developers to build on greenfield sites rather than face the hassle, time, and money of developing projects in the central city. The suburban spread of shops, offices, and jobs continued. In some cities the central cities maintained their centrality. Manhattan survived as a premier retail and commercial center, but in lesser cities the shift outward was more noticeable. In fact, smaller cities, with less capital investment in their downtowns, saw the most marked decentralization.

The downtowns of smaller cities were particularly affected by retail developments that shifted the center of gravity away from the city centers toward the urban fringe. One important icon of this suburban shift was Wal-Mart. The founder, Sam Walton, was born in Kingfisher, Oklahoma. His fraternity newspaper in Columbia, Missouri, referred to him in a 1940 article as "Hustler Walton." He graduated with a business degree in 1940 and worked for a short while for the retail giant J. C. Penney in Des Moines, Iowa. When he got out of the army in 1945 his wife stipulated that she did not want to live in a large town. For someone interested in retail, that condition limited his options. He had visions of himself becoming a big-city department-store owner. Now he focused his attention on small towns. He bought a Ben Franklin variety store in Newport, Arkansas, and opened for business on September 1, 1945. His early experiences told him that cutting prices could increase sales. Although the profit margin was low on any single item, increased turnover meant higher profits. The Walton model was to build cheap and sell cheap. The first Wal-Mart store opened in 1962. Of his third Wal-Mart he wrote:

> The store was only 12,000 square feet, and had an 8-foot ceiling and a concrete floor, with bare-boned wooden plank fixtures. Sterling [a competitor] had a huge variety store in downtown Harrison, with tile on the floor, nice lights. Really good fixtures, and good presentations. Ours was just barely put together—highly promotional, truly ugly, heavy with merchandise—but for 20 percent less than the competition. We were trying to find out if customers in a town of 6,000 people would come to our kind of barn and buy the same merchandise strictly because of price. The answer was yes.[2]

Walton had hit on a winning formula that was perfectly synchronized with the suburbanization of the U.S. population and the development of greenfield suburban sites. The Wal-Mart big box was built big and cheap on a greenfield site; the cheap suburban land enabled the large floor space that enabled the large turnover that generated the profits. It attracted customers away from the downtowns of small and medium cities. It provided easy access, ample parking, and cheap prices. The Wal-Mart model, the big suburban box with discounted merchandise, became a major strategy of U.S. retailing.

Sam Walton's approach paid off. In 1986 he was named the richest man in America by *Forbes*. By 2000 there were 3,302 Wal-Marts in the U.S., including Wal-Mart stores (1,617), Wal-Mart Supercenters (1,140), Sam's Clubs (512), and Wal-Mart Neighborhood Markets (33). The company now has an annual turnover of $220 billion, employs almost 1.4 million people, and has more than 5 million square feet of retail space. In recent years the company has exported the strategy abroad; there are now 1,200 Wal-Mart stores in nine countries around the world. By the summer of 2002 China had 20 Wal-Marts.

The Wal-Mart strategy was soon followed by other variety stores and other retail sectors. Stores like Sterling in Harrison soon felt the competitive pressure and either went out of business or moved to a suburban location. There was a marked disinvestment from the downtown, and the end result was an evisceration of retail from much of the downtowns of the medium- and small-city U.S. Faced with a continuing loss of retail establishments and commercial offices, downtown business interests and city political elites came up with a variety of new responses. Unable to lure back the shopper and office worker, attention shifted to the downtown as a setting for entertainment and recreation and as place for upmarket living. The process has been termed *donning the festival mask.*

Donning the Festival Mask

There have been two waves of urban renewal since 1950. The first, from the late 1940s to the mid-1970s, was developed around federal schemes for slum clearance and motorway construction. It involved the destruction of many low-income neighborhoods as well as the removal of some of the industrial base of the central city. It was the modernist solution. The second, developing slowly in the late 1960s and picking up steam by the 1970s and 1980s, focused more on building than demolition, on entertainment rather than production, and on public-private partnerships rather than on federal programs. It was the postmodern solution in a time of federal fiscal austerity.

A number of plans were established and implemented in this second phase to turn parts of the downtown into festival settings. Alliances of civic leaders, investors, and developers in cities across the nation sought to construct a new iconography of theme retail districts, cultural centers, convention centers, stadia, and festival malls, all in a reimagined downtown that stressed fun and festivity. The goal was to halt the devaluation of the downtown through its promotion as a place of fun, frivolity, shopping, and spectacle. The downtown was sold as a festival setting, as a meeting place and cultural center, all the things that distant suburban malls failed to provide. It was promoted as a cultural centrality in a splintering metropolis. But in order to secure this new writing of the downtown, public money had to underwrite private projects, and citizens had to be convinced that the benefits would ripple through the rest of the urban economy.

There were a few early examples that set the trend. Ghirardelli Square in San Francisco opened in 1964: it involved the conversion of a redbrick factory into an upmarket retail and festival setting. Faneuil Hall in Boston opened in 1976 as a renovation that provided modern retailing in a historic setting. A classic example, and one that has been widely copied and admired, is Baltimore's Inner Harbor. The city of Baltimore had grown up around the port that was founded in 1729. The relatively small ships of the time could sail right into the inner harbor to the heart of the city. By the early twentieth century the city was an industrial powerhouse. But after World War II Baltimore began its long industrial decline, as companies closed, relocated, or shed thousands of jobs. The deindustrialization of the city involved major job losses and a decline of economic vitality. Between 1970 and 1995 the region lost ninety thousand factory jobs. Most of the job losses took place in tidewater branch plants. The port was also losing its economic activity, as the bigger commercial ships could no longer navigate up the narrow harbor. By the 1950s much of the old port, right in the heart of the city, had become an abandoned space. The central city was devalued.

The business elite responded by setting up two committees in the early 1950s, the Committee for Downtown and the Greater Baltimore Committee, which in 1956 produced an urban-renewal plan for the city. In 1959 the Baltimore City Council approved the plan, thus creating a partnership between city government and the downtown business elite. This partnership took the form of the establishment of an entity, the Charles Center Management Office, that had the city's power to generate capital and assemble land while acting like a private corporation, immune from citizen or tax-payer oversight.

In 1964 the City Planning Council outlined a $260 million plan to rede-velop the 230 acres of warehouses, sheds, docks, and derelict spaces in the inner harbor. A proposed promenade along the waterfront created public access to the shoreline. A voter-approved loan of $12 million and a federal grant of $22 million gave the fiscal jump start to the plan's implementation. A cluster of developments built between 1977 and 1981 made the Inner Harbor a festival setting: the World Trade Center and Maryland Science Center were built with state and federal funding; the Convention Center funded with $35 million from state funds attracted business meetings; Harborplace, built by the Rouse Corporation, provided retail and restau-rants in two large pavilions; the National Aquarium was built with $21 million from the city council; and the Hyatt Hotel provided a downtown anchor after a $12 million public grant was made to Hyatt.

The Baltimore plan was unusual, a scheme that was radical in that it was outdoors, downtown, and pedestrian oriented rather than car friendly. Today it appears an obvious plan to make and implement, but at the time the emphasis of urban planning and renewal was on indoor malls and catering to the driver, not the pedestrian. The plan also recycled some buildings rather than simply demolishing everything. The old Baltimore Gas and Electric Company Power Plant, built in 1916, was retained and now houses a Borders bookstore, Hard Rock Café, and ESPN outlet.

Baltimore's Inner Harbor is a good example of public-private partner-ship. In effect, there was a public underwriting of the whole redevelop-ment. Although the Rouse Corporation, Hyatt Regency, and a host of smaller retail outlets invested money, their capital investment was secured by a massive injection of public funds. City, state, and federal funds were used to construct new buildings and refurbish old ones. The plan was suc-cessful. The National Aquarium regularly receives more than a million vis-itors each year. Harborplace has proved a popular destination for visitors and citizens alike for eating and shopping. Nothing succeeds like success. The Inner Harbor model has been used by other cities, such as Camden and Syracuse, eager to revalue their downtowns. "Inner Harborfication" is an awkward name that embodies a popular practice.

Take the case of Syracuse, New York, another industrial powerhouse in the early twentieth century. The city led the world in the manufacture of bicycles and typewriters, but by the mid-1970s the deindustrialization of the local economy meant job losses, a declining population, and a shrinking tax base. The proposed revival of the downtown involved a new downtown mall, a convention center, a science and technology museum, and the creation of "historic" retail and residential districts. The centerpiece of the strategy was the construction of a regional mall. The Carousel Center opened in October 1990 on a toxic dump beside Onondaga Lake. The mall is part of a broader strategy to construct a hotel, housing, retail, and entertainment district from the shores of the lake to an inner waterway. The company was given a holiday from property taxes for twenty-five years in a PILOT (payment in lieu of taxes) scheme. In effect, the developers paid for some of the infrastructural costs but were exempted from property taxes, another example of the public underwriting of private development. In 2001 a new $1.7 billion proposal was launched to turn the 1.4 million–square-foot mall into a 4.6 million–square-foot shopping and destination resort called Destiny USA. It draws its inspiration from the massive Mall of America as well as Baltimore's Inner Harbor. The expansion is predicated on private investment, public subsidies, and $30 million from the state for a tourism center. The developers were looking for full reimbursement of PILOT payments for ten years and partial reimbursements for another five years. The rosy predictions of the consultants suggest nine thousand jobs, $92 million in annual sales and hotel room taxes, and an annual multiplier effect of $4.6 billion. As of 2004 the grand plans were still just plans, as the grandiose scheme had yet to achieve financial traction.

The city of Syracuse is like many other cities with proposed and actual developments dependent upon massive public subsidies to private companies. Critics point to the public subsidization of private developments; supporters argue that there are no feasible alternatives. The cities could refuse to pay the subsidies and see the development go elsewhere and with it perhaps any chance of job growth and increased tax revenue. They could invest in education and housing and hope that investing in the local population will be enough to turn the city's fortunes around. These decisions are tough choices for city politicians and officials looking for ways to revive not only the downtown but also the economic fortune of the whole city. Although not every development can be an Inner Harbor, every city seems to want an Inner Harbor—not because it is a costless benefit, but because there appears to be no alternative.

Many city politicians have tied their reputations and fortunes to the revival of the downtown. A good example is Vincent A. Cianci Jr., known as "Buddy" in the city of Providence, Rhode Island, where he was mayor for more than twenty years. His tenure as mayor is synonymous with the subsequent revival of the downtown. When he first became mayor in 1975 the city seemed in terminal decline. Over the next twenty years he aggressively sought to lure investment back to the city. A new shopping mall replaced the old rail yards, and, developing the water theme of such cities as San Antonio, Texas, rerouted rivers now wend their way through the downtown, complete with gondolas. Investment and people were lured back downtown, and the city began to call itself the Renaissance City. Theater, restaurants, and the zoo attracted people from as far away as Boston. The mayor personified the revival and renewal and staked his power and prestige on accomplishing the transformation. Around the country political reputations were made and destroyed on the backs of downtown revival. In Buddy's case the method of the revival came under some scrutiny. In 2001 he was charged with running a corrupt city hall. As one of the prosecutors said at the time, "The so-called Renaissance City was a city for sale." In the summer of 2002 the mayor was found guilty of racketeering charges.

One of the most favored strategies in the second phase of downtown renewal, the postmodern festival phase, has been the pursuit of professional sports franchises. Sports teams, argue the proponents, generate visitors, cash, and tax revenue. They also create a psychic benefit to the city, especially if the team is winning, and give name recognition to the city. Sports are covered extensively in the national and even international media, and the city name is mentioned regularly during the respective seasons. But all of it comes at a price. Sports franchises are not obtained easily, and they do not come cheaply. In order to lure back the Raiders from Los Angeles, the City of Oakland provided $200 million in incentives. The city also built a ten thousand–seat addition to its stadium and new practice facilities and covered the team's moving costs. The team moved back in 1995. By the time the team played in the 2003 Super Bowl, the City of Oakland and Alameda County were spending $25 million a year just to pay the bonds used to renovate the stadium. In 2003 the owner, Al Davis, who had already moved the team from Oakland to Los Angeles in 1981 because of stalled negotiations over stadium-lease arrangements, was now claiming that he might take the team back to Los Angeles because of poor atten-dance at the Raiders' games. A lawsuit cost the city more than $10 million.

It has been estimated that since 1989 more than $20 billion has been spent on stadium construction, as cities large and small have sought to build downtown sports facilities. A combination of franchises wanting to move, especially into a new stadium with lucrative luxury boxes, and city governments desperate to revalue downtown has created a downtown boom. Sixteen new stadia were built in downtown locations in the period 1995 to 2002. Table 5.2 shows both the absolute and the relative subsidiza-tion of just six National Football League (NFL) franchises that opened new stadia in the 1990s and early 2000s.

Heinz Field in Pittsburgh is a typical example. Home to the Pittsburgh Steelers, it opened in 2002 at a cost of $231 million. The NFL franchise paid $100 million and is ensured a revenue stream from the 127 luxury boxes as well as the stadium and parking facilities. The stadium is owned by the city and Allegheny County, which put up most of the money for construction, financed by local bonds. The city and county pay for most of the costs, whereas most of the revenues go the sports franchise. A typical pattern.

And the name? A recent revenue stream has been the granting of nam-ing rights. H. J. Heinz and Company paid $57 million over twenty years for the right to name the stadium. PSINet paid the Baltimore Ravens $105 mil-lion to name their stadium, but since the company went bankrupt a new name was needed. It is now the M&T Bank Stadium. Invesco paid the Den-ver Broncos $60 million. Stadia, paid for by public funds, are "branded" by high-spending corporations eager for name recognition.

TABLE 5.2

Stadium costs

Team	Stadium total costs ($ million) (A)	Taxpayer subsidy ($ million) (B)	B as % of A
Denver Broncos	401	301	75
Cleveland Browns	300	221	73
Baltimore Ravens	240	206	85
Tennessee Titans	292	220	75
Houston Oilers	449	309	68
Pittsburgh Steelers	231	131	56

New sports stadia have been at the heart of many recent urban-renewal programs. Again Baltimore played a pivotal role. The opening of Oriole Park at Camden Yards in 1992 marked the entry of a baseball-only stadium into the forefront of urban-renewal schemes and dreams. The development was pushed in the mid-1980s by the mayor of the city, William Schaefer, who persuaded the State of Maryland to pay for the scheme from state lottery money. Construction began in June 1989 on an eighty-five-acre site only a few minutes' walk from the Inner Harbor and downtown Baltimore. The site was an old railway yard and some old established businesses that were bought out. The development cost approximately $106 million. Previously, most new post-1960 baseball stadia were on greenfield sites, under domes with artificial turf. Oriole Park was built as a retro baseball park: downtown, open air, brick face, natural turf, alluding to the images and sentiments of Fenway Park and Ebbets Field in a nostalgic reconstruction of an imagined baseball past. The architectural firm of Helmuth, Obata, and Kassabaum (HOK) kept a century-old warehouse as part of the new layout. It is a success. They did build it, and people did come. And again public monies were used to provide facilities for a private company.

A baseball stadium was an integral part of Cleveland's downtown renewal. Jacob's Field opened in 1994 as the new home of the Cleveland Indians. HOK was again employed to design a retro park. The park was partly paid for with public funds, a Cuyahoga County tax on alcohol and cigarettes approved in 1990 that generated $84 million of the total $165 million cost. Also included in downtown Cleveland's urban renewal was a Great Lakes Science Center, a football stadium, a shopping center, a three hundred–room Hyatt, and the Rock and Roll Hall of Fame that opened in 1995 at a cost of $92 million.

Baltimore's example was followed by other cities (table 5.3). In 2002 the State of Missouri and the City of St. Louis agreed to pay for a new stadium for the St. Louis Cardinals baseball team. The stadium, again designed by HOK, is estimated to cost $346 million. The city, state, and county will provide $208 million. The stadium is also a central piece in a much larger redevelopment project, to be named Ballpark Village, which will include 500 residential units, 400,000 square feet of offices, and 120,000 square feet of shops and restaurants.

TABLE 5.3

Major League Baseball stadia built, 1992–present

Stadium (year opened)	Team	Cost ($ million)	Public funds ($ million)	% public funds
Oriole Park (1992)	Baltimore Orioles	314	294	94
Jacobs Field (1994)	Cleveland Indians	221	221	100
Ameriquest Field (1994)	Texas Rangers	242	204	84
Coors Field (1995)	Colorado Rockies	264	207	78
Turner Field (1997)	Atlanta Braves	274	0	0
BankOne Ballpark (1998)	Arizona Diamondbacks	407	291	71
Safeco Field (1999)	Seattle Mariners	601	418	70
AT&T Park (2000)	San Francisco Giants	359	11	3
Minute Maid Park (2000)	Houston Astros	270	184	68
Comerica Park (2000)	Detroit Tigers	327	125	38
PNC Park (2001)	Pittsburgh Pirates	277	227	82
Miller Park (2001)	Milwaukee Brewers	414	324	78
Great American Ballpark (2003)	Cincinnati Reds	353	268	76
Citizen Bank Park (2004)	Philadelphia Phillies	460	228	50
Petco Park (2004)	San Diego Padres	474	301	64
Busch Stadium (2006)	St. Louis Cardinals	346	208	60
? (2008)	Washington Nationals	440	361	82

Note: See *Washington Post,* September 30, 2004, A13.

It is not only in large Rust Belt cities that the festival setting is being used to lure capital back to the downtown. Fresno, California, is spending $30 million over the next decade to lure businesses back. A centerpiece of the effort was the construction of a new stadium downtown for a Triple A baseball team, the Grizzlies. In 2004 it was announced that Washington, D.C., would be the new home of the Montreal Expos. They came at a high price. In order to lure the team, the city, not one of the richest in the country, agreed to build a $440 million stadium. The costs are to be paid for by issuing thirty-year city bonds. These bonds would then be repaid with a new tax on big business in the city; taxes from tickets, concessions, and merchandise sold at the stadium; and rent payments from the team. Estimates were made that the three sources would annually generate $21 million,

$12.2 million, and $5 million, respectively, thus theoretically covering the cost of the bond, estimated at an annual cost of $26 million. Against these very soft estimates a number of critics pointed out that most of the direct benefits would go to the team, conglomerates of rich businesspeople, who would get a free, brand-new, forty-one thousand–seat stadium, naming rights to the stadium, and most of the game-day revenue. And the hoped-for economic spin-off effects to the city? Most independent studies have shown that publicly funded municipal stadia have not had much more than a negligible effect on increasing employment and economic growth in cities. They do not revitalize neighborhoods or generate much economic growth. As one analyst noted, "Basically, you're taxing people who make $30,000 a year to generate a toy for people who make $200,000 and income for people who make millions of dollars a year."[3]

Throughout the country the public subsidization of professional sports franchises has become an important part of the attempted revaluation of the downtown. All independent studies show that sports stadia have no effect on growth of per-capita income, have little or negative effects on employment and overall economic activity, and even the jobs that are created tend to be low-paying, part-time, unskilled jobs. The vast salaries paid to the sports stars tend to leak out of the local economy, as the players are rarely full-time residents or taxpayers of the cities they play in. Sports stadia receive public subsidies without generating public benefits. Moreover, the spending on the stadium represents money that could have been spent on other items such as education. Although downtown developments such as sports stadia are justified as boons to the city as a whole, the economics rarely demonstrate that belief. Instead, most analysts see a net cost to the city and the taxpayers. As more cities compete, they have to offer more in the way of subsidies, direct payments, tax holidays, and write-offs. The benefits rarely match the expenditure of public funds. And for many cities the money used to leverage private money could have been used for building parks, schools, and a better life for ordinary citizens. But these arguments miss the point. The schemes were never intended to improve the lot of ordinary citizens; they were devices to revalue the downtown.

This second wave of urban renewal that began in the 1970s is marked by two elements. The first is the rebuilding of the downtown as a festival setting with the emphasis on retail and leisure, recreation, and entertainment. Sports stadia, restaurant districts, convention centers, themed retail outlets, and science and cultural museums are all important parts of the mix of new developments that transformed the downtown U.S. in the last quarter of the twentieth century. The second is the refurbishment of existing buildings. From Miami's South Beach to Pasadena's Old Town and San Diego's Gaslamp District, downtown renewal involves the transformation of already built environments, fueled in part by the architectural shift from modern to postmodern, which renewed appreciation for the old and the historic. Selected parts of the downtown U.S. were saved from the wrecker's ball and refurbished in a postmodern guise. In South Beach, close to Miami, the one-square-mile Art Deco District was a product of a wave of building in the 1930s and 1940s. From Fifth Street to Twenty-third Street and encompassing the three parallel roads of Ocean Drive, Collins Avenue, and Washington Avenue, hundreds of buildings were built in a speculative boom. Architects such as Henry Hohauser and L. Murray Dixon constructed streamlined buildings decorated with an aestheticized mixture of machine-stamped and exotic hieroglyphics. By the early 1970s, however, the area had deteriorated: the buildings were shabby, the neighborhood was run down, and the whole area was scheduled for demolition. Barbara Capitman and Leonard Horowitz helped to establish the Preservation League that successfully lobbied to get the district on the National Register of Historic Places. Saved from demolition, the area attracted enough new investment so that by the early 1990s most of the buildings in the district were repainted in beautiful cobalt blue, coral pink, and turquoise green that reflect the South Florida sun by day and shimmer at night in the glow of neon lighting. The historic feel of South Beach was part of its charm and contributed to its success in attracting further investment, as hotels were renovated, new hotels were built, a vigorous fashion industry was established, and tourists flocked to both sun on the beach and stroll the streets. Refurbishment had worked.

Part of the success of South Beach and similar examples of urban restoration was because of federal registration. The National Historic Preservation Act of 1966 allowed individual buildings designated as historic buildings to be registered and thus placed under federal protection. Owners were given investment tax credits to maintain their properties in a historically appropriate manner. The passage of the act embodies in legislation a shift in sensibilities away from the modernist belief in progress through destruction and toward a more postmodern sensitivity to the need to save rather than demolish historic buildings. By 2003 more than seventy-seven thousand buildings, sites, and districts had been listed. Although the register has been used to save individual buildings, it has been most significant as an urban-planning tool to save historic districts at a time when demolition was still considered the best way to renew the downtown. Pasadena's Old Town, for example, consisted of buildings constructed during the city's boom from the 1880s to the 1920s. By the 1960s the area had become dilapidated and run down, as retail and shopping had abandoned the location, suburbanizing to strip malls and greenfield sites. The area was due to be demolished, but the Board of City Directors managed to save it and get it listed on the National Register of Historic Places. One scheme in the early 1980s to create a retail center ran out of money, but in the 1990s seventy million dollars' worth of investment and extensive tax credits created the conditions for a genuine urban renewal, based on the recycling of the existing urban fabric. By the early 2000s Pasadena's Old Town had become an important destination for people in the greater Los Angeles region wishing to stroll the old streets and eat in new upmarket restaurants.

Around the country similar tales can be told—some larger than others, some more successful than others. But throughout the country there has been a shift from demolition to refurbishment, from destroying the past to celebrating the (fictitious?) past, as in the case of the Old City District of Charleston, South Carolina, and the French Quarter in New Orleans, and in some cases inventing traditions, as new old-style downtowns were self-consciously created to suggest a sense of history.

In the first wave of urban downtown redevelopment the emphasis was on clearance and rebuilding; in the second an increasing focus was on the preservation of the existing fabric. Historic buildings and the refurbished districts took their place in the second wave of urban renewal as icons and strategies to save and revive the downtown.

In many cities mixed-land-use development involving new building and refurbishment commingled the two waves of downtown revival. In Hollywood, California, a nine-acre, mixed-use development opened in 2001 at the junction of Hollywood Boulevard and Orange Avenue, including a twenty-two-story hotel, a television studio, a shopping center, and the new home of the annual Academy Awards ceremony. When the development opened in a run-down part of the city, *USA Today* reported that the scheme was "expected to launch a revival of the historic area."[4]

In many cities there has been a substantial makeover to the downtown involving new stadia and convention centers, large hotels, refurbished historic districts, and new recreational retail outlets. However, although all of it marks a revaluation of the downtown, it often has little direct connection to the quality of life of inner-city residents. The makeover often masks a continuing deterioration in the economic vitality of the old cities. Although the historic core of Baltimore has been upgraded, the city continues to lose good jobs, and the quality of life in the inner city refuses to improve substantially. William Neill has used the arresting image of "lipstick on the gorilla" to refer to the cosmetic changes that do little to change the brute reality. His comments refer specifically to Detroit but bear wider application. The second wave of urban renewal has saved the downtowns of many cities from further devaluation, but most inner-city residents have seen little direct benefit.[5]

The Third Wave: Business-Improvement Districts

In recent years a more targeted form of downtown renewal has emerged: business-improvement districts (BIDs). BIDs are a state rather than a federal initiative, authorized by state legislation. By the end of 2001 there were close to two thousand BIDs in forty-three states. New York City had almost fifty, while Los Angeles had close to twenty. They vary in detail by state, but in general they share a similar pattern: they are established through a petition process in a designated area and need approval of between 51 percent and 90 percent of local businesses. They are organized as public, nonprofit agencies funded through a mandatory levying of taxes on business in the area. In some states businesses get an investment tax credit. The revenues generated by the BIDs are spent on promotion, consumer marketing, and keeping the area "safe and clean," which involves paying for litter pickup, removal of graffiti, street cleaning, and private security.

Part of the redevelopment of Times Square in New York City was built around a BID. The Times Square BID, established in 1992, stretches north-south from West Fortieth to West Fifty-third Streets and east-west from both sides of Eighth Avenue to Ninth Avenue. Its mission was to make streets clean, safe, and friendly for property owners, tenants, and tourists. The BID was part of the city's more general goal to rid the Times Square area of its lurid image. Tax breaks were given to developers, and zoning was used to push out the sex industry. One hundred and twenty porn stores were targeted. The Times Square BID now contains approximately 399 property owners, 1,500 businesses, 27,000 residents, and 231,000 employees. The annual budget of six million dollars is spent on cleaning the streets, sidewalk lighting, and increased security. The exact role of the BID in the renewal process is difficult to tease out from the general upsurge in investment in the area throughout the 1990s, but it certainly played an important part in shaping business confidence.

BIDs are a worldwide phenomenon found in Australia, Canada, and South Africa. In the U.S. they are the latest in a long line of postwar attempts to revive the downtown. Rather than using the apparatus of the city to make improvements, as with previous strategies, BIDS are a public-private scheme that are largely self-financing and specifically targeted to business interests. They have grown, as local business interests recognize the perceived advantages of targeting dollars to their specific area. There are some who argue that there is a wider social payoff in that BIDs have been successful in broader social terms by reclaiming urban public space from indifference and decay, making streets safer, cleaner, and more accessible to the public. The case has been argued in ideological terms: on the one hand, they are seen as dangerous examples of increased privatization and corporatization of city life; on the other hand, they have been lauded as valiant private-sector attempts to solve problems made intractable by inefficient city governments. There are few studies that empirically address the important questions. Do BIDs make a difference, or would improvements have happened anyway? Have BIDs been successful in raising the quality of urban streets? Are they more efficient than city programs that are ostensibly under more democratic control? However, the debate is marked more by heat than light. One exception is the detailed study of the nine BIDs in Philadelphia by Lorlane Hoyt who showed that they spent two-thirds of their revenue on security and sanitation in order to make the streets safe and clean. The BIDs varied in size from 13 blocks to more than 250 blocks. Hoyt's study turned up some interesting results. Business interests did not predominate in the creation of BIDs; civic association, not-for-profit institutions, and elected officials also played important roles. The BIDs were successful in reducing the crime in their areas. Crime clusters were larger in non-BID commercial spaces even when factoring in contextual differences. In effect, the BIDs were successful in creating cleaner and safer streets.[6]

From urban renewal to business-improvement districts, the history of the downtown U.S. since 1950 has been the search for the solution to long-term decline. The programs have been tailored to meet the perceived needs of local downtown business and property interests. Whereas urban renewal largely failed, more recent examples of refurbishment have been much more successful. In some cases there have been positive benefits for the wider community, but when they have occurred, they are side effects, not the primary goals.

6

Creating a Suburban Society

"A Landscape of Scary Places"

THE UNITED STATES is one of the most suburban societies in the world. At the beginning of the twentieth century only one in twenty Americans lived in suburbs; by the end of the century it was almost one in two. There was nothing inevitable about this process. It was engineered by public policies, underwritten by the federal government, reinforced by market forces, and fostered by powerful interests.

It is not just that a lot of people live in the suburbs; it is that a suburban character has overtaken the nation. Suburbs have shifted from being appendages to cities to being the center of metropolitan gravity. Suburbanization is now one of the most important defining elements of the national character.

Early Suburbs

Suburban growth in the United States, as elsewhere, has a long history. In New York City of the 1770s the Village of Greenwich was two marshy miles from Wall Street. It was a typical suburb of its time, located away from the city in the then countryside. The early suburbs were the domains of the poor rather then the enclaves of the rich. The suburbs of the "walking city" were inconveniently located and were the home of the poor and the marginalized. The rich and wealthy wanted to live close to the center of things.

Early suburbanization was limited and shaped by transportation technology. When walking was the dominant form of personal movement, suburban expansion was limited. Subsequent transportation improvements widened the scope of suburbanization. In the nineteenth century a range of transportation innovations, including the steam ferry, the railroad, the horsecar, and the electric streetcar extended the ability of people to live in one place and work in another. Transportation improvements made commuting possible. Brooklyn on Long Island was one of the first commuter suburbs. Regular steam ferries that allowed people who worked in Manhattan to live across the East River began in 1814. The pace of subsequent growth was tremendous. Brooklyn had a population of only 4,402 in 1810, but by 1850 the population had grown to 96,838. By the end of the nineteenth century Brooklyn was the sixth-largest city in the entire country.

If ferries allowed commuting over water, the railroads extended the commuting range across the land. Railroads were initially designed for long-distance travel, but they also stimulated suburban developments, especially the upper-income suburbs. The New York and New Haven Railroad that ran along Long Island began the tradition of rail commuters from Long Island into the city that continues to this day.

The horse-drawn streetcar was another stimulant to suburban development. First introduced in New York City in 1853, by 1860 it carried 7 million passengers. In Boston, Chicago, and Philadelphia streetcars connected with railroads to provide an integrated urban transportation system. By the 1880s streetcars were carrying 188 million passengers in three hundred cities.

Cable cars also extended the walking city. Companies operated in Chicago, New York, Oakland, and Philadelphia. By their peak in 1890 there were almost three hundred miles of track in twenty-three cities carrying 373 million passengers. Cable cars were expensive to build and operate, especially over flat surfaces. They lasted longer in cities with a steep topography; in San Francisco they survive today, part urban transportation systems, part tourist experience.

The electric streetcar extended the range of commuting. It was cheaper to build than the cable car and more efficient than either the cable or the horse-drawn streetcar. Early experiments in the 1880s in Menlo Park, Cleveland, Montgomery, and New York showed that it was a paying proposition. It involved less initial capital investment, and, traveling at speeds up to twenty miles an hour, it reduced the average cost per passenger mile. By around 1900 there were thirty thousand miles of streetcar lines in large and small cities around the nation.

Often, the new houses in the early suburbs were laid out in the grid of the unimaginative surveyor. In other cases the cult of the winding lane dominated over the straight line. Garden suburbs reinforced the sense of domesticated wilderness by maximizing lot size and the amount of greenery. Frederick Law Olmsted built garden suburbs as well as their larger version, Central Park. Suburban houses came in a variety of sizes and covered the spectrum, from the exclusive suburbs like Westchester and Scarsdale that housed some of New York's wealthiest residents, including the forty-five hundred–acre estate of John D. Rockefeller at Pocantico Hills, west of Tarrytown, to more modest houses on much smaller lots.

Stimulating Postwar Suburbanization

Although there had been suburbanization before World War II, it was limited in size and scale. Suburbs were essentially appendages to a central city. The early suburbs were often new housing developments within the city boundaries. After World War II suburbanization extended beyond traditional municipal boundaries, creating new metropolitan forms.

Suburban growth grew dramatically after 1945 because the federal government successfully stimulated it. The federal government fostered suburban growth through promoting suburban home ownership and highway construction. It began in the New Deal with a Roosevelt administration eager to stimulate employment at a time of mass unemployment. The Federal Housing Administration was established in 1934. It insured mortgages. Home loans thus became safe investments, the risk underwritten by the financial weight and authority of the federal government. Bankers were now willing to lend money to house buyers who in turn purchased homes that required workers to build them. Government involvement helped to reduce interest payments, lessen down payments, and lengthen the repayment period. Prior to the FHA, buyers often needed to put down 50 percent of the loan and pay the loan in five years. Home ownership was thus previously restricted to the affluent who could meet these stringent requirements. A typical FHA loan, in contrast, required just 10 percent down with thirty years to pay. These requirements soon became standard industry practice.

The FHA program had dramatic effects in both the short and the long term. It immediately stimulated the production of housing. Housing starts, which were only 332,000 in 1937, almost doubled to 619,000 by 1941. In the years between 1944 and 1965 between one-quarter and one-third of all mortgages were either FHA or the similar Veterans Administration mortgage program. The VA program was part of the 1944 G.I. Bill, crafted to provide educational and housing opportunities for service families. By 1972 the FHA and VA programs had helped eleven million families buy houses, revolutionized the home-loan industry, and made home ownership more accessible to a wider range of the population. The FHA and VA programs were major factors in the creation of the burgeoning middle class of home owners.

The programs stimulated suburbanization because they had strict lending guidelines that favored the building of single-family homes in suburban areas. The most favorable loans were made available only to new construction. Loans for improvement to existing dwellings were smaller and of a shorter duration. This bias worked against older, inner-city areas. The programs were also racially biased, especially from 1934 to 1965. Between 1945 and 1959, for example, less than 2 percent of all FHA and VA mortgages went to African Americans. The FHA and VA made few loans to minority neighborhoods. Loan guarantees were based on appraisals, and they were explicitly biased toward all-white, single-family neighborhoods and against minority neighborhoods in central cities. Almost 90 percent of loans went to the suburbs. While the FHA made suburbs less the preserve of the affluent and extended the suburban experience to middle- and lower-income households, it supported the white flight to the suburbs and the racial segregation of suburbia. The racial divide between the central city and suburbia is in part the direct result of decades of government lending patterns.

The archetypal postwar suburb was Levittown. The name comes from two brothers, William and Alfred Levitt. They had long been house builders. They first built houses in 1929, and like most home builders of the time they concentrated on small-scale developments for affluent buyers. In 1941 they received a government contract to build more than two thousand houses for workers in Norfolk, Virginia. There they learned the techniques of rapid mass production that they would use to great effect in the immediate post–World War II era.

The two brothers purchased four thousand acres of potato farms, twenty-five miles east of Manhattan on Long Island, and began building homes in July 1947. They standardized house building to a set of assembly procedures. A concrete slab was laid, and in twenty-seven distinct steps the house was built out of composition-rock board and plywood. The Levitts turned house building from a craft industry into a mass-assembly production. With preassembled materials and mass-assembly procedures, they built up to thirty homes in a single day. The result was relatively cheap housing, built to basic standard designs; a typical house sold for $7,990. For many middle-income Americans with FHA or VA mortgages, it was cheaper to buy than to rent. Eventually, 17,400 houses were built in Levittown, and the new suburb became home to 82,000 people. Not all the people. There were racial covenants. Sales contracts barred resale to blacks, and the suburb remained all white until the 1960s.

Other Levittowns were built in Pennsylvania and New Jersey, and many other builders soon adopted the Levitt construction techniques. There was a ready market for the mass-produced houses because of the FHA and VA mortgage programs.

There were other government stimulants to suburbanization. Federal tax rules favored owner-occupation. Mortgage-interest payments were and continue to be tax deductible. By the mid-1960s home-ownership deductions were around $7 billion and by 1984 amounted to $53 billion. Low-income renters receive no parallel tax break. Tax expenditures are skewed toward owner-occupiers. Under a 1951 federal tax law people did not have to pay capital gains on any profits on their home if the money was used to buy another house. This law was a fiscal incentive to the upward spiral in average home size and cost.

Tax breaks did not just aid in the building of houses in the suburbs. Tax breaks also stimulated the construction of nonresidential uses in suburban areas. In 1954 Congress enacted a change in tax law that enabled developers to use the construction of new properties as a tax shelter. Under a complex arrangement the depreciation costs of a commercial structure could be written off in the first years of its life. In other words, developers could build a commercial property and use its depreciation cost to reduce the tax burden. By the mid-1960s this tax break was costing the treasury $700 million per year, as shopping centers, offices, and motels quickly mushroomed on greenfield sites. Accelerated depreciation favored suburbia, as write-offs were greater for new construction than for renovation. The law did not allow depreciation of land on urban sites. These tax breaks also stimulated apartment-dwelling construction. Multifamily homes were only around 6 percent of total housing starts prior to the tax change. By the mid-1960s almost 50 percent were apartments. Some were in the central city, but many were in the suburbs. The tax-law changes thus stimulated nonresidential and apartment construction in the suburbs. By the late 1950s and early 1960s suburbs were becoming more self-contained, with a mix of housing types as well as shopping and commercial facilities. By the 1970s suburbs were important entities in their own right as places of commerce as well as residence.

Postwar suburbia was created around the use of the automobile. Since the end of World War II, there has been a decline in the usage of public transportation and a growing use of the automobile. This change was less a shift in consumer demand and more a conscious manipulation. Car companies such as General Motors bought out streetcar companies and ripped up the tracks. Subsequent large-scale private-auto use in the city was predicated on the construction of highways. In 1944 Congress earmarked 25 percent of all federal highway funds for road construction in urban areas. Half the cost of urban highways was to be paid by the federal government because building new roads in urban areas was expensive and difficult. Land-assembly and construction costs were huge. Few cities attempted urban motorways; New York City was an exception. Under the unelected, but enormously powerful influence of, Robert Moses, motorways sliced through urban neighborhoods. But the big prompt came with the Federal-Aid Highway Act of 1956 when the federal government agreed to pay 90 percent of the costs of interstate highway construction. This federal largesse enabled highways to be blasted through central cities and strung out to distant suburbs and greenfield sites. The federal highway system allowed the wide dispersal of low-density suburbia across the landscape.[1] Massive federal highway spending opened up rural land and kept residential land prices relatively low.

There were other important infrastructural subsidies. In 1956 Congress passed legislation that gave grants for up to 55 percent of the cost of sewer-treatment facilities. This legislation aided all municipalities but particularly helped suburban communities to extend sewage lines deeper into the countryside. In 1972 the federal aid was increased to 75 percent of the cost with an annual appropriation of $6 billion per year. Adequate sewage, like roads and housing, was essential to large-scale suburban development.

By the 1960s there was a growing awareness that the stimulation of the suburbs was leading to the decline of the central cities. Initially, the FHA worked against the minority and inner-city housing market and supported the racial segregation of suburbia. The policy changed only in 1966 by making more loans available to people in inner-city neighborhoods, but in the short term it helped only lower-income white flight to the suburbs. More recently, the FHA has directed funds to the inner city. In 1976 tax breaks were offered for historic preservation that gave sites on the National Register of Historic Places the same treatment as new suburban developments. And in 1977 the Community Reinvestment Act made lending institutions release information on the location of their lending practices to identify discrimination. So even though federal policy was more sensitive to its suburban bias, was it too little, too late? A report by the Brookings Institution on federal spending in metropolitan Chicago showed that although the central cities and older suburbs gain from transfer programs such as food stamps and earned income-tax credits, federal programs that encourage wealth building, such as highways and income-tax subsidies for housing, are concentrated in the newer suburbs. Federal policies continue to lubricate dispersed suburbanization.[2]

It would be wrong to simply blame the federal government. In the early postwar years federal policies played a major role, but so did local municipalities. Given the municipal balkanization of the U.S. metropolis, a topic we will discuss more fully in the next chapter, each separate municipality needed to maximize its tax base. Municipalities compete for tax-revenue-generating developments such as housing, offices, factories, and retail establishments. Rather than metropolitan-wide planning that may have ensured an orderly context for growth, there was a municipal scramble for development; it was zero-sum game, as one municipality's gain was perceived as another's loss. Municipalities were eager, and in some cases desperate, to attract development projects. The consequence was a wide suburban spread of developments.

Federal subsidies for roads, owner-occupation, and greenfield commercial developments plus municipal encouragement for new developments all made the suburbs an attractive place for the private market. House builders and real estate developers all found greater encouragement and resultant profit in the suburbs. Private investment shifted toward suburban districts. Since 1950 the U.S. economy cranked up phenomenal rates of growth, and much of it was in the suburbs. As more growth occurred, more growth was attracted. New housing attracted new commercial developments, such as out-of-town shopping centers that in turn attracted more suburban development. There was an upward cycle of suburban growth. Meanwhile, in another part of the metropolitan universe, the central areas of many cities were becoming the black holes of contemporary capitalism, underfunded and underinvested.

Suburban Sprawl

Lax planning controls, generous federal funding of low-density housing and highways, cheap gasoline, and an almost total lack of an urbane imagination have resulted in the sprawling suburbia that surrounds most U.S. cities. Urban growth in the second half of the twentieth century in the U.S. embraces the suburban strip, the highway system, and the automobile. Linear rather than nucleated developments are the rule, and the emphasis is on mobility and movement rather than stability and community. Although some have wanted to learn from the strip, it is wasteful of space, gasoline, and any sense of civic identity.[3]

The continued use of automobiles extends commuting ranges and a sprawling suburbia of low density. The older forms of transportation, the ferries and trains, tended to disperse population along corridors. The auto, in contrast, allows a wider, more thinly spread sprawl at densities too low to support public transportation schemes.

A defense of suburbia is possible. Safe and affordable homes, high levels of mobility, and relative accessibility to a broad range of goods and services are widely available. But there are costs that include extensive appropriation of rural land and greenfield sites, constant traveling, and a disconnection between residents of the central city and the suburb.

The twentieth-century history of urban planning, such as the Garden City Movement and the Radburn Plan, is full of attempts to reorganize the city along principles of rational efficiency, good design, and encouragement of community. The latest in a long line of urban-design movements is New Urbanism. It is a response to suburban sprawl that emphasizes revitalizing old urban centers; creating mixed-use centers where residences are located close to commercial and office sectors; planning for walkable, high-density, low-rise residential areas that are socially diverse communities; minimizing the speed of autos through urban areas; and making cities more attractive to walking and casual social interaction.[4] There is not anything particularly "New" about these ideas—the century-old Garden City Movement promotes most of these ideals—but for those individuals lacking historical perspective, it sounds unique.

One example of New Urbanism is Seaside, Florida, designed by Andres Duany and Elizabeth Plater-Zyberk, where neotraditional houses conform to a strict code, the houses are at a high density, car traffic is kept to the edges, and the walkways and porches are constructed in order to aid in community interaction. Duany in particular has become a high-profile advocate of New Urbanism. Seaside was the community shown in the movie *The Truman Show.*

Perhaps the most cited example is Celebration, a community initially planned and funded by the Disney Corporation. Walt Disney originally had a plan for an experimental prototype community of tomorrow. However, EPCOT became a theme park rather than a community. Celebration opened in 1996 just outside Orlando, Florida. With its Charles Moore civic center and Ceser Pelli cinema, the place has attracted big-name architects and a lot of attention.[5] There are now almost as many books and articles about Celebration as residents (just over two thousand lived there in 2000, with a planned population of twenty thousand). Celebration has all the design elements of New Urbanism: low-rise, high-density residential areas where garages are at the back of the residences; walkways and porches allow pedestrian movement; and a mixed-use downtown presides. It is also emblematic for the exclusivity that characterizes New Urbanism. The lowest rents are eight hundred dollars per month, and most of the population is upper-income. Although New Urbanism proclaims social heterogeneity, in practice it tends to be restricted to the middle- and upper-income groups.

Underlying New Urbanism is a cozy, nostalgic sense of community and neighborliness, a longing for a lost community. The older high-density cities of the half-remembered, half-created past are often portrayed as places of tight community, whereas more recent suburban growth is seen as a cause of the decline of community. *New Urbanism* is a catchall term that in principle captures the discontent with contemporary developments, especially the nature of low-density sprawl and the alienation felt by many residents. In practice, it means developments that are high-density, pedestrian friendly, and socially exclusive.

New Urbanism is not all that new and is not all that urban. On closer inspection it looks like the latest version of upmarket suburban communities. New Urbanism does little to discourage suburban sprawl since it still produces densities too low to support truly mixed communities, creating instead homogeneous enclaves. It is repackaged urban sprawl, a useful marketing strategy, playing an important role in stimulating debate, but with little practical effect on creating community.[6]

Few would argue the need for some kind of alternative to the standard forms of suburban sprawl. It is wasteful of resources, lacks aesthetic appeal, and produces a series of edges rather than centers. New Urbanism is, at the very least, proposing alternatives to a city dominated by the auto, the highway, and the parking lot. New Urbanism as a design guide is a step in the right direction. However, the claims made for New Urbanism as a source for "recovery of community" are based on a series of assumptions (the community is declining or an urban form can resuscitate this community) that are asserted rather than demonstrated. New Urbanism is a source of interesting design ideas, but as a method of re-creating community, the verdict is still out.

Suburban sprawl has increased as housing densities have fallen and average lot sizes have increased. In many cities in the U.S., the suburban frontier consists of McMansions on large lots. Metropolitan areas extend their reach farther out into the countryside and small towns, and the metropolitan sphere of influence deepens its shadow across the landscape. Farmland turns into tract housing, woods into subdivisions, and the prairie into gated communities. One response is the Smart Growth initiative emerging from urban planners and municipalities. It is very similar to New Urbanism: it stresses mixed land uses, compact building designs that create high density, and low environmental impact. Smart Growth has emerged as a strategy to deal with the constant pull of development toward greenfield sites on the city's edge; it focuses on existing developments in order to utilize their infrastructures and to preserve open space and farmland. Smart Growth is a mantra for municipalities facing heavy development pressure and looking for principles and policies to halt the abandonment of the urban infrastructure and the costly rebuilding on greenfield sites.

In 1996 the Smart Growth Network enunciated a number of principles: mix land uses; design more compact building design; construct walkable communities; create a sense of place; preserve open space; direct development toward existing communities; provide a variety of transportation choices; make fair, predictable, and cost-effective decisions; and encourage community involvement in development decisions. The Federal Environmental Protection Agency recommends Smart Growth policy. It is still too early to say whether it will become an effective policy to halt the seemingly relentless expansion of the suburban fringe into open spaces.

New Urbanism and Smart Growth are responses to suburban sprawl that emphasize revitalizing old urban centers and creating mixed-use centers where residences are located close to commercial and office sectors. The sprawling suburbs, endless strips, and burgeoning malls represent the matter of suburbanization; Smart Growth and New Urbanism are the blueprints of the antimatter of suburbanization.

Edge Cities

As the suburban border continually expands, central cities see a marked reduction in the population, economic activity, and political influence. The suburban rings are no longer appendages to the central city. The term *edge city* refers to this change in metropolitan dynamics. Joel Garreau uses the term to refer to centers with more than five million square feet of office space, six hundred thousand square feet of retail space, and more jobs than bedrooms situated on a greenfield site. He claims to identify 120 edge cities around the country. It is interesting to note that most of the edge cities he identifies are at the junction of interstate highways, reinforcing the point that there has been a federal underwriting of suburban expansion and edge-city developments.[7]

The continued suburbanization of people, jobs, and political power reverses the traditional central city–peripheral suburban relationship. Office parks on motorway junctions, out-of-town shopping centers, and distant subdivisions of rural land are reshaping the traditional metropolis. And as more people spend most of their lives in the suburbs, the idea of a traditional metropolitan center is less tenable. As more of the economic activity takes place in the suburbs, the metropolis is more a place of edge connections than central city–suburban relations. The central city retains the name, attracting people for events and spectacles, but the beating heart of the metropolis is in the suburbs. The edge city has replaced the central city as the pivot of the metropolitan economy.

The scale of suburbanization now makes it difficult for us to consider suburbs as a single category. There are now a range of suburban types: the old streetcar suburbs, the FHA- or VA-financed houses of the immediate postwar suburbs, the speculative developments of the 1970s, and the very dispersed and recently constructed monster homes strung out along rural roads. Suburbs vary in size and population from the modest to the exclusively rich and from the racially homogeneous to the ethnically diverse. Suburbs are now less homogeneous and more varied, and, as the center of metropolitan gravity moves farther out, even the inner suburbs experience population and job loss.

Suburbanization as the Motor of the Economy

Suburbanization is more than just the physical extension of the city. Suburban expansion is a key element in the growth of the U.S. economy because it is intimately bound up with road construction, car ownership, and conspicuous consumption. People in suburbs tend to live in single-family dwellings; buy a range of goods including cars, furniture, refrigerators, and washing machines; and either purchase garden equipment or hire someone to do the gardening. They need at least one car and invariably more. Suburbanization is intimately involved in key economic sectors of construction, manufacturing, and retailing. Suburbanization, with its attendant patterns of spending, borrowing, and consumption, is now a major element in economic growth and prosperity. Initially stimulated by federal and local governments, it has a life of its own. The numbers of houses built and cars purchased are vital statistics, signs of consumer willingness to buy durable goods that are taken as a bellwether of economic trends. Suburbs and suburbanization are deeply embedded in the economic fabric of society. Economic growth is, in turn, dependent on continued patterns and levels of suburbanization. Economic levers that affect suburbanization, such as bank interest rates that influence the purchase of big-ticket items like houses, cars, and expensive consumer durables, are used by the federal government to either promote or deflate growth. The impressive rates of economic growth in the postwar U.S. are related directly to the patterns and levels of suburbanization with their attendant patterns of high mass consumption. Suburbs and economic growth have gone hand in hand in the U.S.

The Suburbs and Cultural Criticism

The suburbs play a role in the cultural discourse of the nation. They are blamed for a variety of social ills. Although the criticism has varied over the years, the intellectual's distaste for the suburbs remains a constant. Intellectual critiques of the suburbs in the 1950s and 1960s focused on the idea that they are sites of conformity. Lewis Mumford sees the suburbs of Levittown as an ocean of conformity,

> a multitude of uniform, unidentifiable houses, lined up in inflexibly, at uniform distances, on uniform roads, in treeless communal waste, inhabited by people of the same class, the same income, the same age group, witnessing the same television performances, eating the same tasteless pre-fabricated foods, from the same freezers, conforming in every outward and inward respect to a common mold, manufactured in the central metropolis. Thus the ultimate effect of suburban escape in our time is, ironically, a low-grade environment from which escape is impossible.[8]

Suburban conformity was further detailed in William H. Whyte's 1956 book *The Organization Man* that described the corporate conformity of the postwar U.S. For many intellectuals of the 1950s and 1960s conformity and the new suburbs went hand in hand as, in order to live in suburbia, people had to inhibit individualism in the quest for normalcy.

Later criticisms take a completely different tack, arguing that suburbs are places where rampant individuality replaces social cohesion. These suburbs cause the decline of community. In Vance Packard's 1972 book *A Nation of Strangers*, suburban sprawl is to blame for the decline of community, although the exact causal mechanisms are never fully outlined.

Suburban sprawl has been blamed for a loss of community. James Howard Kunstler is the latest in a long line of critics who use the contemporary suburban landscape to marshal a critique of U.S. society. For Kunstler, the landscape of strip developments, shopping malls, dead city centers, and congested suburbs embodies the overwhelming power of the profit motive and the lack of aesthetic sensitivity. Urban form is a text that tells a story of environmental degradation, social fracturing, and loss of community. He writes:

> Born in 1948, I have lived my entire life in America's high imperial moment. During this epoch of stupendous wealth and power, we have managed to ruin our greatest cities, throw away our small towns, and impose over the countryside a joyless junk habitat of which we can no longer support. Indulging in a fetish of commercialized individualism, we did away with our public realm, and with nothing left but our private life in our private homes and private car, we wonder what happened to the spirit of community. We created a landscape of scary places and became a nation of scary people.[9]

Robert Putnam has called attention to civic disengagement. He documents the process of disengagement from 1970 to 2001, as formal membership in civic organizations declined 10–20 percent. People are now less likely to join coworkers in formal organizations, and even such informal social connections as eating with friends declined. Although there were some countertrends such as the rise in youth volunteering, grassroots activity among evangelical conservatives, and the growth of self-help groups and cyber communities on the Internet, the process seems one of inexorable civic disengagement. The reasons given in a rough guesstimate include: pressures of time and money (10 percent), suburbanization and sprawl (10 percent), television (25 percent), and what he calls a "generational shift" (50 percent). The pre–baby boomers were a civic generation, joiners and community builders. The baby boomers, in contrast, are more individual than group oriented. Suburban sprawl is an important cause of civic unraveling.[10]

The notion of suburbia as detrimental to community is a popular but precarious position to hold. The connection between low-density suburbia and the lack of community is not exactly clear. Though Putnam has done a wonderful job in documenting civic disengagement, he is much less successful in explaining it. His explanations are more suggestive, vague headings than causal connections. Suburban communities, for example, have also spawned a rich mix of civic associations and neighborhood groups. Although they are of the horizontal kind and refer to the local community rather than the wider metropolis, they are still an active form of civic engagement. The suburban landscape does shape the context for social interaction. People spend more time in their cars driving from disconnected nodes of shopping, school, and work, which means we have less time with each other for leisurely, casual interaction, but the supposed causal chain that links suburban sprawl to loss of community and civic disengagement has not been convincingly demonstrated. The argument is more of a vague hypothesis lacking empirical evidence than a fully argued case. Much more serious work needs to be done.

The former sites of conformity are now settings for rampant individualism: the same suburbs but now wildly differing interpretations. What is going on? The causal connection between the suburbs and social ills is never demonstrated, merely asserted, allowing so much leeway that contradictory views of the suburbs can be held. *Suburbs* is a general term referring to middle-class life and its attendant woes that in the 1950s were criticized for leading to social conformity, whereas in the 1990s they were described as settings for rampant individualism. *Suburbs* is a free-floating signifier of a variety of ills, a deep container of social malaise, anomie, and civic disengagement. From 1950 to 2000 there was a huge expansion in the absolute and relative number of suburbanites and the spaces they inhabited—not only the physical space but also the space they occupied in the national discourse. As the U.S. became a nation of suburbs and more American lives were lived in single-family homes where journeys to work and play were made in automobiles, the term *suburbs* is used as a shorthand for general critiques of mainstream U.S. society.

The Suburbanization of Politics

Suburbs and suburbanization play an important role in the shifting political attitudes in the U.S. To take just one example, congressional representatives from predominantly suburban districts are more likely to be Republican, and more right-wing Republican at that. The suburbs, especially the faster-growing, more affluent ones, tend to be more right wing. The new suburbs are the incubators of the rise of the Republican Right. The extensive suburbanization of U.S. society in the context of metropolitan fragmentation cordons off different social and racial groups into different administrative spaces. Though the suburban U.S. in general is more heterogeneous, individual suburbs are still very segregated by race and income. The segregated nature of suburbs reinforces the political attitudes of small government regarding limitations on redistributional policies. Suburban residents tend to be more supportive of the Republican Party and Republican candidates and less supportive of government spending than city residents. This trend is changed only with racial differences. If the suburb has more African Americans than average, there is a proportional decline in Republican support.[11]

It is not simply that suburbs are causing this political shift. Those individuals with certain political attitudes have a tendency to move to the suburbs. But neither are the suburbs neutral containers of movers with specific political attitudes. Political attitudes are shaped by our friends and neighbors, the complex tissue of relationships that maintain political attitudes and local political cultures. Metropolitan fragmentation compartmentalizes distinct groups, thus allowing the easier maintenance of local political discourses that stress local autonomy, restricted federal government, and a more limited role for redistributional policies.

Suburbs are more Republican in the double sense that more registered Republicans live there and that the suburban experience of a fragmented metropolis creates the preconditions for a Republican ideology with a range of political opinions, including spending tax dollars locally in the community rather than in transferring them to other communities. The appeal of small government is that it localizes government.

As both political parties appeal to the suburban voter it has become a platitude that big government is bad and small government is good. Suburban municipalities want to keep their tax dollars and spend them locally and not have them taken away to spend on (undeserving) central-city residents. The suburbs are the setting for the growing rhetoric of small government, the decline of support for welfare spending, and a growing distrust of socially progressive redistributional policies. The suburbs are the setting *and* the crucible for the rise of a particular faction of the Republican Right. As both parties now appeal to the suburban majority, national political debates are foreshadowing the needs and attitudes of the suburbs, often at the expense of the central cities.

In 2005 a study by the *Congressional Quarterly* showed that of the 435 congressional districts, 220, or just over 50 percent, had a majority of residents in suburbs. Population shifts and congressional redistricting have created a suburban majority. Control of the House is now impossible without ensuring the political support of suburbanites. Appealing to suburban voters is now the surest route to political success and political power.[12]

7

New Suburban Realities

"Trouble in Paradise"

A CURRENT, PERSISTENT, AND POPULAR representation of the metropolitan U.S. is a declining urban core and growing homogenous suburbs. The existence of working-class suburbs and more recently of "suburbs as slums" has been recognized and documented as well as the more general articulation of the notion of suburban ills as "trouble in paradise." However, the simple dichotomous model persists in many academic studies and newspaper articles. I will term it the traditional metropolitan model of central cities contrasted with essentially homogenous suburbs. It is still the dominant structure for interpreting and collecting data at the metropolitan scale and has a continuing hold over scholarly and popular thinking.[1]

The conventional method of organizing data reinforces the stereotypes. The U.S. Census continues to provide data in terms of central cities and suburban counties. This coarse-grained mesh bolsters the simple dichotomies and does not allow for a more nuanced analysis of the metropolitan variation.

The Analysis

In order to show that American suburbs are not monolithic and homogenous entities, I will use more finely grained, place-level data to examine the suburban areas of selected metropolitan areas. The census defines a metropolitan statistical area as an area comprising a core city that contains a minimum population of fifty thousand and "adjacent communities" that have social and economic integration with that nucleus. Our analysis is of those "adjacent communities" that are defined by the census as "places."

According to the census, there are three types of places: census-designated places (CDPs), consolidated places, and incorporated places. CDPs are concentrations of population, housing, and commercial sites with a degree of local identity. A consolidated place is a unit of local government for which the functions of an incorporated place and its county or minor civil division unit have merged. An incorporated place is established to provide governmental functions for a concentration of people as opposed to a minor civil division unit, which is generally created to provide services or administer an area without regard to population. I have combined these three designations to identify suburban places. This consolidation provides a finer-grained analysis of suburban communities than the traditional city-county divide. The even finer-grained mesh of census tracts is troublesome for our purposes since tracts have to be aggregated to identify suburban communities: they often change from one census to the next, and they often cross political boundaries between the central city and the suburban ring. It distorts the data needed to specifically capture population and employment dynamics unique to suburban entities.

The boundaries for suburban places, as census tracts, can change from one census to the next. However, such boundary changes occur only for incorporated places where there has been municipal annexation, detachment, or mergers of two or more places. I believe that such minor boundary changes that have occurred in my sample of suburban places since 1980 do not invalidate my comparative analysis.

The primary data source is HUD's *State of the Cities Data System, 1970–2000*. I have identified 13 metropolitan areas for this study. All such selections can be criticized. The aim is to provide a representative sample rather than undertake the enormous task of looking at all metro areas in the country. The sample is relatively small to make data analysis manageable but large enough to capture the major sources of metro variation in the country. These areas provide a representative sample of the major socioeconomic trends across the nation. They can be classified by regional growth and decline patterns based on the transition to a service-based economy.

First, I have included Baltimore and Philadelphia to capture the experience of older Rust Belt cities along the northeastern corridor. Second, midwestern cities such as Cleveland, Cincinnati, and St. Louis are included because they have experienced manufacturing decline and share similar economic functions. Third, I include Atlanta and Phoenix since they are both sprawling Sun Belt cities that have witnessed high population growth during the past two decades. Fourth, San Francisco, Oakland, and San Jose represent the West Coast. Last, Boston, Chicago, and Washington, D.C., are large regions with highly specialized service economies that contain substantial interdependence between their suburbs and central cities. Table 7.1 lists the metropolitan regions and the respective number of places I have identified in their suburban areas. In total, 13 metropolitan areas were examined containing 1,652 places (13 central cities and 1,639 suburbs). I identify four key variables to explore the socioeconomic mosaic of suburban areas: income, employment, race, and immigration.

TABLE 7.1

Suburban places of selected metropolitan areas

Metropolitan area	Number of suburbs
Atlanta MSA	126
Baltimore PMSA	91
Boston PMSA	128
Chicago PMSA	299
Cincinnati PMSA	133
Cleveland PMSA	117
Oakland PMSA	44
Philadelphia PMSA	188
Phoenix MSA	36
San Francisco PMSA	40
San Jose PMSA	18
St. Louis PMSA	223
Washington, D.C. PMSA	196

Notes: MSA = Metropolitan Statistical Area; PMSA = Primary Metropolitan Statistical Area. The number of suburbs is based on places that existed in 1980.

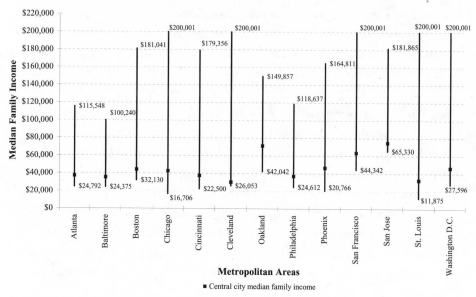

7.1. Income variation in selected metropolitan areas, 2000.

Rich and Poor Suburbs

The traditional model of metropolitan America posits a poor city and wealthier suburban ring. However, when we use the finer-grained mesh of place data, a more complex pattern emerges. Figure 7.1 shows income data for the sample of 13 metropolitan areas. The vertical lines for each metro area represent the range of median family incomes. There is substantial variation in the median family income of suburban places, and although the central-city median income is always at the lower end of the scale, in all cases the poorest suburban place has a lower median family income than the central city.

Let us consider two cities in some more detail. Figure 7.2 shows the spatial distribution of median family income in the Atlanta metropolitan area. Whereas richer suburban places can be found along a southeast-northwest axis from the central city, significant numbers of moderate-income places can be found in the outer periphery. One such suburb of Atlanta is Griffin, located in Spalding County, approximately forty miles south of the city of Atlanta. Traditionally a manufacturing town, it still has almost 24 percent of its population employed in manufacturing. The suburb has grown considerably to a population of twenty-three thousand. As

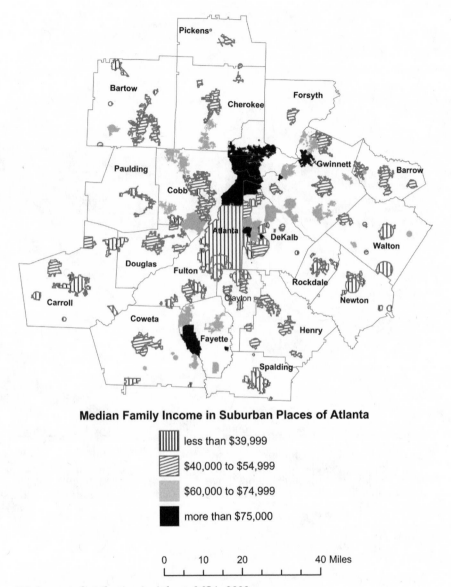

Median Family Income in Suburban Places of Atlanta

▓ less than $39,999

▨ $40,000 to $54,999

▨ $60,000 to $74,999

■ more than $75,000

0   10   20   40 Miles

7.2. Income distribution in Atlanta MSA, 2000.

well as having a substantially lower median family income, Griffin is below the state average for the percentage of population with a bachelor's degree and for median house value. Atlanta's suburban expansion now encompasses poor as well as rich places. Figure 7.3 provides a visual expression of this income diversity.

A similar pattern can be noted for Chicago (fig. 7.4). Again, the expan-

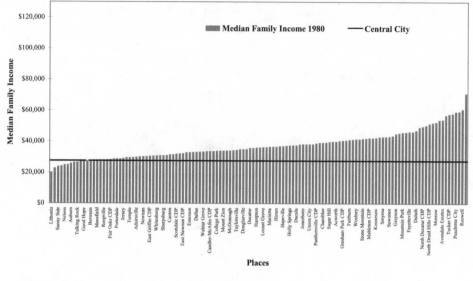

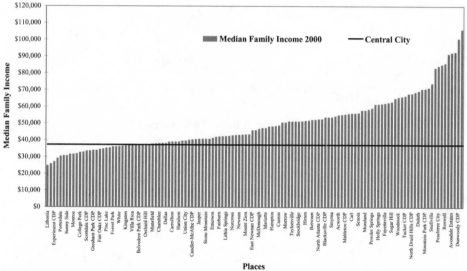

7.3. Income diversity in Atlanta MSA, 1980 and 2000.

sion of the metro area now includes places of modest income on the metropolitan periphery. For instance, Morris, once a small village in rural Illinois, is now part of Chicago's suburban diversity. Its median family income of $54,987 has consistently lagged $15,000 behind the rest of Chicago's suburbs from 1980 to 2000. As in Atlanta, Chicago's suburban landscape now encompasses both rich and poor places scattered across the metropolitan area.

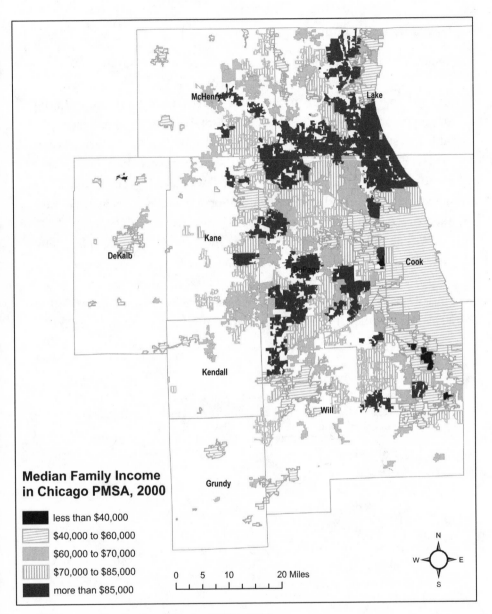

7.4. Income distribution, Chicago PMSA, 2000.

Metropolitan areas are now expanding to incorporate places with modest economic opportunities. Poor places outside of the central city are now becoming part of the metro landscape. There are now low-income as well as high-income suburbs, and we need now to include the presence of poor places in our models of metropolitan America.

Poor, Blue-Collar Suburbs

The traditional model emphasizes the geographic concentration of manufacturing and industrial workers in the central city, a declining urban core, and an expanding suburban periphery. However, there is manufacturing employment in the suburbs. I identified a total of 748 suburban places that had at least 25 percent of residents employed in the manufacturing sector in 1980. In other words, almost half of all suburban places had considerable manufacturing employment in 1980. The finer place-level mesh allows us to see that the simple divide of the traditional model was, even in 1980, inadequate for understanding metropolitan regions.

We can follow the track of some of these manufacturing suburbs by identifying the subset that experienced an increase in poverty levels. Table 7.2 lists those suburban places that had at least 25 percent manufacturing employment in 1980 and had an increase in poverty level from 1980 to 2000. The traditional manufacturing Rust Belt cities of St. Louis, Cincin-

TABLE 7.2

Poor blue-collar suburbs

Metropolitan area	Number of suburbs	%
Atlanta MSA	14	11.1
Baltimore PMSA	8	8.7
Boston PMSA	2	1.5
Chicago PMSA	52	17.3
Cincinnati PMSA	30	22.5
Cleveland PMSA	23	19.6
Oakland PMSA	1	2.2
Philadelphia PMSA	24	12.7
Phoenix MSA	0	0
San Francisco PMSA	0	0
San Jose PMSA	0	0
St. Louis PMSA	55	24.6
Washington, D.C. PMSA	1	0.5

Note: We define these suburbs as places that had at least 25% manufacturing employment in 1980 and had an increase in poverty levels from 1980 to 2000.

nati, Cleveland, and Chicago had a significant proportion of their suburban places in this category. Almost one in four of all suburban places in metro St. Louis fit into this category, whereas for Cincinnati and Cleveland it is closer to one in five. In the old established manufacturing metro regions, a significant proportion of the suburban places can be characterized as blue-collar suburbs experiencing increased levels of poverty from 1980 to 2000. Dundalk, a suburb of Baltimore County and home to a Bethlehem Steel plant, is a prime example of a traditional blue-collar suburb where local industry, because of economic restructuring and advances in technology, is no longer employing local residents. In 1970 the percentage of employed residents of Dundalk working in manufacturing was almost 48 percent, compared to only 16 percent in 2000. The loss of manufacturing employment was not offset by alternative employment opportunities. The poverty rate in this suburb increased from 5.5 percent in 1980 to 9.1 percent in 2000. The trends we normally associate with metro cores are also found in selected suburban places.

Black Suburbs

The traditional model assumes a racial divide of essentially white suburbs and central cities more dominated by minority populations. The place-level data allow us to see a more complex picture. Out of the total of 1,639 suburban places over the period 1980 to 2000, 1,245 increased their black population, in 227 places by more than 10 percent and in 114 places by more than 25 percent. The absolute figures are also revealing. By 2000 there were 252 suburban places where the black population was more than 25 percent and 132 suburbs where it was more than 50 percent. Thirty-five of these suburbs are in the St. Louis metro area, and 33 of them are in the Washington, D.C., metro area. Furthermore, the Washington, D.C., metro area is interesting because whereas the central city's black population declined from 70 percent to 59 percent, it increased in such suburban places as New Carrollton and Woodlawn from 21 percent to 67 percent and from 27 percent to 71 percent, respectively.

This trend is not simply the suburbanization of poor blacks. I also identified what I have termed black middle-class suburbs, which by 2000 had more than 25 percent black populations and median family incomes greater than the national average (table 7.3). The truly outstanding metro area in this regard is Washington, D.C., which has almost one-third of its

TABLE 7.3

Black middle-class suburbs

Metropolitan area	Number of suburbs	%
Atlanta MSA	8	6.3
Baltimore PMSA	10	10.9
Boston PMSA	0	0
Chicago PMSA	20	6.6
Cincinnati PMSA	3	2.2
Cleveland PMSA	3	2.5
Oakland PMSA	0	0
Philadelphia PMSA	6	3.1
Phoenix MSA	0	0
San Francisco PMSA	0	0
San Jose PMSA	0	0
St. Louis PMSA	10	4.4
Washington, D.C. PMSA	59	30.1

Note: We define these suburbs as places that had at least 25% black population and an income of at least $50,046 (U.S. median family income) in 2000.

suburbs classified as black middle class. This categorization is not the result of a statistical aberration caused by a small population size. Some of the suburbs have substantial populations. Bowie in 2000, for example, had a total population of 50,269 that was 30.3 percent black with a median family income of $82,403. The federal government has led the way in affirmative action. And the growth of federal employment and the creation of a substantial middle class have gone hand in hand in the suburbs of Washington. The two suburbs of Washington noted above, New Carrollton and Woodlawn, for example, had median family incomes of $56,000 and $60,392, respectively.

Although there is a growing segment of middle-class black families in the suburbs, it is interesting to note that many live in majority-black areas (fig. 7.5). Despite my assertion that the suburbs are becoming more varied, racial segregation still appears to be the reality in suburban America.

A similar trend for Hispanic populations can be noted. Out of a total of 1,639 suburban places, there are 1,410 places where the Hispanic popula-

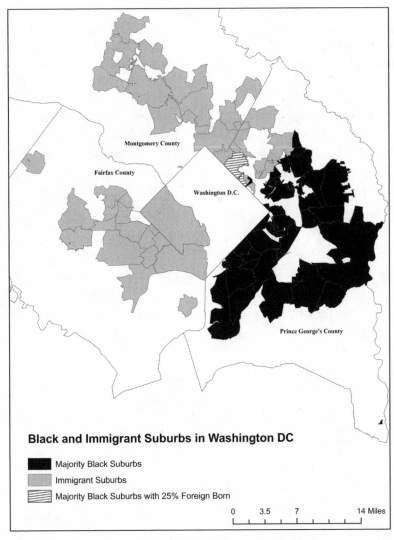

Black and Immigrant Suburbs in Washington DC

■ Majority Black Suburbs

▨ Immigrant Suburbs

▧ Majority Black Suburbs with 25% Foreign Born

0   3.5   7   14 Miles

7.5. Black and immigrant suburbs in Washington, D.C., 2000.

tion increased between 1980 and 2000. Moreover, there are 153 places where population grew by more than 10 percent and 32 places where it grew by 25 percent or more. In 2000 there were 81 suburban places with a Hispanic population of more than 25 percent and 18 with a population of more than 50 percent.

Since the 1970s, suburban areas have become more racially and ethnically diverse. The suburbs are largely white but with increasing population diversity. The suburbs are changing color and taking on a more multicultural flavor. In 2000 racial and ethnic minorities constituted 27 percent of suburban populations as compared to only 19 percent in 1990.[2]

Immigrant Suburbs

The traditional model assumes that the majority of foreign-born citizens will be located in the metro centers, often depicted as the main receiving point for immigrant streams. In large measure this traditional model still holds true. The central areas of growing metro regions such as Boston, San Francisco, and San Jose still attract significant numbers of foreign-born residents. However, I was able to identify suburban places of significant foreign immigration, designated as those places having more than 25 percent of their 2000 population born overseas (table 7.4).

Some of the suburban places had substantial foreign-born populations in 2000, such as Chamblee in Atlanta (64.1 percent), Union City in Oakland (44 percent), Daly City in San Francisco (52.3 percent), and Langley Park in Washington, D.C. (64.5 percent). Immigration is still directed toward the more economically dynamic metro areas; the Californian metro areas have

TABLE 7.4

Immigrant suburbs

Metropolitan area	Number of suburbs	%
Atlanta MSA	7	5.5
Baltimore PMSA	0	0
Boston PMSA	5	3.9
Chicago PMSA	29	9.6
Cincinnati PMSA	0	0
Cleveland PMSA	0	0
Oakland PMSA	14	31.8
Philadelphia PMSA	3	1.5
Phoenix MSA	1	2.7
San Francisco PMSA	11	27.5
San Jose PMSA	8	44.4
St. Louis PMSA	1	10.4
Washington, D.C. PMSA	42	21.4

Note: We define these suburbs as places that had at least 25% foreign-born population in 2000.

significant amounts of immigrant suburbs, whereas the Rust Belt cities of Ohio have none. In some cities, there is a distinct clustering of immigrant suburbs. Figure 7.5, for example, plots the distribution of black suburbs and immigrant suburbs in the Washington, D.C., metro area. Note that there is a distinct "Black Belt" that stretches east from the city into Prince George's County, whereas the immigrant suburbs are clustered in Fairfax County in northern Virginia and Montgomery County in central Maryland. If early-twentieth-century immigration into the U.S. was concentrated in the central areas, early-twenty-first-century foreign immigration has a distinctly more suburban flavor.

Revising the Model

Suburbs come in various shapes and sizes with different demographics and economies. The analysis reveals that the variation between suburban places is often more striking than the difference between the central city and its surrounding suburbs. This variation differs regionally. In the Baltimore MSA, for example, the difference between the suburbs with the highest and lowest median family income is $75,865, whereas in the St. Louis MSA the income gap is $188,126. It is time to develop alternative models that account for the differences between and within metro regions.

The new metropolitan reality is of heterogeneous suburbs. The traditional "city-suburb divide" no longer suffices as a standard measure of comparison. I have identified poor suburbs, manufacturing suburbs, black suburbs, and immigrant suburbs that undermine the simplicity of the traditional model (table 7.5). The analysis of suburban places found pockets of poverty and decline, dispelling the myth of suburban uniformity. The analysis showed that 10 percent of 1,639 suburban places in 13 metropolitan areas had median family incomes less than their central city in 2000 (table 7.6). These findings are consistent with W. H. Lucy and D. L. Phillips's examination of 554 suburbs in twenty-four states. They found that, from the 1960s to the 1990s, 20 percent of suburbs declined faster in median-family-income ratios than their central cities. And it is in line with the study by T. Swanstrom et al. that showed a widening gap between the richest and poorest suburbs since 1980.[3]

Suburban decline is most prevalent in the first-tier or inner-ring suburbs. In particular, the first-tier suburbs of the Rust Belt cities in the Northeast and Midwest are aging, with a housing stock that is no longer

TABLE 7.5

Summary of findings for suburban places

Number of suburbs (% of sample)	Summary analysis
169 (10.3)	Median family incomes less than central city in 2000
210 (12.8)	Manufacturing employment greater than 25% in 1980 and increase in poverty levels from 1980 to 2000
748 (45.6)	25% manufacturing employment in 1980
252 (15.3)	Black population of at least 25% in 2000
125 (7.6)	Foreign born greater than 25% in 2000

Note: The number of suburbs reflects the sample of 1,639 places in 13 metropolitan areas.

TABLE 7.6

Low-income suburbs lagging behind central city

Metropolitan area	Number of suburbs	%	Central-city income ($)
Atlanta MSA	29	22.3	37,231
Baltimore PMSA	1	1.0	35,438
Boston PMSA	1	0	44,151
Chicago PMSA	13	4.1	42,724
Cincinnati PMSA	19	11.3	37,543
Cleveland PMSA	1	0	30,286
Oakland PMSA	1	1.6	44,384
Philadelphia PMSA	14	5.6	37,036
Phoenix MSA	28	54.9	46,467
San Francisco PMSA	7	12.5	63,545
San Jose PMSA	7	25.9	74,813
St. Louis PMSA	23	9.2	32,585
Washington, D.C. PMSA	25	10.2	46,283

Note: The number of suburbs within metropolitan areas represents how many places have median family incomes below their respective central city in 2000.

marketable, infrastructure that is in need of repair, and residents that are dying off with no younger generation to replace them. Furthermore, many of these suburbs experience economic and social problems normally associated with central cities such as rising crime rates and poor school performance. Yet most public policies and revitalization efforts focus on central cities to the neglect of declining suburbs. There is a great deal of suburban diversity, and there are "suburbs in crisis."

8

Metropolitan Fragmentation

"Obsolescent Structure of Urban Government"

THE TYPICAL U.S. METROPOLIS is a balkanized arrangement of numerous municipal governments. In this chapter I want to answer two questions: How did this come about? And what are the consequences?

The History

An important feature of civic life in the U.S. has been the relative ease by which local self-rule was possible. Through the course of the nineteenth century, municipal incorporation, the formal creation of civic government, had become a right rather than a privilege. Permissive state incorporation laws allowed the easy and quick creation of municipalities. In many states the minimum population requirement was low: California allowed a minimum of just 200 residents, Illinois 150, and Tennessee just 100. Developers eager to make their town the next Chicago, residents eager to distance themselves from other social and ethnic groups, and small suburbs eager to avoid the costs of big cities could, with relative ease, break away from existing civic arrangements to establish separate municipalities.

Throughout most of the nineteenth century, business interests wanted metropolitan annexation, the name given to the capturing of suburban municipalities by the central-city government because it allowed for easier business expansion and growth. But when manufacturing industries, in particular, began to move out of the central cities in the late nineteenth and early twentieth centuries to avoid unionized workers and higher wage costs, businesses began to resist annexation by central cities and supported municipal incorporation. Business interests could benefit from the metropolitan fragmentation by locating in suburban areas where they could avoid the higher taxes and the more militant labor of the central cities.[1]

There was a rich mix of factors encouraging the U.S. city to be less of a unitary political structure and more of a fragmented metropolis. Among the many social forces behind political fragmentation were the desire for social homogeneity, lower taxes and improved services, the drive for class and ethnic separation, and the creation of suburban communities around "moral" principles such as antidrinking and even "immoral" principles such as gambling that were not permitted in the city. The U.S. metropolis became a political mosaic of differing homogeneous communities—enclaves of sin as well as islands of morality. The result was central cities hemmed in by suburban municipalities.

There is now a multiplicity of local government units. According to the U.S. Census of Governments, published in 2002, there were 87,849 units of local government in the U.S. (table 8.1). There has been some decline in the past fifty years, a function of a reduction in the number of school districts. There has been a major consolidation of school districts in the past fifty years as the unified school district replaced the one-room schoolhouse. The number of municipalities has, in the same period, increased from 16,807 to 19,431. Some units, such as special districts organized around specific goals like flood prevention, come under the control of other local government authorities.

There are many local government units responsible for taxing and spending. Figure 8.1 shows the diversity of political jurisdictions for the

TABLE 8.1

Number of government units in the United States

Type of local government	1952	2002
County	3,052	3,034
Municipal	16,807	19,431
Township and town	17,202	16,506
School district	67,355	13,522
Special district	12,340	35,356
Total	116,756	87,849

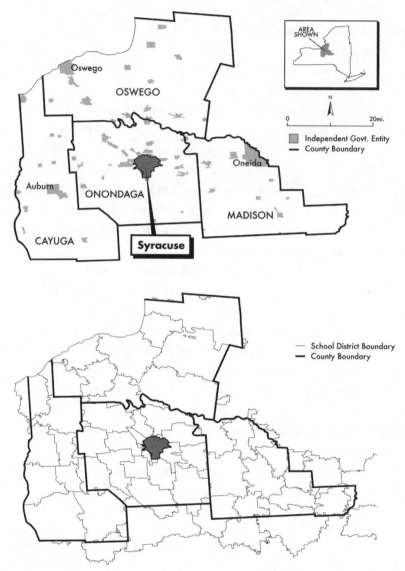

8.1. Syracuse, New York, metropolitan area and school districts.

Syracuse metropolitan area. The metro area consists of a central city and four separate counties, and within these counties are a variety of governmental entities. On average, there are approximately 121 units of local government in each metropolitan area in the U.S. This average figure is useful to indicate the overall picture of metropolitan fragmentation but ignores the wide variation for individual metropolitan areas. New York has more than 1,400 units and Chicago more than 1,000. The issue of fragmentation provides the explanatory metaphor of some classic urban studies. Robert Fogelson's study of Los Angeles, for example, is titled *The Fragmented Metropolis.*

The large number of local government units is, in itself, not a problem. There are some, public-choice theorists being the most vocal, who would argue that this situation is a healthy state of affairs. A large number of different municipalities in a city region allows residents to choose a variety of tax loads, school districts, and forms of government. When households have the opportunity to choose between many different local governments, these governments have to be more sensitive to citizen demands and preferences. The fragmented city can be the city of choice that allows different forms of municipal government to be tried and tested. To be more accurate, however, we should note that not all households have the luxury of such choice. The lower-income households have a restricted choice, and low-income minorities have the least choice. There is an important equity issue of opening up the suburbs to low-income households effectively trapped in the central city.

There are other arguments in favor of multiple municipalities. They tend to be smaller, and small municipalities are closer to the needs of individual citizens, more accessible, more responsive. Smaller municipalities allow ordinary residents and citizens to be engaged. These arguments for the status quo are convincing and cannot be easily dismissed. However, there are also problems associated with this fragmentation. We can consider three.

The first is a central city-suburban fiscal-disparity problem. Central cities, especially ones with shrinking populations, have a declining tax base and lower-income population, whereas the suburbs have an expanded tax base and a relatively affluent population. Central cities have to deal with the politics of economic decline, while many suburbs get to contend with the management of growth. This situation creates a tremendous inequity in municipal funding. This problem has been exacerbated by the decline of federal funding for many social programs. Whereas central cities may witness a downward spiral of low tax base, leading to poor services that cause more people to leave, thus reducing the tax base even further, the growing suburban communities may experience a benign cycle of new population, generating more tax revenue, thus allowing better services, thus attracting even more people. Municipal fragmentation that separates out poor cities from affluent suburbs reinforces the inequalities in U.S. society.

The increasing concentration of poverty in certain municipalities has a negative fiscal effect. A recent study of southern California, for example, showed a severe fiscal stress in the old industrial suburbs of Los Angeles County and the poorer cities of San Bernardino and Riverside where there was a concentration of poor people. The decline in welfare provision and its move from a federal to a more local responsibility meant that intergovernmental transfers did not make up for local differences in resources. The study shows that cities with a concentration of poverty were unable to provide the local services that could enable residents to escape from poverty.[2]

A second problem is the case of public education. Figure 8.1 shows a typical example. In the Syracuse metro area the central city is one school district surrounded by a range of suburban school districts. In the United States the federal government, in contrast to countries like France, has a very limited role in providing funding and resources to public schools. School funding is dominated by state and municipal sources. States provide an average of 50 percent of total school budgets, local districts around 45 percent based on local property taxes, while the federal government contributes only 5 percent. Rich states such as California spend more on education than poor states such as Mississippi. But even here statistics need some careful interpretation. California spends more on average than other states but has 25 percent fewer teachers per pupil than other states and spends 9 percent less per pupil. Bigger states tend to have more students, larger class sizes, and sometimes more problematic performance. At the school-district level disparities in wealth feed directly into educational standards and performance. Poor school districts cannot afford to spend the same as richer school districts. The poorest 25 percent of school districts in the U.S. receive approximately one thousand dollars less per student per year than the richest 25 percent.

In his 1991 book *Savage Inequalities*, Jonathan Kozol provides the most detailed and accessible description of differences in educational spending. In the fiscal year 1988–1989, for example, two school districts in New Jersey, Princeton and Camden, spent $7,725 and $3,538 per student, respectively. It almost goes without saying that Princeton is an affluent suburban district, whereas Camden is a poor urban district. In New York State the disparities were just as pronounced. In 1989–1990 New York City could afford to spend only $7,299 per student, but the affluent suburb Manhasset could spend $15,084. This disparity translates to marked differences in the amount and quality of teachers, facilities, and resources that in turn lead to different levels of educational attainment. Spending on education is an important component of educational attainment that in turn is an important predictor of future income levels. Although there are some who say that you cannot throw money at social problems, education is one of the exceptions. The more you spend per pupil, in most cases but not all, the higher their educational attainment and the greater their choices in the job market. How well you do in school is an excellent predictor of future earnings, household income, and personal wealth. The fragmentation of school districts is reinforcing inequalities. Students who come from poor households generally need more spending to make up for their home lives. In most of the U.S. they receive less. For many already affluent households public education may provide an escalator to affluence, but for most low-income households trapped in poor school districts, public education is a funnel of failure.

Formulas to achieve equality have in large measure failed. Most states guarantee some form of schooling for all the children in the state, but the quality of this education varies dramatically among school districts because of the differential tax base. Although there was a concern with increasing equality from the 1950s to the mid-1970s, since then there has been renewed concern with local control. In San Antonio, Texas, for example, a federal district court ruled that the disparity in educational spending was in violation of the U.S. Constitution. Even with state subsidies, differences in spending per pupil in the metro area ranged from $543 in the affluent districts to $231 in the poor districts. However, a Supreme Court decision overruled the decision of the lower court. Disparities will persist as long as the emphasis on local control deflects issues of social justice.

The third problem is a lack of metropolitan-wide civic engagement. Metropolitan fragmentation reinforces divisions, differences, and fracture lines in U.S. society. Take the case of metropolitan Los Angeles that includes the city of Los Angeles with a population of 3.4 million, only 37 percent classified as white, as well as the municipality of Rolling Hills, with a population of just over 1,800, 85 percent white. To be involved in the civic life of Rolling Hills is important, but it is not civic engagement in the wider sense. It even could be an integral part of the polarization of the metropolis. Full civic engagement means a connection with the wider world of a diverse metropolis. The contemporary American city has a metropolitan fragmentation that separates out cities from suburbs, blacks from whites, rich from poor. As the city becomes more balkanized, architecturally into gated communities and politically into exclusive suburbs and abandoned inner cities, simply calling for more civic engagement in the local community is to miss this wider structural context. To be actively involved in your all-white suburban neighborhood, or predominantly Latino neighborhood, may be public involvement, but it is not civic engagement in the sense of engaging a variety of metropolitan experiences.

Metropolitan reform was a significant feature of social-policy debates in the 1960s and early 1970s. In 1969, for example, Daniel Patrick Moynihan could write that "part of the ineffectiveness of the effects of urban government to respond to urban problems derives from the fragmented and obsolescent structure of urban government itself."[3] Since then the notions of national urban policy and metropolitan reform have faded from view. There are exceptions. David Rusk is the latest in a long line of writers promoting metropolitan reform. In *Cities Without Suburbs* he argues that the lack of metropolitan reform condemns central cities to limited futures, promotes segregation, and reinforces income disparities between city and suburb. In a later book, *Inside Game Outside Game,* he points to policy solutions, including regional land-use planning, metropolitan-wide public-housing programs, and mandated city-regional revenue-sharing programs.

Metropolitan government occurs to varying degree in Miami and Portland, and city-county consolidation has occurred in Nashville, Jacksonville, and Indianapolis. Portland is one of the few metro areas with a directly elected regional government. It was a long, hard struggle. A recommendation was first made to the Oregon Legislative Assembly in 1926 to consolidate the city and a neighboring county. A metropolitan planning commission was established thirty years later. A series of reports and recommendations finally led in 1992 to the creation of a metropolitan political authority now responsible for three counties and twenty-four cities. The authority is responsible for land-use planning, and it is not inci-dental that Portland has one of the most restrictive urban-growth policies in the country.

It is unlikely, however, that the annexation of suburbs into a regional government is a serious contender for implementation. Suburban resist-ance is too strong, and most state legislatures reflect rural and suburban in-terests rather than big-city concerns. More likely are regional forms of collaboration and state- and federally mandated programs of revenue sharing. But there is also an important role for civic organizations to adopt a more metropolitan-wide vision and thus promote a more vertical form of engagement. Extending our sense of community from the local municipal-ity to the metropolitan area will allow a wider range of issues to be ex-plored and greater diversity to be encountered, taking civic engagement away from the local and parochial before it reaches the more distant na-tional citizenship. The most effective and meaningful forms of civic en-gagement are more likely to be the ones that encompass the whole metropolis rather than divisive suburbs. Civic engagement at the metro-politan level may not reunite the Republic, but is a useful first step in the creation of a connected citizenry.

PART THREE

The Social Dynamics
of the Metropolis

9

Urban Economies

"All That Is Solid Melts into Air"

IN 1950 SCHENECTADY, New York, and San Jose, California, had similar population sizes: 92,061 and 95,280, respectively. At that time Schenectady's economy seemed secured. More than 27,000 people worked for General Electric. The city was flourishing, with a vibrant downtown and a buoyant job market. Corporations such as American Locomotive Company provided employment for thousands of workers as well as a way of life. Social clubs and softball teams grew up around the connections workers made in the factory. Fifty years later most of those jobs are gone. The locomotive company closed in 1968, and General Electric shed more than 90 percent of its jobs in the city. The city's population shrank to just over 61,821; the houses lost value, and the credit rating of the city, always a sharp-eyed fiscal view of a city's economic health, was downgraded by Moody's Investors Service to the lowest in the state. The median household income in 2004 was $29,378.

By 2000 San Jose, in deep contrast, had a population of 894,943 and was one of the larger cities in the U.S. Decades of spectacular growth fueled in particular by the Silicon Valley boom in high technology and computer-related industries make San Jose one of the most prosperous and economically dynamic cities in the country. In 2004 the median household income was $70,243. Among the companies headquartered in the city are Adobe, Cisco, and eBay.

Schenectady and San Jose—close in population size in 1950, but by

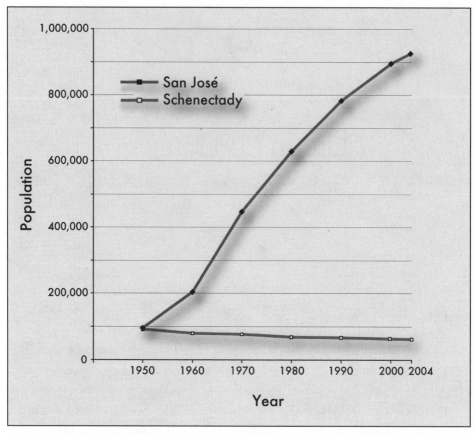

9.1. A tale of two cities: San Jose and Schenectady.

2000 they were on two different trajectories, one spiraling downward and the other trending upward (fig. 9.1). Although they have different recent economic histories, they are linked by the dynamism of the U.S. economy that over the past fifty years has transformed every town and city in the nation.

The U.S.'s capitalist economy, one of the largest and most capitalistic of economies, is responsible for both the Schenectadys and the San Joses. "All that is solid melts into air," Karl Marx once wrote about the restless dynamism of the capitalist economic system. Joseph Schumpeter used the term *creative destruction* to describe the forward drive of capitalism with its continual technological changes and innovations, ongoing striving for market dominance, and endless searching for more profits and greater market share. This dynamic is nowhere more apparent than in the restless landscapes of the urban U.S. where the booming economy of a city like Schenectady can disappear within a single generation while a San Jose can rise from relative obscurity to global prominence. Creative destructive is full of ambiguities, dangers, and unforeseen economic, cultural, and political consequences.[1]

The forces of capitalism have reached their full potential in the U.S. A relatively new country shaped in the image of a bourgeois, property-owning class created an ideal social and political container to harness the awesome economic power of capitalism. There was and continues to be an attendant ideology of a belief in the future. Americans share an over-whelming trust in the future, in developments, in change. Less burdened by feudal legacies or socialist ideologies, the U.S. experiences the forces of capitalist creative destruction at their strongest. And these changes are writ large in the contrasting economic fortunes of cities across the nation. Four broad urban economic trends have influenced these fortunes: deindustrialization, the growth of the service and information economies, the steady rise of the public sector, and the changing importance of retail.

Losing Blue-Collar Jobs

In 1950 the U.S. was the single largest manufacturing center in the world with a distinct competitive advantage in the immediate aftermath of World War II. Unlike its major economic competitors, such as Britain, Germany, and Japan, the U.S. did not experience wartime destruction of its manufacturing base. During the war a military-industrial complex was established to provide ships, guns, and tanks. This complex was to remain at the heart of the economic growth in postwar America.

In the immediate postwar decades, manufacturing employment grew from around 15 million in 1960 to its peak of more than 19.5 million in 1979. Since 1979, though there has been some fluctuation, the general trend has been downward, with a very marked decline since 2000. In January 2004 the number of manufacturing jobs stood at 14.3 million, a loss of 3 million from 2000.

From 1950 to 1979 there was an expansion of manufacturing employ-ment, and from 1979 to the present day there has been a marked decline. In total, more than 5 million manufacturing jobs were lost from 1979 to 2004, and manufacturing as a share of the nation's economic output fell from 21 percent to 14 percent. Behind this change lie important social implications as a heavily unionized workforce in relatively high-paying, secure jobs expanded, then contracted, and traditional industrial districts and cities lost jobs and economic rationale.

The growth period from 1950 to 1979 witnessed both an increase in manufacturing employment in traditional centers in the Northeast and Midwest such as Baltimore and Chicago and the emergence of newer manufacturing centers in the West and South. There was also a suburbanization of manufacturing employment, as factories and jobs moved to the newer greenfield sites in the suburbs. Behind the spread was a change in the balance of power between capital and labor. The older urban factories in the Northeast were traditionally unionized and were the foundation of the power of organized labor in the U.S. The shift to the West and South and to the suburbs was a move to less unionized plants. The full implications of this movement were masked in the growth period from 1945 to 1979 since there was an increase in manufacturing employment and a corresponding increase in organized labor. In 1983, the earliest comparable data point, 25.4 million workers in the private sector were either union members or covered by unions, 35 percent of all private-sector workers. Organized labor was a powerful force not only in shaping wage levels and conditions of employment inside the factory gates but also in promoting a social-welfare agenda in the broader political sphere through its strong connections with the Democratic Party. Organized labor's success is apparent in the steadily increasing real-wage increases over the growth period and the establishment of welfare programs, especially under the Democratic administrations of Truman, Kennedy, and particularly Johnson. The rising living standards were expressed, for a white working-class at least, in increasing levels of home ownership in the expanding suburbs.

There were limits on this social agenda because of the peculiar nature of U.S. politics. The Democratic Party until the late 1970s was entrenched in the South, where it was part of a racist creed that limited the civil rights of blacks. Powerful southern Democrats worked against programs that established national standards of prolabor and pro-social welfare legislation, all in order to maintain their white power base. The southern wing of the Democrats ensured that the party never became a labor party like the British Labour Party.[2]

The growth in manufacturing employment contributed to the expansion of existing plants, the construction of new plants, and the creation of an organized working class whose relative economic success was translated into both material goods and an ideology that chimed in harmony with the capitalist economy. Whereas Europe of the nineteenth and early twentieth centuries saw the emergence of a working class as a point of resistance to the capitalist society, in the U.S. of the third quarter of the twentieth century the working class was part of the very fabric of contemporary capitalism, sharing the values of consumerism, private property, and free markets. This U.S. working class of relatively well-paid owner-occupiers sought to benefit from, not to overthrow, capitalism. Even the term *working class* seemed inappropriate, as the term *blue collar* with its less threatening connotation gained currency. The blue-collar suburbs that sprouted around central cities embodied this profound transformation.

The year 1979 marks the high point of manufacturing employment in the U.S. There are three main reasons behind the subsequent decline in manufacturing employment. First, there was a slower rate of growth in the demand for manufactured goods. As consumers' income rose and the economy matured, there was a shift from spending on goods to services such as health care. In 1979 52 percent of consumer spending was on goods, but by 2000 it was only 42 percent. Second, there has been an enormous increase in manufacturing productivity. Each year since 1979 the productivity of manufacturing workers has increased by 3.3 percent, which compares favorably with the rest of the economy, where productivity growth rates are closer to 2 percent. As machines replace people, fewer workers are needed to produce the same amount of goods. The automation of production reduces the power and influence of skilled manufacturing workers. Third, there was growing competition from overseas manufacturers. Goods formerly produced in the U.S. were and are being made more cheaply offshore, especially in countries where wage rates are substantially below U.S. levels. There has been a global shift in manufacturing employment from western Europe and North America to Asia. There has been a deindustrialization of the advanced economies and a rapid industrialization in a small group of developing countries such as China, Singapore, Taiwan, and South Korea.

Behind this general decline was the growth of manufacturing employment in selected parts of the U.S. In parts of Los Angeles and New York, for example, clothing manufacturing continues to employ people, mainly immigrant women. And new car factories have sprung up in the small towns of the South and Midwest. Whereas many older automobile manufacturing plants closed, new automobile production and assembly plants were opened along a seventy-mile band running alongside Interstates 65 and 75 from Michigan through Indiana and Ohio into Kentucky and Tennessee. Between 1980 and 1991, twenty new vehicle-assembly plants were built in this corridor to minimize freight costs and located in small towns to avoid heavily unionized areas. However, if we divide the economy into manufacturing and nonmanufacturing, then almost 82 percent, in terms of both employment and the gross domestic product, of the U.S. economy can de described as nonmanufacturing. The factories have disappeared and with them the jobs of the blue-collar middle class.

At the national level, this long-term decline meant a contraction of manufacturing employment and a weakening of the power of organized labor. In 1983 25.4 million workers in the private sector were either union members or covered by unions. By 2004 this figure had fallen to 15.5 million, and the respective percentage figures for all private-sector workers had fallen from 35 percent to 12.5 percent. Even as the total number of private-sector workers increased, the numbers of those employees associated with unions declined in both absolute and relative terms. The contraction of manufacturing employment varied. The largest declines were in the old established urban centers of the Northeast and Midwest, traditionally union places, whereas the largest relative and absolute increases were in the Sun Belt states, many of them with antiunion laws and regulations. The decline of manufacturing in the old established cities effectively weakened the hand of organized labor and strengthened the hand of capital. The result was a squeeze on the living standards of industrial workers and a general depression of middle-class incomes. The average weekly earnings of all private-industry employees declined from $275 in 1982 to $274 in 2001 (in constant 1982 dollars). The squeezing of the middle class, a popular trope of political rhetoric, reflects the declining power of organized labor, the globalization of economic activities, and the weakness of a social-democratic political force similar to what exists in western Europe that can more effectively control market forces to aid the general population.

Up until the 1970s manufacturing was still dominated by Fordist techniques, which involved the mass production of goods on fixed assembly lines. Since the 1970s manufacturing has shifted more toward flexible specialization involving shorter production runs, more automation, and less-skilled workers. Although this alteration makes industry much more sensitive to changing consumer preferences, it has reduced the number and skill levels of manufacturing workers. And this decline in turn has led to a decrease in labor's bargaining power, with resultant effects on wages. The more jobs are deskilled, the more easily they are shipped offshore to unskilled labor pools in third-world countries.

There has been a shift from the power of the producers to the dominance of the consumer. Under the so-called Fordist regime, customers could have any color Model T Ford as long as it was black. Now consumers can demand a wider range of choice. The consumer has emerged as the dominant player, further weakening the power of the worker. The large retailers can impose more stringent cost controls on producers eager to gain access to the consumer market. Since most of us are both workers and consumers, this shift is evident in our own lives, as our consumer choices widen while our work lives speed up and are devalorized. As consumers we are kings and queens, but as workers we are becoming more like paupers.

From 1950 to the early 1970s the growth of high-wage, unionized jobs dominated the economy. Since then cuts in real wages, resistance to union organizing, and the shifting of production to lower-wage sites in the nation and overseas marked the economy very differently. Though capital was more footloose, able to locate in others parts of the county or even the world, labor was caught in place. Deindustrialization involves the closure of plants, especially in the urban cores, the reduction of workers in existing plants, and a net shift in manufacturing employment away from the central city to the suburbs of the Sun Belt. In vibrant urban economies the loss of manufacturing jobs is offset in aggregate terms by the growth of jobs in other sectors. However, in neighborhoods and cities where there is little alternative employment growth, the loss of manufacturing employment is devastating. Traditional small industrial cities such as Schenectady, Syracuse, or Flint saw the lifeblood of the local economy drained away without the transfusion of new jobs. In selected inner-city neighborhoods jobs have gone, not to be replaced. Dundalk, a blue-collar Baltimore suburb, saw a decline in manufacturing from 48 percent in 1970 to 16 percent in 2000. With few employment opportunities, the poverty rate doubled from 5 percent to 10 percent. William Julius Wilson charts the effects of such employment loss on minority neighborhoods in cities like Chicago where deindustrialization impacts significantly on African American urban communities.[3]

The city of Detroit embodies the process of deindustrialization and job loss. The city grew in the first two-thirds of the twentieth century on the back of the car industry. Its very nickname, Motor City, was associated with car production. In 1960 there were 642,704 jobs in the city, and the population was 1.6 million. In the last third of the twentieth century the city fell apart as the jobs disappeared. By 2000 there were only 345,424 jobs in the city, the population declined to just over 1 million, vast swaths of the city became vacant, and an endemic fiscal crisis limited the effectiveness of city government. Motor City became Vacant City as seventeen thousand acres out of the city's total of eight-six thousand lay vacant and derelict. One proposal by an official in 1993 even suggested a form of urban triage involving moving residents from the most derelict parts of the city and fencing off and landscaping the vacant areas.

The loss of blue-collar jobs is an important seismic shift in the U.S. that signals not only an economic transformation from a manufacturing to a service-dominated economy but also a social transformation because manufacturing jobs were the backbone of a secure blue-collar middle class. Jobs in the manufacturing sector were the platform for an expanded middle class of owner-occupiers with relatively high standards of living. Many high school graduates, unable to attend college, now face a bleaker future without the availability of traditional manufacturing employment. And the weakening of organized labor led to declining or stagnant wages and harsher working conditions for many Americans. Deindustrialization results not simply in a loss of blue-collar job but also in a death knell for the blue-collar middle class.

The Growth of the Service Sector

Compared to the decline in manufacturing, there has been an increase in services, which now account for one in every three U.S. workers and almost 30 percent of the gross domestic product. The term *services* covers a wide range, from jobs in health care and financial consultancy to computer information companies. The sector includes a range of wildly differing job experiences. At one end are the high-paying Wall Street brokers working in high finance and international currency dealing, all making good wages and lucrative annual bonuses that have fueled the local housing markets. At the other end are the contract cleaners of the offices that house these executives. One particularly dynamic sector of services is the knowledge-based industries, so-called producer services such as banking, financial and business consultancies, and information technology. Together these sectors constitute the dynamic edge of the U.S. capitalist economy. Since 1980 a city's success rests less on manufacturing employment and more on the extent to which it can generate, retain, and attract such employment. Financial services continue to be concentrated especially in the global cities such as New York, where the economics of agglomeration and the importance of face-to-face contact continue to make big cities attractive places. Manhattan continues to resist deconcentration and loss of population in large part because of the continuing need of advanced financial services to have a downtown location. High-tech industries have aggregated around a number of innovative centers such as Austin, Silicon Valley, and Route 128 in Boston. Here the pull is other firms, local linkages with universities and government research labs, and a pool of highly skilled labor.

The main growth in the more high-paying service jobs is business services in a very small number of very large cities such as New York and high-tech jobs in a small number of urban centers such as Austin and San Jose. Former manufacturing cities such as Schenectady, too small to attract significant business services and not attractive enough for a significant influx of high-tech industries, show the downward spiral of job loss leading to outmigration, leading to further job loss. San Jose is at the other end of the spectrum. The city, close to San Francisco, became an attractive destination for companies leaving the higher-tax city. Stanford University, located close by, provides the intellectual power that was the basis for new high-tech companies building upon the Hewlett Packard Company, which was started by graduates of the university. And success bred success, especially in the 1980s and 1990s, when information technology seemed to be on an upward spiral of continued growth. As the capital of Silicon Valley, San Jose continues to expand, attracting young, highly skilled people who in turn provide both pools of labor and sources of intellectual capital and personal connections that allow even more new companies to emerge and flourish. In the city alone Cisco employs 14,800, Adobe 2,000, and eBay 1,400. San Jose is to high tech in 2000 what Schenectady was to manufacturing in 1950.

A key barometer of urban economic success is the ability to attract and retain young educated workers. Growing cities such as San Jose attract educated young people, and declining cities such as Schenectady lose educated young people. As the economy shifts to more information-based, knowledge-orientated jobs, then educated young professionals become both the barometer and the means of economic success.

The growth of the service sector produces a more polarized job market with, on the one hand, high-paying jobs with full benefits and, on the other, minimum-wage jobs with few benefits. At the core of the new service economy are the highly paid knowledge-based professionals, the symbolic analysts such as business consultants and investment bankers. Paid generously, they have employment security, good working conditions, and generous benefits. They often work long hours with brutal deadlines, but they are firmly located in the middle to upper-middle class, and they can ensure their children's similar economic success by being able to buy good private education or by being able to make the right residential choices to ensure the best public education. At the very upper levels of this sector is a world of affluence that is often represented but rarely experienced. It is the world of the corporate jet and the million-dollar-plus stock options that provide the deep financial cushioning from the vagaries of life. Outside of this core group there are two peripheries. The first consists of full-time workers with less income, status, and prestige. Their jobs are less secure, and too often they are able to hang on to middle-class status only when more than one person in the household is working. The second group comprises people on short-term or part-time contracts. They may work from home on their computer and relish the flexibility of such work or may be picked up on a daily basis at the street corner by landscape gardeners to manicure the lawns of the wealthy.

There is an economic struggle in the penumbra of the service-sector economy. It is rarely given much voice in public debates or political campaigns. The concerns of the wealthy and the affluent dominate the media. In a market-dominated political economy the wealthier consumers carry more economic muscle, wield more political power, and have greater cultural prominence. The poor suffer from economic, political, and cultural invisibility. In the 1960s there was a rediscovery of poverty in the U.S., as commentators identified those Americans left behind in the increasing age of affluence. Michael Harrington's 1962 book *The Other America* drew attention to the poor, those individuals outside the formal economy, unable to get jobs. In the first decade of the twenty-first century a number of observers noted the precarious lives of those citizens close to the bottom of the low-wage service economy. Barbara Ehrenreich's 2001 book *Nickel and Dimed* is a well-written first-person participant account that tells the story of the people at the wrong end of the service economy. She worked as a waitress, hotel maid, nursing-home aide, and sales clerk. Whatever the different job, it was a depressingly similar story of little pay for hours of hard work, with few benefits and punishing work schedules. David Shipler also highlights the plight of the working poor in his 2004 book *The Working Poor.* The title is resonant because it reminds us that you can be working and still poor. Poverty is not simply a function of unemployment. According to federal guidelines, a family of four in 2002 earning $18,500 was above the poverty line, yet one-fifth of Americans now have a median net worth of $7,900. However, this bar is very low, and for those individuals in expensive housing areas it is barely enough to keep body and soul together. People who live in poverty live on the edge, their lives marginalized and precarious. And the official response? It is dominated by a profound lack of concern; the minimum wage, for example, has remained unchanged since 1997 at $5.15 an hour. Working a forty-hour week gives an annual income of $9,888. In 2000 dollars the minimum-wage equivalent in 1950 was $5.36. The highest it ever reached was $7.92 in 1968. It has been below $6 since 1982. Weak or nonexistent unions and high levels of unskilled immigration, both legal and illegal, have undercut the power of labor. Congress responds enthusiastically to the rich and powerful yet effectively ignores the plight of the working poor.

In 2004 almost 7.5 million workers received the minimum wage, or 6 percent of the total workforce. This low minimum wage suppresses other low-wage workers. Another 8.2 million, or 6.6 percent of the total workforce, earn only $1 an hour more than the minimum wage. Jason Deparle's 2004 book *American Dream* follows the experience of three women in Milwaukee who were moved off welfare in the wake of the 1996 welfare-reform legislation. Though one fell into crack addiction, the other two retrained and got jobs that earned almost $10 an hour. However, it was just enough for them to keep their heads above water. They are, in their own words, "just making it," leading a precarious existence above the subsistence level, always liable to collapse in the wake of major expenditure needs such as health care or education.

Low wages are not in themselves problematic. In other capitalist countries, life chances are in part shaped by what we might call the social wage, the services and benefits we receive through citizenship or residency in a country, such as welfare, health benefits, and educational opportunities. The problem with low wages in the U.S. is that they combine with a relatively low social wage; universal health insurance seems impossible to achieve, and educational quality varies dramatically between rich and poor school districts. Low wages in the U.S. mean minimum or no health care and poor education, creating cycles of poverty across generations. Pockets of concentrated poverty and multiple deprivation occur across the country in rural as well as urban places, but they are most starkly visible in the low-income ghettos of inner-city America.

The shift from a manufacturing-based economy to a service-based economy has profound effects on income distribution. A strong manufacturing base allowed low-skilled workers to obtain relatively good wages. The service economy, in contrast, provides high-paying jobs for those individuals with marketable skills, but more limited opportunities for low-skilled workers. For those workers lacking high educational attainment, the opportunities shrink to the low-wage service sector. The substitution of well-paying manufacturing jobs for lower-paying service jobs makes the lives of those service workers more difficult. The "squeezing of the middle class" is not just political rhetoric; it is a brute economic fact, as the more poorly educated see their earnings deflate in real terms.

The shift from manufacturing to a more service-oriented economy also goes hand in hand with an increase in female employment. In 1950 the female participation rate in the formal economy was only 30 percent, but by 2001 it had increased to almost 60 percent. By 2001 out of a total employed labor force of 135 million, 63 million were women. The workforce was feminized. In the 1950s older married women led the way back to the workforce; in the 1970s and 1980s it was younger married women. The 1980s also saw women with infants entering the paid workforce in substantial numbers. Female participation rates now include married and unmarried, childless and with children, and black and white, yet increasing employment in the formal economy failed to reduce gender inequalities. The average female earns only about three-quarters of what a similar male worker earns. And women's participation in the world of paid work does not come, except at the upper income levels, with release from domestic responsibility and child care.

There are a number of reasons behind this increase in female employment. More women want to work outside the home. There has been a gender revolution since the 1950s, with middle-class female identity in particular no longer simply anchored to the role of domestic labor and child rearing. Lower-income women have always been in the labor market, but it is now more acceptable for middle-class women to work outside the home. Child rearing is delayed or ignored, as more women seek identities in the workplace rather than in the realm of domestic reproduction. More women have to work. The stark realities of declining middle-income wages means that most households now need more than just one person to work. Six out of every ten married women are in paid employment, whereas two out of every three single women are. Almost 70 percent of single women with children are in the workforce.

The Role of the Public Sector

One important change in the national economic picture is the rise of government and the corresponding increase in the importance of the public sector. The federal government is a major money machine, collecting taxes and spending revenues that in turn have major implications for urban economies. Federal spending in 2001 totaled $1,863,900,000,000. Though some goes to transfer payments, a little less than a half is spent on goods and services. Government spending through direct procurements (buying tanks and airplanes) and fixed-asset investment (building highways) plays a significant role in shaping the urban economy. At the national level the military-industrial complex is an important shaper of urban-regional economic health. The rise of the Sun Belt cities, such as Los Angeles and San Diego, is in large part a direct function of military-defense government spending. Regional industrial complexes have been built upon sustained government spending, especially in the areas of military-defense spending where lucrative contracts have allowed heavy investments that have laid the basis for long-term economic growth. Government spending is critical to both the genesis and the continued buoyancy of the urban economies of such Sun Belt cities as Dallas, Houston, and Phoenix as well as the Baltimore-Washington corridor.

The particularity of U.S. politics has also played a large part in guiding the geographic distribution of government spending. Compared to smaller countries where government expenditure tends to favor a narrow range of regions such as the southeast of England, the U.S. is a large country with a federal system of government designed to secure the power of smaller states. California and New York with 2001 populations of 34 million and 19 million, respectively, had two senators each, and so did Wyoming and North Dakota, with 490,000 and 634,000, respectively. Power in both the Senate and the House also derives from seniority based upon the number of years served so that long-serving politicians from small states can chair powerful committees. This system allows government pork barrel to be spread across the country and especially to the districts and states of powerful committee chairs. Government expenditure reflects political power rather than population size. The end result is that government money flows not to areas of greatest need or maximum economic efficiency but to places of political patronage. And as the country shifts to the suburbs and to the political Right, the big cities lose their political power.

At a more local level the location of federal government fixed-asset investments such as military bases, research centers, highways, and airports has a huge influence on local urban economies. The location of public highways, for example, has guided the form and level of private investment in suburban areas. The edge cities of out-of-town shopping malls and bedroom communities are as much creations of public spending as they are functions of private investment. Public investment provides an important container for private investment.

Government procurements, at the federal, state, and local levels, also lead the way in giving encouragement and preference to female-owned and minority-owned businesses. In the past twenty years these programs enabled a more diverse group of people to benefit from government contracts. The creation of a female and minority entrepreneurial class has been enormously aided by preferential treatment in the awarding of government contracts.

The public sector is also an important employer in its own right. Immediately after World War II the government's employment share of total employment fell to almost 9 percent. Since then it has remained around 10 percent, with minor oscillations. Between 1947 and 1981 federal employment rose by less than 1 million workers, and since 1980 the number of federal workers has remained at around 3 million. This figure hides a growing use of outsourced labor by the federal government. Many basic services such as cleaning, security, and data entry are now done by private contractors.

The largest increase in public-sector employment is at the state and local levels. In 1980 there were 3.7 million state employees and 9.5 million local-government employees, and by 2000 the respective figures had increased to 4.8 million and 13 million. As with the federal government, much of the services have been outsourced to private contractors, so these employment figures undercount the amount of "government-related" work.

Since the public sector is more unionized than the private sector, public-sector employment acts as a counterweight to the decline of union membership in the private sector. Public-sector employees are four times more likely to be in a union than private-sector employees. The heavy unionization of the public sector, along with relatively good working conditions and employment security, reinforces the outsourcing of work, as cash-strapped governments seek cheaper, more pliable workers.

Government employment, at least since the 1970s, is more open to women and minorities. Data for state and local employment show that, for 1999, 44.8 percent were women and 30.1 percent were minorities. Public employment has been an important platform for the creation of a black middle class and a significant source of female employment.

Public employment is a significant element in city finances and urban politics. New York City alone employs almost a half-million people, with an annual payroll of $1.7 billion. The cities with the largest payrolls are listed in table 9.1. Notice how city employment is a significant source of

TABLE 9.1

Public-sector employment in 2001

City	Public employment	Per 10,000 population	Annual payroll ($ million)
New York	458,100	579	1,708
Los Angeles	49,200	134	230
Chicago	41,300	145	171
Detroit	40,700	372	132
Washington, D.C.	37,700	192	48
Philadelphia	31,100	209	109
Baltimore	30,800	452	95
Memphis	28,200	446	80
Boston	23,300	396	80

work and income in many of the larger and poorer cities of the nation. The increasing size of city payrolls is in part a function of rising demand for municipal services. However, it is not a simple case of municipal employment growing in line with rising needs. There is also pressure from public-sector unions to win jobs and better conditions, and there are mounting political claims from urban constituencies eager to benefit from municipal largesse. There is a long tradition in U.S. urban politics of ethnic constituencies coming into political power and sharing the spoils of political patronage. Frances Fox Piven and Richard Cloward make a convincing claim that the urban fiscal crisis of the 1970s and 1980s was caused in part by cities being "unable to raise revenues commensurate with . . . expenditures; and they are unable to resist the claims that underlie rising expenditures."[4] What makes their case so strong is that they are not the usual right-wing conservatives eager to beat up on the public sector. They have well-deserved reputations as promoters of a liberal welfare agenda. Thus, their argument that the fiscal crisis in part was caused by the rising demands of public-sector unions and political constituencies wanting to gain access to secure public employment has all that much more power and legitimacy. Municipal employment is part of the political compromise worked out by business elites and community leaders to maintain political peace and lubricate the smooth workings of urban regimes.

Municipal employment is also a part of the conflict and compromise in the urban political arena. We can identify a number of diverse interests, including the concerns of taxpayers, users of services, and municipal workers. The groups are not mutually exclusive; some people can easily fit into all three categories. Parents of schoolchildren complain of poor-quality education; the same people as taxpayers balk at the rising tax demands; and they also may be teachers who want to keep their jobs and get more teachers employed to lighten their load. There are sources of conflict among the groups. Users of services want efficient, good-quality services. Taxpayers want to keep taxes low. Municipal workers want protected, high-paying jobs. In some cases all these interests can be held together, but in many other cases there is a conflict of interests, as often the tensions bubble up into direct conflict. Municipal employment is not just another job category; it is an important element in the ongoing struggle in the urban political arena.

The Rise of Retail

As the U.S. has changed from a manufacturing to a service-dominated economy, one particular sector has emerged as a very important economic and cultural phenomenon: retail. The selling of goods to individual customers not only plays a significant role in the economy but also acts as powerful economic engine, a transformer of urban-suburban landscapes, and a significant cultural marker.

In 2001 just over 23.4 million people were employed in retail, or approximately 17.8 percent of the total workforce. Retail constitutes one of the single biggest employment sectors, larger than the manufacturing or government sectors and second only to the service sector. One of the most significant features of this sector is its low relative wage. Whereas the average hourly earning in 2001 for production workers in manufacturing was $14.84, the comparable figure for retail was $9.82. The rise of retail goes hand in hand with the re-creation of a low-wage service economy.

Household-consumption patterns now constitute almost one-third of all aggregate demand in the economy. The U.S. consumer not only drives the national economic motor but is also one of the prime movers of the global economy. Many of the goods and services produced around the world find their way onto the shelves and floors of stores in the U.S., and their consumption is vital to the long-term stability of an increasingly interconnected global economy. U.S. consumers constitute one of the single biggest sources of effective demand in the entire world; their purchasing patterns filter through worldwide production chains into the distant corners of the world, from textile factories in Sri Lanka and Vietnam to electronic factories in mainland China.

Retailing is a central feature of economic organization. Retail now dominates production. The old push economy of the first three-quarters of the twentieth century in which companies made things and retailers then sold the items to consumers is now a pull economy where large retailers so dominate the consumer market that they tell producers what to produce and at what cost. The "big box" retailers such as Wal-Mart, Target, Kmart, Sears, and Home Depot have so much power in the marketplace that they dictate to manufacturers the cost, style, and delivery schedule of goods. The relentless drive toward reducing costs by such powerful companies as Wal-Mart is central to the staggering productivity increases in the manufacturing of consumer goods and to the globalization of manufactured goods. As Wal-Mart forces producers into intense competition to trim costs, it compels many U.S. economies to follow the route to China in order to keep up with its Asian suppliers. The large retailers have so much power that they force manufacturers not only into reducing costs but also into moving production offshore. Wal-Mart's inventory is now dominated by cheap imports from Asia, and although it gives lower prices to U.S. consumers, it also disciplines manufacturers and ultimately U.S. workers. Wal-Mart provides a platform for Asian goods and acts as a lubricant to the globalization of manufacturing toward the lower-cost producers.

The three iconic firms of the past hundred years are U.S. Steel, Ford, and Wal-Mart. Their individual trajectories indicate the changing nature of the U.S. economy. U.S. Steel was typical of early industry, producing the iron and steel sinews of an industrializing economy, with antagonistic relations between labor and capital. The Ford model was of high-paying jobs in standardized production that laid the basis for high mass consumption. The Wal-Mart model is bargain-basement retailing with costs kept low by a global search for cheap products and poorly paid jobs in the stores. The U.S. economic history of the past hundred years is the story of the shift from basic industrial companies through the age of mass production-consumption to the era of mass retailing.

Retail has been one of the most powerful centrifugal forces of American urbanization. The downtown department store of the 1950s has been replaced by the strip mall along the arteries of the metropolis and by the out-of-town huge shopping mall in distant greenfield sites. In this competitive market the earlier strip malls and shopping centers are experiencing stiff competition from the newer centers and discount malls. As retailers search for capturing either the bargain-driven or the fashion-driven consumers, the middle-of-the-road malls in unattractive strips are finding it more difficult to compete. The creative destruction that is the hallmark of the American city also applies to retail. The spatial organization of retailing changed profoundly in the past fifty years, moving from downtown to suburban-mall dominance. The competition for savvy consumers involves constant makeovers and new mall developments: it is not only that shopping malls follow the suburbs; now suburbs are following the malls, as residential developments on a city's far-distant edges are often anchored by shopping malls.

The mall itself is now a site of competing forces. A place to make money, it must also entice and entertain, enclose without threatening, control yet give the appearance of freedom. The shopping experience for fickle, sophisticated consumers must always be new yet always within the confines of the safely predictable, the comforting repeatable. As Jon Goss has noted:

> The shopping center appears to be everything that it is not. It contrives to be a public civic place even though it is private and run for profit; a place to commune and recreate, while it seeks retail dollars; and it borrows signs of other places and times to obscure its rootedness in contemporary capitalism. The shopping center sells paradoxical experiences to its customers, who can safely experience danger, confront the Other as a familiar, be tourists without going on vacation, go to the beach in the depths of winter, and be outside when in. It is quite literally a fantastic place . . . a space conceptualized, planned scientifically and realized through strict technical control, pretending to be a space imaginatively created by its inhabitants. The alienation of commodity consumption is concealed by the mask of carnival, the patina of nostalgia, and the iconic essences of everywhere.[5]

Lizabeth Cohen has identified three consequent major effects of the suburban shift to enclosed malls: the commercialization of public space, the privatizing of public space, and the feminization of public space. The construction of postwar shopping centers is more than just the making of new places to shop. It involves the creation of new public spaces where parking is ensured, the weather is controlled, and most consumer needs can be met. The unpredictability and anarchy of open, public-street shopping are rendered predictable and safe. The centers envelop consumers in more than just shopping choices. Restaurants and gyms, banks and movie theaters now sit side by side in specially designed places to keep the customer satisfied, entrapped in a totalizing experience. Shopping centers are the new sites of civil society, the new meeting places, the new third space between work and home where consumption is connected to a wider range of leisure activities. Shopping malls involve the commercialization of public space, the creation of privately controlled places that are hubs of social life. But it is a controlled and managed public life. The privatization of public space involves restricted access and a limited range of behavior. Unlike public space where open access and free speech are, in theory, allowed, these new commercialized public spaces have restrictions and controls. Most ban overt political campaigning, placing limitations on the ability to exercise free speech, monitoring behavior. Although the shopping-center managers want to make their sites public, they need passive consumers, not active citizens. The rise of specifically engineered shopping places also involves the feminization of public space, with the encouragement of female-orchestrated consumption. Women are often the most active consumers in typical family households, and shopping centers are planned and managed with women in mind.[6]

A new science of shopping now exists to make us buy more things more often. The design of retail spaces is finely tuned to maximize our spending. Tables are placed in the center of such stores as the Gap and Banana Republic so that people can more easily touch the sweaters and shirts. The more able we are to touch clothes, the more likely we are to buy them. Chocolate and candies entice at checkouts, so those shoppers waiting in line can make impromptu purchases with less guilt and children can annoy their parents enough so that they buy the chocolate. The makers of cereals pay the stores extra to have their products located at eye level where they are more visible and more likely to be bought than those cereal boxes languishing on the bottom shelf.[7]

The more pervasive rise of retail involves the permeation of the language and mind-set of consumption throughout everyday lives. Citizens were reconfigured as consumers. In my own area of work, universities are no longer just teaching students; they are "meeting the needs" of educational consumers. The notion of "selling the product" escaped the narrow confines of retail strategy to become a new mantra for activities well beyond the shop and the store. Modes of consumption enter the fabric of everyday life, just as the jokey slogans enter the language: "When the going gets tough, the tough go shopping," "Shop till you drop," and "retail therapy," my favorite because it combines the two popular discourses of psychobabble and consumption. The language and practice of retail infuse the soul of the nation.

Consumption is now a defining experience for individual and group identity. It is perhaps glib to say that fashion consciousness has replaced class consciousness, but it is not too far off the mark. Commodities are embedded in wider meaning systems. Emotional branding links people in their buying patterns to communities of fact and fantasy. Consumption is a dominant organizational focus of people's lives. To buy a certain brand of sunglasses is not simply to buy protection for your eyes; it is to make a statement about who you are as well as who you long to be. A whole language of persuasion is enacted to make us buy certain brands rather than others. The language of advertising is now the dominant discourse. Marketing makes us not only buy things but also accept a particular view of the world. A consumer ideological apparatus composed of signs and symbols, images and narratives fills the airwaves, public spaces, and private lives.

Consumption is now so pervasive that both rebellion and acceptance are mediated through its lens. The term *ghetto* in the 1960s U.S. meant the predominantly black, low-income part of town. By the early 2000s the term designated a style, the rapper's articulated act of rebellion as just one more musical or clothing choice with such qualifiers as *ghetto fabulous* to describe a particular variant. The ghetto is no longer a place; it is a fashion statement.

The Other Economies

The four economic trends that I have outlined refer to the world of the formal economy. There are other economies, including the informal economy, the illegal economy, and the domestic economy.

The informal economy is the world of unrecorded economic transactions. If I employ my neighbor's son to cut my grass and pay him twenty dollars, the transaction is rarely recorded. A great deal of such economic activity takes place beyond the realm of official records. In many poor communities the informal economy is often the way many people get by. The informal economy works best when there are strong networks of friends and neighbors and where the role of trust can substitute for the formal or legal.

The illegal economy is the dark side of economic transactions. Incursions into illegality can range from the minor (taking copying paper or paper clips from your place of employment for personal use) to the major (such as the making, distributing, and selling of illegal substances). In many cases there is no hard-and-fast line between legal and illegal economies. In the financial world, for example, sharp practice can soon turn into downright illegal in the blink of an eye. Recent corporate scandals highlight the fine line between savvy business practices and illegal transactions. There is often a distinction between white-collar crime, such as financial manipulations, which seems to be treated more leniently, and blue-collar crime, such as auto theft. Although financial scandals can cost investors millions, the criminals rarely receive the extensive jail time or harsh treatment that car thieves sometimes get.

The drug trade is perhaps the largest and most extensive illegal economy in the U.S. The crack trade of inner-city America is matched by the methamphetamine industry in small-town rural America. Estimates of billions of dollars of trade are simply guesses; we have no accurate figures. In certain communities the economic opportunities in the illegal drug trade offer a powerful option in the employment choices of young people. There is an arbitrariness to the definition of drug illegality. Whereas alcohol producers and tobacco growers receive government subsidies, marijuana growers and cannabis distributors receive jail time. Yet where there is economic opportunity and the possibility of supply and demand in a high-profit venture, the illegal drug trade will continue to play an important role in the informal economies of the urban U.S.

The domestic economy refers to the amount, type, and division of labor within the home. In the past fifty years there has been a changing relationship between the formal and the domestic economies. In 1950 fewer middle-income women worked outside the home; their labor was often unpaid domestic labor. Female participation rates in the formal economy were little more than 30 percent. By 2000 most women were working in the formal economy while still also responsible for many of the domestic chores and for raising children. Women in particular face a double burden of participation in both the formal and the domestic economies.

There has been steady decline in leisure time, with an increase in both the amount and the pace of work. People spend more time on the job, working harder. Paid holidays in the U.S. are substantially fewer than they are in Europe. The European tradition of paid summer holidays and long breaks at Christmas is unknown in much of the U.S. This time crunch induces people to spend less time with children and on relationship maintenance, and the net effect produces what Juliet Schor describes in her book of the same title as "the overworked American," a close relative to another described by the title of her later book, "the overspent American." She argues that middle-class Americans are maintaining and expanding lifestyles only through working long and arduous hours and by extending credit.

Mass consumption at the beginning of the twenty-first century recalls patterns of elite consumption at the end of the nineteenth century. Writing at a time of increased inequality and the amassing of personal fortunes in the U.S., Thorstein Veblen's 1899 book *The Theory of the Leisure Class* describes a leisure class whose wealth freed them from the need for employment. Their consumption patterns were connected not so much to basic needs as to the desire to create what he described as a "decorous" appearance. The leisure class was thus recognizable not by occupation or even ownership of the means of production but by its patterns of consumption. Of particular importance was *conspicuous consumption,* whereby the super-rich flaunted their exemption from the need to work. Examples of such ostentation include the construction of large holiday mansions and villas, the acquisition of arcane and redundant artifacts, an interest in elite sports, and a tendency to accumulate a staff of servants—groundskeepers and the like—to further indicate a distance from the world of work. There has been a spectacular rise in luxury consumption in recent years, with the consumption patterns of the global elite continuing to act as a marker for those individuals further down the income scale. In his 2000 book of the same title Robert Frank describes this spiraling process as "luxury fever." Consumption expectations are ratcheted up all across the income scale. The very wealthy are raising people's expectations and assumptions. In the U.S. the average size of a house has doubled in square footage in the past thirty years. In part it is a function of the positional nature of consumption. We consume in order to position ourselves relative to other people. People are no longer keeping up with the people next door, but with the people they see on television and in magazines. It is not so much keeping up with the Joneses as it is "keeping up with the Gateses." In order to maintain these raised consumption standards, people are working harder and longer as well as taking on more debt. The increase in luxury consumption has raised consumption expectations further down the income scale, which in order to be funded has involved increased workloads and increased indebtedness. As a nation we have become more affluent, but have we become richer?

10

Race and Ethnicity

"E Pluribus Unum"

IN 1963 NATHAN GLAZER and Daniel Patrick Moynihan published their classic work on ethnicity, *Beyond the Melting Pot*. It was primarily a study of New York City and the extent to which various ethnic groups sturdily maintained their distinctiveness. Their work was a conscious intellectual intervention, a spirited counterargument to the Marxian notion that urbanization would lead to class identity superseding ethnic ties. Their detailed work of different immigrant groups in the city showed that urban living did not diminish the ethnic identities, but reinforced them.

Glazer and Moynihan's work, while responding to the assumptions of their old ideological adversaries, was also expressing a long obsession with race and ethnicity in the United States. The motto of the Republic, "E pluribus unum" (One from the many), makes the observation that there are many, with the hope that from the variety a singular national identity and consciousness will be formed. Behind that hope lies a fear that the many may fail to become one. The city long has been singled out as one of the primary sources of this fear. Ever since the nineteenth century, the urban concentrations of ethnic and racial difference have been a source of continuing disquiet in the Republic.

The Glazer and Moynihan book was published at a critical juncture in the immigration history of the U.S. The period from the end of World War II to 1965, two years after their book was first published, was a period of limited immigration into the U.S. New groups had appeared in northern cities, especially African Americans, but foreign immigration was limited in size and origin. Two years after their book came out, a new immigration era was inaugurated that marked the beginning of a major influx of foreign immigrants into U.S. cities. Prior to the publication of *Beyond the Melting Pot*, the dominant concern was the continuing resilience of traditional ethnic identities; after the book was established as a classic, the abiding narrative was a celebration of hybrid new identities in the U.S. city.

The Problem of Words

Race and *ethnicity* are not so much descriptive devices as linguistic land mines, ready to go off in response to even the most gentle of pressures. We need to spend some time with the words themselves.

According to *Webster's Dictionary, race* can be defined as a "group of persons related by common descent, blood or heredity." Even this definition is hazy, conflating as it does history, biology, and genetics. But it is just this combination that is commonly assumed. Races are biologically different, and this difference, so the common assumptions run, both causes and embodies the separate histories. Although we can in most cases make ready distinction between men and women, racial categories such as black, white, or Asian, on closer inspection, are like fingers grasping water: the subject itself is fluid. Race is not so much a fact of biology as a social construct, partly adopted, partly imposed, and always constructed and defined in relation to others. Black is defined in relation to white, and Asian to non-Asian. There is no separate biological fact of race other than the relative, socially constructed definitions that we use. Race is the name we give to perceived social differences based on a shifting and unclear combination of half-understood genetics and half-remembered history. We can more accurately consider "race" as a fluid, relational concept rather than a fixed, eternal, biological fact.

Races are identified in relation to other races, and this categorization is not innocent of political and economic considerations. We classify in order to count, to demarcate, and ultimately to control. The term *racialized groups* refers to this social construction and use of racial categories; it reminds us that races are artificial constructs that embody political power and exact a social cost on those individuals in the least-favored, nonhegemonic categories. Though race may be fluid in theory, the most persistent fact in the racial practices of the U.S. has been the obdurate persistence of the basic black-white classification and division.

Ethnicity, on closer linguistic attention, is even more vague. *Webster's* defines it as "pertaining to or characteristic of a people" and, it goes on, "belonging to or deriving from the cultural, racial, religious or linguistic traditions of a people or country." *Ethnicity* is a more general term for different collective identities that are in part imposed and in part adopted. We can distinguish between *imposed ethnicity*, when a group of people are named and treated as ethnically different, and *adopted* or *symbolic ethnicity*, when individuals choose to express an ethnic identity.

Race and ethnicity slide into one another in common discourse. And there are some categories such as Hispanic that combine both. In the rest of this chapter I will use the term *race* to refer to the "racial" categories of white and black. I will use *ethnicity* to refer to a range of national origins such as Italian and Irish, as well as the more problematic categories of Asian and Hispanic. The term *race/ethnicity* will be used for the combination of race and ethnic categories.

Race: Categories and Numbers

Race and ethnicity do exist separately from the classifications we use and the ways that we count social difference. The classifications used in the U.S. Census both express race and ethnicity as well as construct racial and ethnic categories.

In the U.S. the main racial categorization has been the distinction between black and white. In the early nineteenth century, the census drew a distinction between free whites, free blacks, and slaves. From 1850 a more finely grained racial distinction of this basic black-white dichotomy was used, with the introduction of the term *mulatto*. The census of 1890 made an even finer distinction between "mulatto," "quadroon," and "octoroon." In 1930 these distinctions were dropped in favor of the "one-drop-of-blood" idea that placed anyone with a trace of "Negro" blood as Negro.

Other classifications were introduced and used in the wake of racial anxieties. After a wave of Chinese immigration and subsequent increase in anti-Chinese sentiment, the 1870 census introduced "Chinese" as a racial category. In 1970 the category of "Korean" first appeared. Races are defined less in relation to objective criteria and more in terms of national concerns about "floods" of immigrants and the invasion of the "other." The racial categories in turn take on a social reality. In the 1950 census seven racial categories were identified: white, Negro, American Indian, Japanese,

Chinese, Filipino, and other. This categorization uses both race (black and white) and nationality (Japanese and Filipino), thus adding to some of the confusion and reflecting the enduring concern with the black-white racial divide and the persistent anxiety with Asian immigration.

In 1950 89.5 percent of the population was classified as white, 10 percent as Negro, with the other groups making up less than 1 percent (fig. 10.1). The Chinese formed a small though significant population, highly segregated in largely urban enclaves, such as the Chinatowns of Los Angeles, New York City, and San Francisco. The prime racial cleavage was between black and white. Whites predominated in almost every city in every part of the country. Blacks were located in the South, with significant concentrations in selected northern cities. Many schools, public offices, and residential neighborhoods excluded blacks, as institutionalized racism prevailed in much of the nation's public life. It is to the lasting shame of the U.S. that for so long after the ending of slavery politicians of both major parties—while espousing general notions of freedom—tacitly supported the segregation and the second-class treatment of black Americans in this deeply racialized country. The treatment of blacks undermined the nation's claim to be the home of liberty and democracy and a shining light to the world and reinforced a global perception of the U.S. as a place of hypocrisy.

The black population in 1950 was concentrated in two distinct areas of the country. First was the South, where its distribution reflected the historic pattern of slave labor along the southeast coast and the banks of the lower Mississippi. There was and still is a concentration of black population from east Texas through the states of the Deep South up through Georgia and

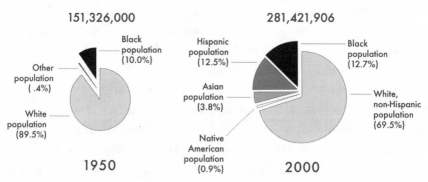

10.1. U.S. population by percentage of race and ethnicity.

the Carolinas to Maryland, a population marker for the historic distribution of slave labor in the cotton fields and on the tobacco plantations. Second, there was also a marked concentration in selected cities in the North, Midwest, and West. A predominantly rural population in 1900 had by 1950 become more urban, as people had begun to move from the rural South in search of greater economic and social freedoms. Between 1915 and 1940 almost 1.7 million blacks moved from the South to the urban North. New York City was home to almost 17 percent of the blacks outside of the South. Almost half of all blacks outside of the South lived in the six cities of Chicago, Cleveland, Detroit, New York, Philadelphia, and Pittsburgh. Neighborhoods such as Harlem in New York became recognizably black areas.

Fast-forward to 2000, and there are still seven races: white, black or African American, Asian, American Indian, Alaska Native, native Hawaiian, or Pacific islander. Census respondents could also select some other race and even put themselves down as belonging to more than one race. More than 98.6 percent of people reported in the 2000 census that they belonged to one racial category. In the fifty-year period from 1950 to 2000, the most important changes in racial categories were an increase in the Asian population, from around 0.2 percent to 4.1 percent; a small increase in the black or African American population, from 10 percent to 12.9 percent; and a relative decline in the white population, from almost 90 percent to 77 percent. The largest single increase was in the number of Hispanics, which were not counted in the 1950 census but constituted more than 11 percent in 2000. This category spans the racial divide as people who consider themselves either black or white can signify Hispanic status.[1]

From 1950 to 2000 the U.S. became more racially diverse, although it is still predominantly white, with this group's numerical importance reflected in their social, cultural, and economic dominance. In the rest of this chapter I will explore the urban dimension to the experience of the main racial and ethnic categories.

The Racialized City

From the late 1940s to the mid-1960s there was a massive population redistribution, as blacks from the southern states made their way to the cities of the North and West (figs. 10.2 and 10.3). Almost five million black people

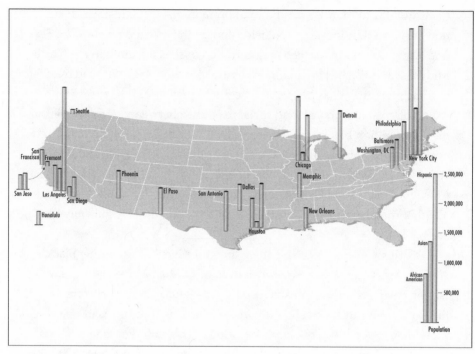

10.2. Top ten U.S. city populations, 2000 (for African American or black, Asian, and Hispanic or Latino).

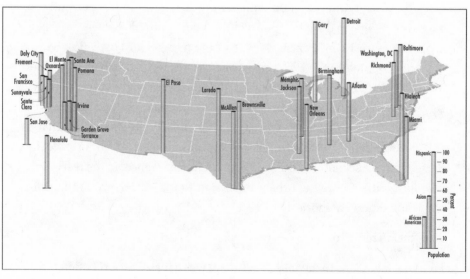

10.3. Top ten U.S. city populations by percentage, 2000 (for African American or black, Asian, and Hispanic or Latino).

left the rural South for the urban North. The migration was fueled by the search for social freedom and better economic opportunities. People left the cotton fields for the inner-city neighborhoods, and a predominantly rural population became more urban. Cities were changed in the process. In 1950 the West Side of Chicago was mostly white; by 1960 it had become mostly black. One neighborhood in the area, Lawndale, changed from 13 percent black in 1950 to 91 percent black in 1960. As blacks moved in, whites moved out; and as more whites moved out, more blacks moved in. Racial prejudices and outright discrimination herded the incoming black population into the poorest neighborhoods where houses were subdivided and further subdivided to meet the increased demand. Housing discrimination, involving the steering of real estate professionals and the lending practices of banks, restricted black households to "black areas" of the city.

In one sense the black migration to the cities was part of a long tradition of minority groups moving to the central city. Other groups also had a hard time in a white Protestant country: the Irish, Italians, and Jews all faced hostility and discrimination, yet whereas the other groups eventually moved out of the central city, the blacks tended to remain. There were complex factors at work. Institutionalized racism was different, more pervasive and damaging than mere ethnic hostility. Racial discrimination was woven into the fabric of U.S. society. The racial divide was wider and deeper than ethnic differences. Blacks were formally discriminated against in a housing market that restricted their housing choices. Households were denied access to nonblack areas and forced into increasingly black areas of the city.

As blacks moved into the central cities, the good blue-collar jobs started to move out. The long deindustrialization of central-city America began just after the blacks arrived there. The well-paying jobs suburbanized, while the blacks were restricted to the central city. The declining fiscal health of the cities, in part a function of the job loss, also made it difficult to provide the range of services, especially education, that could enable the next generation to move up and out. Funnels of failures were created in central-city America. The result was a growing concentration of blacks in selected central-city areas just as central cities were losing jobs and experiencing cutbacks in government expenditure.

For a range of large cities table 10.1 reveals a marked concentration of

TABLE 10.1

Black populations in central cities, 1950, 1970, and 2000

City	1950 %	1970 %	2000 %
Baltimore	23.8	46.4	64.3
Boston	5.3	16.3	25.3
Chicago	14.1	32.7	36.8
Detroit	16.4	43.6	81.6
Gary	29.4	49.2	84.0
Los Angeles	10.7	17.9	11.2
New York City	9.8	21.1	26.6

blacks in central cities over the period 1950 to 1970 and increased concentration over the period 1970 to 2000. This process occurred in traditional black cities such as Baltimore as well as cities with a relatively small black population in 1950 such as Boston. In effect, the central cities became more black, both in absolute and in relative terms. Three broad categories can be noted. There is a concentration of blacks in cities with a marked economic downturn such as Baltimore, Detroit, and Gary. In these cities manufacturing job loss has been very marked. There has been a increase but not numerical dominance of blacks in cities with a more buoyant economic base such as Boston, Chicago, and New York where there has been manufacturing job loss but economic growth in other sectors offset general economic decline. And there are a few cities, such as Los Angeles, where other racial and ethnic groups moved into the central city, and the black population declined in relative terms. Tables 10.2 and 10.3 list the cities with the largest black populations and the largest percentage of blacks. The cities cited in Table 10.2 include almost one out of every four blacks in the U.S. The black cities identified in Table 10.3 are predominantly declining industrial cites and southern cities.[2]

The growing concentration of blacks in central-city areas had two consequences. The first was the creation of an urban black identity, clearly revealed in the dominant musical forms. In 1943 Muddy Waters moved from the Mississippi Delta to Chicago. A musician well versed in the traditional blues of the rural South, his 1951 recording "Still a Fool" marked the beginning of a new urban blues, an electric musical form associated with the streets of Chicago and not the cotton fields of Mississippi. In the 1950s the

TABLE 10.2

Cities of more than 100,000 population with
the largest black populations in 2000

City	Number of blacks
New York City	2,129,762
Chicago	1,065,009
Detroit	775,772
Philadelphia	655,824
Houston	494,496
Baltimore	418,951
Los Angeles	415,195
Memphis	399,208
Washington, D.C.	343,312
New Orleans	325,947

TABLE 10.3

Cities of more than 100,000 population with
the largest percentage of blacks in 2000

City	% black
Gary	84
Detroit	81
Birmingham	73
Jackson	70
New Orleans	67
Baltimore	64
Atlanta	61
Memphis	61
Washington, D.C.	60
Richmond	57

rural blues became the urban blues. From then on, black music has always been associated with the urban experience. The harsh anguish of the marginalized urban dwellers replaced the haunting lament of the rural poor. From Muddy Waters to contemporary rappers, black musical voices are an important element in the cultural articulation of the U.S. urban experience.

The second consequence is an urban articulation of black political power fueled in part by a capture of the formal levers of power. The most obvious feature of this success was the election of black mayors. In 1967 two black mayors were elected: Carl Stokes in Cleveland and Richard Hatcher in Gary. Subsequently, blacks won mayoral elections in a series of cities: Harold Washington in Chicago, David Dinkins in New York, Tom Bradley in Los Angeles, Andrew Young in Atlanta, and Coleman Young in Detroit were just some of the high-profile black mayors of major cities. Of 218 cities with a population of more than 100,000, 29 had black mayors by 1998, and almost half of them did not have a majority black population. Black mayors embody black political power, but two provisos need to be made. The first is that the election of black mayors, especially in the biggest cities, required a coalition of a large black turnout and the support of significant white voters and business interests. Black mayors represent more of a coalition of interests than simply black power. The second is that even white mayors in major cities have to pay some attention to black constituencies. When Richard Daley replaced Harold Washington as the mayor of Chicago, black interests were neither marginalized nor ignored. Instead, they were a vital part of a coalition of support and patronage that crossed ethnic and racial lines. In the long tradition of U.S. urban politics, blacks, like other groups before them, have gained access to municipal power and city government largesse.

On the other hand, black political power also operates at an informal street level. The urban riots that shook the country are significant in this regard. There is a rich history of urban rioting in the U.S.: the politics of the street rarely breaks through the normal political discourse, but it has a significant place since the founding of the Republic, which in part owes its establishment to urban rioting. However, since 1945 urban riots have become synonymous with the perceived expression of black rage.

On August 11, 1965, a white policeman arrested a young black man for drunken driving in Watts, the black ghetto of Los Angeles. A scuffle broke out that quickly turned into a confrontation between a large black crowd and white policemen. Later that evening, passing white motorists were attacked by a rock-hurling crowd. For the next six days looting, arson, and assault were rampant in the area. The National Guard was called in, a curfew imposed, and order eventually restored. Over a six-day period, thirty-four people died, one thousand sustained injuries, and more than four thousand were arrested.

Watts was a taste of things to come. In the summer of 1967 civil disorder broke out in twenty-three cities, in large cities such as Detroit but also in smaller cities such as Newark and New Brunswick, New Jersey. The scenes of urban disorder prompted President Johnson to establish the National Advisory Commission on Civil Disorders, popularly known as the Kerner Commission after the name of its chair, Otto Kerner. The president charged the commission with finding out what happened and what could be done to prevent it from happening again. The commission report, published in 1968, signaled an official recognition of the deep-seated problems that underlay the civil disturbances. "Discrimination and segregation," the report noted, "have long permeated much of American life; they now threaten the future of every American." The commission cited pervasive discrimination and segregation, growing concentrations of poor blacks in the central cities, and the existence of black ghettos, where segregation and poverty converged, as the basic causes of the riots. The disturbances were the outcome of the frustrations of the powerless left aside in the wake of growing national affluence. The commission recommended increased aid to cities, a federal program to increase employment in the central cities, a review of police procedures, and active promotion of antidiscrimination measures, especially in the housing market.

The Kerner Commission marks a high-water mark of concern. It was the latest in a long line of reports of urban riots, from the 1910 riot in Chicago to the Harlem riots of 1935 and of 1943. The very litany of riots and their subsequent reports provide an indication of the underlying and persistent racial tension at the heart of U.S. cities. The Kerner report, written in a more liberal time of Keynesian economics and belief in the federal government's ability and duty to redress social and racial inequalities, was different, however, in that it assumed an interventionist federal government and national commitment to solving the underlying problems. There were some immediate actions. The 1968 Fair Housing Act, for example, banned the formal discrimination in the sale and renting of housing. The 1977 Community Reinvestment Act was a delayed response to criticisms of bank lending practices.

Since the Kerner report was published, many U.S. cities continue to be sites of concentrated and segregated black poverty, homes to the "underclass." This group is the subject of some discussion, producing two broad theories. On the one hand, there is a right-wing view that, at its crudest, tends to blame the victims. Their personal characteristics are the reason they are the underclass. This underclass is unconnected to a culture of work and saving, the very values that would enable them to improve their position. Poverty is created, so this argument goes, because the poor have a culture of poverty. Criticisms of the welfare system that promotes and sustains a culture of dependence add to this basic argument. On the other hand, there are those individuals who argue that the loss of jobs in the central city is a key feature in the creation of the underclass. The steady erosion of the economic opportunities to people trapped in the central city is the brute economic reality of the persistence of the underclass.

More sophisticated analyses now comprise both cultural and economic arguments. The loss of well-paying jobs from a population trapped in the central city reinforces the poverty of that community. The cultural norms of a poor, disadvantaged community, cut off from mainstream values, in turn reinforce that poverty. A community that condones out-of-wedlock births to young, poor women is not a community that is equipping its members to move out of poverty. Attitudes to education, for example, can help people do well at school or do poorly. In this more sophisticated theorization, structural arguments and cultural arguments are intertwined. Job loss, restricted economic opportunities, and continuing discrimination have all played important parts in ghetto formation.

In their book *American Apartheid: Segregation and the Making of the Underclass*, D. Massey and N. A. Denton make a convincing argument that segregation and poverty created the racial ghetto. They argue that blacks are segregated at all levels of income more than any other racial or ethnic group in the U.S., but for the very poorest there is what they term *hypersegregation*, which defines areas with more than 90 percent black people. More than one-third of all blacks live in extremely segregated communities. And not through choice. When the vast majority of black people are asked to state their preferences, they prefer to live in more integrated neighborhoods. In the ghettolike conditions an oppositional culture may emerge that will not celebrate educational attainment but will promote oppositional role models instead. Crime, delinquency, heavy drug use, teenage illegitimacy, and broken homes all become standard fare. Extreme residential segregation and restricted economic opportunities form the linchpin of the black underclass in U.S. cities.

Massey and Denton provide a recipe for the underclass. Take a group recognizably different from the majority population, generally perceived in a negative, inferior light; contain them in distinct areas with both formal and informal systems of housing discrimination; take away the jobs so that poverty results; underfund their social services; limit their educational attainment; isolate them so that normative behavior of joblessness, crime, and drugs establishes a culture of resistant poverty; and continue to keep them isolated in decaying neighborhoods. Then add to the mix a censorious blame for their problems.

Martin Luther King Jr. described a riot as "the language of the unheard." The interesting question is not why riots occur, but given the dreadful state of affairs why more riots don't occur. There have been only isolated riots since the ones that produced the Kerner report. On March 3, 1991, three black men drove through a red light on California Highway 210. Police cars followed. Eventually, there were twenty-one Los Angeles police officers surrounding the car. Rodney King stepped out and was savagely beaten, an act caught on tape by an amateur videographer. The police struck him again and again as he lay prostrate. He tried to get up and fell down again under the crushing weight of the blows. The imagery is as symbolic as it is dramatic: a black man mercilessly beaten by white policemen. Later, in the trial in the predominantly white community of Simi Valley, the police officers were found not guilty. South Central Los Angeles erupted; in equally dramatic footage black thugs beat a white truck driver. Stores were looted, and the National Guard was called into action. In one sense it was all depressingly familiar—the same scenes of shops being looted, flames flickering into the warm night, arrests, commentary, debate, and then silence again. It was just one more eruption at the most extreme point in the jagged relationship between poor, black, inner-city communities and police officers, a conflict fueled by a mixture of benign neglect and casual indifference on the part of mainstream white society and a resulting festering, sullen resentment on the other side of the racial divide. Yet among all this heartrendering familiarity, new racial dramas were also enacted in Los Angeles. Koreatown, for example, was badly looted during the riots. More than just black-white hostilities played out in the city this time around.

The Kerner report was produced at a time of belief in the federal government's willingness and ability to do something. In subsequent decades the government moved from active intervention to containment. No major federal programs have been forthcoming. The most significant trend is a rightward shift away from seeing the federal government as the solution and more toward it as the source of the problem. This shifting political culture reflects the rise of small government suburbanites eager to minimize taxes and the redistributional spending that helped the inner cities. The result is a continuing separation in the fortunes of the inner city and the affluent suburbs. The major government initiative of a Democratic presidency in the 1990s was the overhaul of welfare that made it more difficult to stay on welfare. While U.S. foreign policy was making a slow shift from containment to intervention, domestic policy moved in the opposite direction and away from the central cities.

Race continues to fracture the social life in the U.S. The black-white divide informs almost any social indicator you might care to mention. There is a persistent racial division in the separate lives led by black and white Americans, reinforced by the patterns of residential segregation and extremely divergent neighborhood conditions. More than one-third of blacks live in conditions of hypersegregation, while most blacks live in segregated communities. The basic conclusion of the Kerner report was "Our Nation is moving towards two societies, one black, one white—separate and unequal." This statement is nearly as true today as when the report was first published in 1968, despite some legal challenges and federal legislation. Consider the case of education.

Since 1950 schools have been officially desegregated. Following the decision of the Supreme Court on May 17, 1954, in *Brown v. Board of Education*, schools were mandated to end racial segregation of black and white children with "all deliberate speed," ruling the educational system to have been "inherently unequal." The case involved five school districts, Summerton, South Carolina; Washington, D.C.; Topeka, Kansas; Delaware; and Prince Edward County, Virginia. The name of the case derives from the Reverend Oliver Brown who along with twelve other families in Topeka filed suit to allow their children to attend the local whites-only school.

Although the 1954 decision made segregation illegal, there was resistance to the ruling. Prince Edward County simply closed its schools entirely rather than implement the ruling. Desegregation was slow. Black lawyers went back to court in Topeka in 1979 to speed up the painfully slow pace of desegregation, and in 1994 a federal judge ordered the closure of thirteen predominantly black schools in the Topeka School District to eliminate segregation.

Brown and the 1964 Civil Rights Act that gave further legal bite to the 1954 ruling did make a difference. In 1950 not one of the more than one million black children in the southern states of Alabama, Georgia, Louisiana, Mississippi, and South Carolina attended a racially mixed school. This figure remained the same in 1960, six years after the *Brown* decision. Even fifty years after *Brown* more than one-third of all black students in the South attend a school that is more than 90 percent black.

There has been some improvement. By 1988 school integration nationally reached a high, with 45 percent of black students enrolled in majority-white schools. Yet segregation continues: 41 percent of white children are in schools that are almost 100 percent white, whereas more than one-third of black and Hispanic children are in schools with 90 percent minority population.[3]

The legal mandate to desegregate schools is offset by the selective suburbanization that siphons off white families to suburban school districts, leaving many central-city school districts increasingly and overwhelmingly populated by minority students. In the South suburbanization trends have also been reinforced by the privatization of education.

On the fifty-year anniversary of the *Brown* decision, the *Washington Post* did a follow-up on the school districts involved in the landmark case. In Summerton white families left the school district, sending their children to a new private school, and the public school system was 98 percent black. In Washington, D.C., white families fled to the suburbs, and the public schools remain overwhelmingly black, considered by most to be dismal failures at educating children. In Topeka and Delaware (one rural and one urban district) the school districts are integrated, with the average black child attending a school that is 51 percent black. Prince Edward County closed its schools from 1959 to 1964, but by 2004 the average black child attended a school that was 40 percent white.[4]

The story of school districts from 1950 to 2000 is one of explicit segregation, of resisted legal rulings to promote desegregation and differential processes of suburbanization that reinforce segregation. Although there has been some desegregation in certain school districts, schooling in this country is still a racialized, segregated activity, especially in the South.

The Ethnic City

There never was a melting pot. Ethnic pluralism is always the exception rather than the rule. Although there has been a slow blending among broadly similar groups, differences persist. Rather than a melting pot, a more appropriate metaphor would be of a lumpy stew with a shared gravy.

From 1950 to 2000 ethnicity became more pronounced. In 1950 the U.S. was still in a period of very limited immigration dating from the 1920s. Immigration is a pendulum that swings one way and then creates the forces that swing the other way. This era of limited immigration had its roots in the previous era of massive immigration. There were two waves of mass immigration: the first in 1860–1890, when more than 10 million immigrants arrived in the U.S. mainly from northwest Europe, and the second in 1890–1914, when almost 15 million immigrants came from southern and eastern Europe. Waves of non-English-speaking non-Protestants into a country whose elite were English-speaking Protestants fueled nativist sentiments. The Immigration Restriction League was established in Boston in 1894. The Chinese were essentially denied further entry into the country by legislation in 1882 and 1902. Immigration dried up during World War I; it briefly revived in the early twenties, when approximately 800,000 people came in 1921, but by the end of the 1920s the immigrant wave subsided. A literacy test was introduced in 1917 and a quota system implemented in 1921. The Immigration Act of 1924 established a ceiling of 150,000 immigrants per year, and the total was divided into quotas that favored the British and other northern and western Europeans, which the *Los Angeles Times* declared at the time as a "Nordic victory."

The period 1950 to 2000, the focus of our attention, may be considered as two distinct immigration periods. The first, from 1950 to the mid-1960s, was part of the era of limited immigration. Immigrant numbers fell dramatically, and there were no longer streams of new immigrants to fuel the existing ethnic stocks of the first and second periods of mass immigration. The previous immigrant groups such as the Irish and the Italians prospered and, to an extent, Americanized. In the postwar world, as the economy boomed and policies restricted immigration, the ethnics moved out of the old neighborhoods and into the new suburbs. Though Glazer and Moynihan could still write about ethnic neighborhoods and attitudes in their 1963 book, they were writing just as the move out of these neighborhoods to the suburbs assumed momentum in the pursuit of the myth of a U.S. journey signaling Americanization, success, and integration—a myth always tinged, however, with nostalgic regret, as a kind of "invention of tradition" took hold. The old neighborhoods were romanticized as bastions and citadels of community and frugality that favorably contrasted with the conspicuous consumption in the new suburbs. *The Godfather*—the book and the movie trilogy—embodies these tensions as the Corleone family moves from the dense inner-city neighborhood of the first generation to the Long Island suburbs of the second, then out west to Nevada. The collapse of the family, in both senses of the term, is an arc of Americanization.

In this first period, from 1950 to the mid-1960s, with the lifeblood of new immigration closed off and the economy booming, the white ethnics took their place in mainstream American life. Second- and third-generation households moved into the new houses of the expanding suburbs. They stopped being "ethnics" and became just "white." Italian Americans, for example, moved from the margins toward the center of national cultural and economic life. The "Italian" in "Italian American" became a token of cultural heritage rather than a restricted economic niche. Given the enduring racial divide, the notion of a white identity became more apparent. As Italian Americans mainstreamed, white rather than Italian became a source of identity and political mobilization in many metropolitan areas.

The Immigration and Nationality Act of 1952 eliminated racial barriers to naturalization and immigration but still established a system of fixed quotas that favored northern and western Europeans. Immigration policy was subsequently transformed by amendments to this act in 1965, which abolished national quotas and moved to a first-come, first-served system. Immigration policy was transformed. Emphasis on family reunification guaranteed increased immigration, especially among the traditionally larger extended Asian and Hispanic households. Between 1971 and 1980 4.5 million immigrants came to the U.S., with increasing numbers coming from Asia and Latin America. The 1990 Immigration Act set a target of around 675,000 immigrants per year, with preference for relatives of U.S. citizens as well as employment-based considerations that favored professional and skilled workers. The effect of the 1965 and 1990 legislation was to increase and widen the immigrant streams to the U.S. From the mid-1960s immigration levels increased to more than 400,000 per year, rising to more than 1 million per year in the early 1990s.

This third wave of mass immigration, from 1965 to the present day, is ethnically diverse. In the first two decades of the twentieth century the top five countries sending immigrants were, in order, Italy, Austria-Hungary, Russia, Canada, and the UK. In the last two decades the respective countries were Mexico, the Philippines, China/Taiwan, the Dominican Republic, and India.

In the past fifty years the U.S. has again become an immigrant nation. Between 1961 and 2000 more than 24 million immigrants were admitted to the U.S.; 15 million immigrants were admitted in the period 1980 to 2000, with 5.7 million from Asia and 7.7 million from Central and South Americas. The percentage of foreign born increased from 6.9 percent in 1950 to 11.1 percent in 2000; also by this latter date more than 31 million people in the U.S. were born outside its borders. Almost 56 million people in the U.S., around 1 in every 4 persons, were either born outside or had at least one parent born outside the U.S.

From 2000 to 2004 another 4.3 million immigrants arrived in the U.S. Estimates now place the total number of immigrants at 34.2 million, or almost 12 percent of the total population. Table 10.4 highlights the main metropolitan destination points for foreign migrants. The Los Angeles and New York metro areas have very large absolute amounts, followed by San Francisco, Miami-Dade, Chicago, and Baltimore-Washington. The highest-percentage figures are recorded in Miami-Dade, where more than 1 out of every 3 people in the metropolitan area are foreign immigrants.

From 1950 to the present the "foreign other" is a much larger element in the national picture as well as significant in selected metropolitan areas. The truly remarkable feature of this ethnic transformation is the extent to which the debate is, with a few notable exceptions, handled with extreme care in the public arena. The benefits of multiculturalism are widely proclaimed, and the trumpeting of the positive influences of a varied ethnic mix is now an integral part of mainstream, established political discourses.

TABLE 10.4

Immigration and metropolitan areas in 2004

Metro area	Number of immigrants (000s)	As % of total population
Los Angeles	5,507	31.9
New York	5,217	24.3
San Francisco	1,970	28.5
Miami-Dade	1,611	38.8
Chicago	1,370	15.4
Washington-Baltimore	1,281	15.4
Dallas	1,140	17.7
Houston	947	19.3
Boston	827	13.8
Seattle	524	14.2

Note: See S. A. Camarota, Economy Slowed but Immigration Didn't.

Nativist sentiments have gone underground to the realm of anecdotal gossip, sullen resentment, and a generally unarticulated sense of the "country's changing for the worse." Relatively few ethnic backlashes occur. Indeed, ethnic slurs are now considered unacceptable in most polite conversation. Compared to much of the rest of the world, the U.S. handled a profound change in the ethnic makeup of the country with remarkably few social tensions. In the U.S. the formal separation of church and state that has allowed a rich religious diversity to blossom with the emphasis on individual rights rather than the elaboration of a singular ethnic identity has created a fertile ground for the flourishing of a multiethnic society.

The two largest racial/ethnic categories are Asian and Hispanic. There has been an Asian presence in selected cities of the U.S. for more than a hundred years. The oldest were the traditional Chinatowns of San Francisco and New York. From the 1960s immigration from Asian countries expanded the Asian presence beyond the traditional centers of concentration. "Asian" immigration comprises a broad category of countries, including Lebanon as well as Laos, Turkey, and Thailand. The largest streams are from China, India, Korea, and the Philippines. Together these four countries contributed more than 50 percent of Asian immigrants. The cities with the largest Asian populations are noted in table 10.5. The largest

TABLE 10.5

Cities of more than 100,000 population with
the largest number of Asians in 2000

City	Number of Asians
New York	787,047
Los Angeles	369,254
San Jose	240,375
San Francisco	239,565
Honolulu	207,588
San Diego	166,968
Chicago	125,974
Houston	103,694
Fremont	75,165
Seattle	73,910

cities attract the most Asians, but there is also a bias toward the economically dynamic cities of the Rain Belt and Sun Belt such as Seattle and San Jose. As with most migrant streams, Asians move toward the places where there are the most employment opportunities.

People classified as Asian tend to come from a variety of educational backgrounds, but one important element is the preponderance of entrepreneurial and skilled workers among them. Whereas only 3.3 percent of Hispanics have advanced degrees, the comparable figure for Asians is 15.3 percent. Whereas 22.1 percent of blacks live below the poverty line, only 10.8 percent of Asians do. Compared to the rest of the population, Asians are better educated and more likely to own a business. As table 10.6 shows, the places where Asians dominate are, apart from the case of Honolulu, all in California (see also figs. 10.2 and 10.3). Asian immigration follows the tracks of economic growth in the national economy, both reflecting and embodying the patterns of recent economic dynamism. Asian migration is also associated with particular niches of the economy: Korean grocery stores in New York City, Indian engineers, and "Asian" doctors and dentists.

There are differences within the general category of "Asian." Southeast Asians typically fare worse than East Asians (Chinese and Koreans)

TABLE 10.6

Cities of more than 100,000 population
with largest percentage of Asians in 2000

City	% Asian
Honolulu	55.9
Daly City	50.7
Fremont	37.0
Sunnyvale	32.3
Garden Grove	30.9
San Francisco	30.8
Irvine	29.8
Santa Clara	29.3
Torrance	28.6
San Jose	26.9

owing to the different kinds of immigrants, with refugees forming a larger proportion of the Southeast Asian numbers.

The number of Hispanics was recorded only since the 1970 census, when a question on Spanish/Hispanic origin first occurred on the long form distributed to a sample of the population. By 1980 the Hispanic-origin question appeared on the short form distributed to the entire population. The name itself is problematic: in recent years some complain of its European bias, preferring Latin or Latino/Latina to indicate a more New World emphasis. The term *Hispanic* is also a hybrid racial category, as it includes both blacks and whites. Hispanics come in all shades of skin color, although color coding often implies differences in class and social status. In this chapter I will continue to use the term *Hispanic* while acknowledging its difficulties.

Since the 1980 census the number of Hispanics rose in both relative and absolute amounts. This increase is in part a function of the census allowing the designation of a Hispanic identity as well as a function of increasing immigration from Central and South Americas. By 2001 almost 37 million people in the U.S. were designated as Hispanic, constituting 13 percent of the national population. By 2000 the largest national category of foreign born was Mexico with 9.1 million, easily dwarfing the next four

TABLE 10.7

**Cities of more than 100,000 population
with largest number of Hispanics in 2000**

City	Number of Hispanics
New York	2,160,554
Los Angeles	1,719,073
Chicago	753,644
Houston	730,865
San Antonio	671,394
Phoenix	449,972
El Paso	431,875
Dallas	422,587
San Diego	310,752
San Jose	269,989

largest sources: the Philippines 1.4 million, India 1 million, China 989,000, and Vietnam 988,000. The largest concentrations of Hispanics are in the three largest metro areas—New York, Los Angles, and Chicago—with a significant representation in large cities of the West and Southwest (table 10.7). The cities with the largest percentage of Hispanics, shown in table 10.8, are all in Texas or California, with the exception of Hialeah in Florida (see also figs. 10.2 and 10.3).

The term *Hispanic* lumps together very different ethnic groups. In much of the West and Southwest the dominant stream is from Mexico, whereas the Hispanic presence in Miami is predominantly Cuban. Hispanic immigrants comprise a wide variety of types, from poor, unskilled laborers, concentrated in the Southwest, to middle-class professionals. Although Hispanics form an underclass in many Texas and California cities, in Miami and Hialeah they constitute a dominant economic and political majority.

Immigrant Cities and Suburban Concentrations

The large-scale immigration of the past thirty years turned a significant number of cities into multiethnic sites. New York City, for example, is the destination for almost 15 percent of all the new immigrants since 1965, and

TABLE 10.8

Cities of more than 100,000 population
with largest percentage of Hispanics in 2000

City	% Hispanic
Laredo, Texas	94.1
Brownsville, Texas	91.3
Hialeah, Florida	90.3
McAllen City, Texas	80.3
El Paso, Texas	76.6
Santa Ana, California	76.1
El Monte, California	72.4
Oxnard, California	66.2
Miami, Florida	65.8
Pomona, California	64.5

the city changed as the percentage of foreign born increased to more than 35 percent by 2001, a figure not seen since 1910. The city is again an immigrant city. The most recent wave of mass immigration transformed the look, feel, language, sounds, and smells of the largest cities. However, unlike the previous waves' concentration, there are wider spreads of immigrants throughout the metropolitan areas. Although some settle in the central cities, many of the more recent Asian immigrants are widely scattered through the suburban areas of major metropolitan regions. Thus, whereas the Chinatowns of the nineteenth century were highly visible and dense, the "Little Saigons" are likely to be situated in suburban settings with people more widely dispersed, coming together for events such as weddings, dining, and shopping rather than living together in tightly demarcated ethnic neighborhoods.

A Brookings Institution research paper presents evidence of increasing integration in metropolitan neighborhoods in the decade from 1990 to 2000. The data show that for the ten largest metro areas, the number of predominantly white neighborhoods fell by 30 percent, all but one of the metro areas witnessed an increase in mixed-race neighborhoods, and among the neighborhoods that changed from homogenous to mixed race, most were in the suburbs.[5]

Race, Ethnicity, and Class

For someone who grew up in the class-dominated society of Britain, the lack of discussion of class in relation to race and ethnicity in the U.S. is bewildering. Much of the debate makes no mention of class or class differences, as if race and ethnicity trump any other form of social identity. If this assumption were ever true, it is becoming less so. If we consider race for a moment, class differences are more, not less, important. With the decline of formal segregation and the creation of greater employment opportunities, especially in the government-employment sector, the creation of substantial black middle and upper-middle classes whose economic horizons have broadened attains greater significance. Meanwhile, the position of low-income blacks with few formal skills and trapped in decrepit, hypersegregated, inner-city neighborhoods has worsened. As Henry Louis Gates Jr. noted:

> A theoretical politics of solidarity—of unity of sacred covenants—must inevitably run up against the hard facts of political economy. . . . [B]lack America isn't as fissured as white America; it is more so. . . . [T]he black middle-class has never been larger. And never before have so many blacks done poorly. . . . [W]e need something we do not yet have: a way of speaking about black poverty that does not falsify the reality of black advancement; a way of speaking about black advancement that does not distort the enduring realities of black poverty.[6]

The way to speak about these things is to add a class dimension to debates about race. Not all blacks are inner-city ghetto dwellers, and not all affluent middle-class suburbanites are white.

In the past fifty years class differences overlay, undermined, and sometimes reinforced racial and ethnic categories in complex ways. Immigration, for example, is not just the entry of low-income job seekers. There has been a substantial influx of middle-class immigrants from Latin American countries that is ignored by the dominant portrayal of peasants flooding the southern borders. Hispanic immigrants include both farmworkers in California orchards as well as the successful businesspeople holding positions of social, economic, and political power in Miami.

There is some movement toward a more nuanced awareness. In 1988

Jesse Jackson managed to galvanize many African American, as well as non–African American, voters in his bid for the presidency. Drawing on all the rhetoric of the civil rights movement, Jesse Jackson presented himself as the voice of black America. He won nearly seven million votes. In 1993–1994 Al Sharpton also ran for president, but with much less success. He failed miserably even in states such as South Carolina with substantial numbers of African American voters. There are many reasons behind Jackson's success and Sharpton's failure, but a significant one is the decline of a monolithic "black" vote. Many more blacks are registered Republicans and independents, and the notion of a singular "black vote" is now much less compelling. Class as much as race plays a significant role. And as racial and ethnic groups enter mainstream America, class will increasingly trump racial and ethnic identity. Race and ethnicity do continue to play significant roles in the mobilization and articulation of political power. However, when presidential candidates learn a few words of Spanish or attend a black Southern Baptist church, racial and ethnic differences are not so much attended to as reinforced. The more different the subgroup is from the rest of the population, whether by skin color, religion, or cultural values, the more these differences will be heightened under certain circumstances. To some extent these differences are maintained and even created by the practice of multiculturalism, which pervades the cultural discourse of the U.S. Ethnic entrepreneurs whose raison d'être involves promoting racial and ethnic differences have reinforced these differences. Even such ostensibly race- and ethnicity-neutral promoters such as Clarence Thomas and Linda Chavez, who built their reputations on challenging the old reliance on quotas and racial and ethnic identities, reverted to the race and ethnicity cards, respectively, when their political nominations were in trouble, Thomas to the Supreme Court in the Bush the Elder's administration, and Chavez to a cabinet post in the Bush the Younger's first administration.

The forces of globalization also maintain and reinforce diasporic identities. In the first decades of the twentieth century, immigrants to the U.S. faced massive journeys that effectively cut them off from their homelands. International travel was difficult and expensive; communication was fitful at best. Now people can keep in touch with their homelands much more easily; they can travel back home more frequently and make regular contact with their places of origin. The latest musical videos from the Bombay film studios quickly find their way into the homes of many Indian immigrants in the U.S. By such means ethnic identities are maintained.

Nathan Glazer and Daniel Patrick Moynihan present a picture of the continuing importance of race and ethnicity, exposing the "melting pot" notion as always something of a fiction. But so is the idea that identities are unchanging, singular. The immigrant experience dramatically transformed the U.S. into a pluralistic, multiethnic society. However, as the society changed, so too did the immigrants: although they may not have folded into an amorphous, banal mix, neither have they remained unaffected. Second- and third-generation immigrants both adopt and add to U.S. ways. There is a complex social interaction as newcomers and natives interact with one another, changing each in turn. Rather than a multicultural society, a condition that implies unchanging groups remaining separate from each other, there are different forms of polyculturalism, as various groups interact and change each other.

11

Housing and the City

"Shaky Palaces"

THE U.S. IS A NATION of owner-occupiers. In 1945 only 43 percent of all households lived in owner-occupied housing. And that percentage included some of the very poor as well as the very rich. Most of the urban middle class resided in private, rented accommodations in high-density neighborhoods. By 2005 the home ownership rate was 69 percent, with more than two out of every three households living in owner-occupied housing. The creation of a mass middle class and the government commitment to home ownership went hand in hand to create single-family owner-occupation as the dominant embodied form of the American dream.

The Rental Sector

There are two main housing types: renting, in which households rent dwelling space from a landlord, and owner-occupation, in which people purchase the property rights. In the case of private renting, landlords take the risks of purchasing property and finding tenants, but they get the benefits of increasing property values. Tenants get housing, the amount and quality depending on supply and their purchasing ability. There is often a conflict between landlords and tenants, as landlords seek to maximize rents and minimize improvements that cost money and thus reduce profits, while tenants want to minimize rents and maximize property improvements. The housing market is studded with conflicts between tenants and landlords. These conflicts tend to remain at the level of very local, often intensely personal conflicts. The government tends to get involved only when public health and social peace are threatened. In the crowded cities and overheated housing markets of the nineteenth century U.S., landlords were renting poor-quality spaces that were public-health hazards. In 1901 New York City passed the Tenement House Laws that set minimum standards, and other localities soon followed. The legislation was supported by urban elites not only for the health of the poor but also for their own self-interest. The diseases and viruses in the poor districts could and did spill over into the neighborhoods of the rich and powerful. The 1908 Housing Commission, established by President Theodore Roosevelt, suggested federal acquisition of slum rental properties in order to minimize the public-health problems. The proposal was never realized, as the power of property interests obstructed any federal involvement.

The need to halt inflationary pressures under wartime conditions resulted in rent control at the federal level in 1943. Rent control blocked rapid rent increases in a time of artificial scarcity. Rent controls are still in operation in 140 municipalities around the country. New York State alone has rent controls in operation in 55 municipalities that cover more than 1.2 million rental units. Rent control in New York City has been in operation since 1943. Originally, the system covered all rental units built before 1947; currently, it covers around 185,000 apartments. In addition, rent stabilization exists for apartments built after the war, around 1 million apartments. The controls limit the rent levels a landlord can charge compared to what could be achieved on the open market. For proponents, controls keep housing affordable, and in New York City there is an argument that it retains the low- to middle-income people essential to the smooth workings of the city. For the critics, the arguments against rent controls hinge around issues of investment, rent levels, and equity. Rent controls, it is argued, artificially keep rents so low that they reduce landlord profits, which inhibits further investment and the construction of new rental units. The controls create a scarcity that keeps rent levels artificially high in the noncontrolled, nonregulated apartments. The equity argument stems from the belief that some very rich people are benefiting from rent control. A policy designed to help the low- to middle-income renter may effectively subsidize the rich. In New York City some very rich people live in rent-controlled apartments. "Luxury decontrol" in 1997 lifted rent controls for households with incomes of more than $250,000 paying rents of more than $2,000. Both conditions had to be met; thus, a person earning $5 million per year but with a rent controlled at $670 would be exempt. Rent control limits rent levels, which benefits those individuals already in the apartments. If they are poor or middle-income, the policy works, but if they are rich, the policy is a boon to the wealthy. Other arguments against rent control, such as asserting that rent control contributes to housing abandonment, is simply not borne out by the fact that rates of housing abandonment are often greater in such cities as Detroit where there is no rent control.

The lack of investment in private renting is not, however, a function of rent controls in New York City. Housing choices are structured in the U.S. such that owner-occupation is the desired housing category. Why? Simply put, there are more benefits to be gained from owner-occupation than private renting. If you are a renter you are simply buying dwelling space. But when you buy a property you are buying not only dwelling space but also property rights and the potential ability to benefit from the increase in property prices. Owner-occupiers do not simply get dwelling space; they also get the possibility of capital gains.

Private renting is still important in three sectors of the market: in the very low-income sector where many households are unable to afford the down payment and mortgage payments associated with owner-occupation, among the more transient population who require quick access and exit from housing, and for those individuals who through choice prefer to live in rented accommodations. Though becoming of less significance nationally, private renting is still very important in the central areas of the larger metropolitan regions where a substantial rental stock continues to exist. Table 11.1 lists the most important cities for renting. New York City dominates the national scene, with more than two out of every three households renting from a landlord. Renting continues to play a role in the larger older cities where there are more single-person and nonchild households as well as a significant stock of apartments and rented accommodation suitable for both mobile professionals and lower-income households unable to afford owner-occupation. Renting is also a more dominant tenure type for nontraditional households. Whereas more than 18.8 percent of married couples are renting, just over 55.3 percent of nonfamily households are in private renting.

TABLE 11.1

Renting in U.S. cities, 2000

City	% renters	Population (millions)
New York	69.8	8.00
Los Angeles	61.4	3.69
Chicago	56.2	1.95
Houston	54.2	1.51
Philadelphia	40.7	1.31
Phoenix	39.3	1.22
San Diego	50.5	1.18
Dallas	56.8	1.14
San Antonio	41.9	0.95
Detroit	45.1	0.90

Encouraging Owner-Occupation

Because housing is very expensive in relation to average income, immediate house purchase is beyond all but the wealthiest. Mass owner-occupation requires financial institutions to lend large amounts of money and accept relatively small repayments over long periods of time. It is not the most attractive proposition for profit-minded lenders. Mass owner-occupation is made possible only in those countries where the central government plays an important role in reducing the risks to private lenders. Prior to World War II only about half of all owner-occupiers held mortgages, and they were typically three- to five-year loans covering only 40 percent of the total property value. These mortgage arrangements excluded large sections of the middle class from owner-occupation. As with many social policies in the U.S., the new framework was established in the New Deal. After the stock market crashed in 1929, the mortgage market essentially dried up. As part of a general effort to stimulate the economy, Franklin Roosevelt's New Deal established the Home Owners Loan Association to encourage the housing market by refinancing mortgages and introducing the fifteen-year mortgage, revolutionizing the housing finance system to make it easier for ordinary households to become owner-occupiers. In 1934 the Federal Housing Administration was established.

The new agency insured long-term mortgages and helped to establish lending practices based on 20 percent down payments for twenty-year mortgages. The government also provided mortgages directly. From 1944 to 1952 the Veterans Administration alone funded four million mortgages at very low interest rates with long repayment periods.

After World War II the government continued to make mortgage lending a relatively risk-free operation. The federal government insured mortgages, and legislation was crafted to create a very fluid market for the selling and reselling of mortgages. In 1968 Congress rechartered the Federal National Mortgage Association (Fannie Mae) as a private institution to provide liquidity in the mortgage market. Fannie Mae generates capital from around the world that is then used to buy up mortgages: in 2003 it purchased $5.7 billion worth of mortgages. Fannie Mae provides a vast pool of money to minimize the risk to lending institutions of lending large amounts of money in house-purchase loans. Through its various tax, fiscal, and housing policies the federal government takes away the risk of mortgage lending and makes house purchases an attractive proposition for households. Mortgage-interest payments are tax deductible, and, since 1951, taxpayers are allowed to make profits from the sale of their houses free from capital-gains tax. Tax expenditures are revenue losses attributable to federal legislation. Housing tax expenditures now constitute an important part of government fiscal affairs. In 2003 the tax expenditures on the deductibility of mortgage interest on owner-occupied homes amounted to a staggering $66 billion, while capital-gains exclusion on home sales was a healthy $20 billion. In terms of overall rank, these two items were the second- and twelfth-largest tax expenditures in the whole federal budget.

In the postwar period a benign cycle of increasing owner-occupation reigned as the risks were taken out of lending long-term mortgages for lenders, while the tax code benefited mortgage borrowers. Rates of owner-occupation continued to increase, reaching 60 percent by 1960 and 69 percent by 2005. A huge building boom emerged as low-density owner-occupied suburbs sprouted around the edges of every town and city in the U.S.

This encouragement of owner-occupation gives huge power to mortgage-lending institutions to shape the housing market. The risk-aversion

strategies of the lenders and their racial and socioeconomic biases operated in the first half of the postwar era to starve both inner-city neighborhoods and minority households of easy access to mortgage financing. It
was easier and cheaper for whites than blacks to get a mortgage and easier
and cheaper to get a mortgage for a new suburban property than an older
property in the central city. Such lending practices promoted the white
flight to the suburbs and laid the basis for the decline of the inner city.

The Housing and Urban Development Act of 1968 marked something
of a turning point in official policy, since the legislation made it easier for
lower-income households to obtain mortgages and allowed the FHA to in-
sure mortgages in older areas. The Civil Rights Act outlawed housing discrimination. No longer was it possible to legally discriminate against racial
minorities. The days of formal racial covenants were over. The question remains, however, does discrimination still exist? Moving from merely anecdotal stories to firmer empirical basis has been made possible by the 1975
Home Mortgage Disclosure Act (HMDA) that provides information on
mortgage approvals and denials by race and ethnicity of applicants and
type of property. Using and supplementing these data, the Federal Reserve
Bank of Boston undertook a study of mortgage applications in 1991 in the
greater Boston area, finding that the loan-rejection rate for minorities was
more than twice the rate for whites. Race and ethnicity are closely tied to
income and housing choices. One argument contradicting claims of mortgage discrimination indicts differences in the income and available housing to low-income households; thus, the high rate of rejection is measuring
income, not race. However, when the researchers took income differences
into account, they found that black and Hispanic households were still 80
percent more likely to be rejected for a loan. A careful follow-up study con-
firmed the validity of the results and also found across a range of other
cities that discrimination occurs at all levels of the mortgage process, including the receiving of less information on mortgage choices, higher rates
of rejection, and being quoted higher interest rates when accepted for a
loan. An even more recent study of housing discrimination, by the Department of Housing and Urban Development, using paired testing in which
identical applicants, except one is white and the other a minority, applied
to buy or rent accommodation, found that between 1989 and 2000 discrimination against African Americans and Hispanic home buyers declined

significantly, yet remained significantly high. Discrimination was in the form of denial of information about the availability of housing opportunities and agents sometimes steering African American households to less predominantly white areas.[1]

Discrimination may also occur against neighborhoods as well as individual households. The term *redlining* refers to this practice; the name derives from the former practice of some financial institutions to draw red lines on city maps to identify areas where they would not provide mortgages. Redlining was commonly practiced in most U.S. cities. A detailed study of mortgage allocation in Philadelphia from 1940 to 1950 identified different areas in the city. Those areas that had more than a 25 percent nonwhite population were graded "hazardous" by the Home Owner Loan Corporation (HOLC) and tended either to receive fewer mortgages than expected or to be awarded mortgages that had higher interest rates. The areas either starved of mortgages or denied access to cheap mortgages subsequently tended to deteriorate.[2]

Under the Community Reinvestment Act (CRA) of 1977, financial institutions must provide mortgages in areas from which they accept deposits, thus rendering redlining effectively illegal. The evidence on contemporary redlining is mixed, with some studies finding evidence for its continuance, while others do not. However, even if redlining is no longer widely practiced, the damage has been done, with the consequent decline and abandonment of areas previously starved of mortgage financing.[3]

Money Machines and Shaky Palaces

Owner-occupation is not only a housing choice but also an investment decision. By 2003 households invested almost $25 trillion in their housing. For most households mortgage payments constitute their single largest expenditure, and their dwelling is their largest wealth asset. When house prices rise, existing owner-occupiers see an increase in their equity. From just 2000 to 2003 home owners in the U.S. gained $2.6 trillion in home-equity wealth. A combination of rising house prices and declining interest rates allowed many households to remortgage and cash in. In 2003 $60 billion of this newfound money was spent on goods and services. The realized wealth of owner-occupation enriches households and is a significant element in the general economy. The home-equity spending of recent years did much to offset a sluggish economy.

Against this story of rising levels of housing wealth, it should be noted that increases in home equity are possible only with a combination of rising house prices and low interest rates. When house prices decline, equity is lost. Declining equity is most common in inner-city neighborhoods at risk of further deterioration and in housing markets where job loss and economic decline result in a slump in housing demand, which leads to a further bifurcation, as households in growing parts of the country and in affluent parts of the city tend to gain more housing equity than households in declining regions and poorer inner-city neighborhoods. Matthew Edel, Elliott D. Scalar, and Daniel Luria undertook a comprehensive study of home ownership in Boston working-class communities from 1890 to 1970. They found that rather than being an escalator to middle-class status, home ownership involved problems of rising taxes and maintenance costs and declining property values, making suburban "dream houses" more like "shaky palaces."[4]

The relentless dynamism of the U.S. housing market and the continuing extension of the suburban frontier place central-city and even inner-ring suburban neighborhoods on shaky foundations for sustained property-value increase. New houses are continually being constructed as newer housing forms achieve fashionable acceptance, while older, unfashionable dwellings in the traditional areas of the city are effectively devalorized. Uncertain property values threaten households that face rising maintenance costs, increasing taxes, and often declining services such as transportation links, schooling, and the range of public services necessary for a high quality of urban life. The dark side to the rosy picture of new properties in the outer suburbs and the occasional windfall gains of selected gentrifying neighborhoods is the steady devalorization of much of the older housing stock, especially minority neighborhoods in declining urban economies. In order to halt disinvestment and increasing vacancy rates, the City of Syracuse introduced an insurance program for buyers against loss of equity. Even in the boom years of the 1990s, the Syracuse economy was so bad that continual population loss meant declining housing demand that led to a fall in housing prices in the inner city. The average price of a house in the city fell from $63,601 in 1997 to $61,974 in 1999. The respective averages for the suburban areas were $98,409 and $104,207. The local congressman, who also happened to be chair of the House Subcommittee on Housing, secured $5 million of federal monies for the program in 2001.

The encouragement of owner-occupation remains the dominant housing policy, despite the higher risks to lower-income home owners, as they stretch their incomes to meet mortgage payments. Predatory lending practices to low-income households in central-city neighborhoods are increasingly common, as successive administrations promote owner-occupation for low-income households. These practices involving higher-than-average interest rates create a particularly vulnerable set of owner-occupiers. Predatory lending is the new form of redlining. At the extreme there is "house flipping," which is a practice followed by unscrupulous lenders. It works like this: a seller buys a house in a low-income inner-city neighborhood for a low price, makes some cosmetic repairs, and then sells it to a householder. The seller arranges the mortgage, often using dubious accountancy to make the buyer seem like a good financial prospect, and inflates the house price for good measure. The seller is often in cahoots with a subprime lender who charges very high interest rates. The seller makes a profit on the difference between the original price he or she paid and the increased resale price, and the lender makes money on the mortgage, which is federally guaranteed. The new buyers are left at the edge of their financial capabilities with a deteriorating house and declining equity. After a short while, the new owner cannot make the mortgage repayments, and the property is foreclosed.

House flipping was a major reason for the dramatic increase in mortgage foreclosures in the 1990s; they increased by almost 70 percent in a decade when relatively low interest rates were the norm rather than the exception. The city of Baltimore became a hot zone for house flipping, with 5,000 foreclosures in 1999 alone and a default rate of almost 18 percent overall in the period 1996 to 2000. Mortgages classified as more than ninety days late are considered in default. Whereas the FHA average default rate was 6.4 percent, some of the more notorious lenders in Baltimore such as Capitol Mortgage Bankers had a rate of 35.4 percent. House flipping was a common practice in a number of inner-city housing markets in Atlanta, Baltimore, Chicago, Los Angeles, New York, and Washington, D.C. In 1998 the Federal Trade Commission (FTC) filed suit against Capital City Mortgage Company for predatory lending practices. The FTC alleged that most Capital borrowers in the Washington, D.C., area paid annual interest rates of approximately 25 percent. The company foreclosed on one of every three of its loans in 1990. House-flipping practices were not restricted only to the fly-by-night financial companies. The Baltimore-based consumer-lending division of Citigroup, the nation's largest financial institution, neither admitted nor denied improper practices in its mortgage-lending program in the city, but in 2004 it still agreed to pay a $70 million fine and restitution.

Housing affordability is directly linked to interest rates. Low interest rates stimulate the economy in general and especially the housing market, as households can borrow cheaper mortgages and builders can take out bigger loans to finance their operations. Conversely, sharp increases in interest rates choke off housing demand and house building. The higher the rate, the more expensive are the mortgage-repayment costs. Table 11.2 and figure 11.1 show the general relationship between mortgage rates and housing affordability. The index of affordability is the ratio of median family income to qualifying income with values of more than 100 indicating that the typical family has more than sufficient income to purchase the median-priced house. Values of less than 100 indicate an insufficient income. These national figures show that affordability is in line with mortgage rates, with the most marked downturn in affordability associated with the high interest rates of the early 1980s. The data show an increase in housing affordability at the national level. However, households operate in the

TABLE 11.2

Housing affordability

Year	Mortgage rate	Housing-affordability index
1971	7.6	151
1975	9.2	123
1980	12.9	79
1985	11.7	94
1990	10.0	109
1994	7.8	129
2000	8.0	129
2002	6.5	136

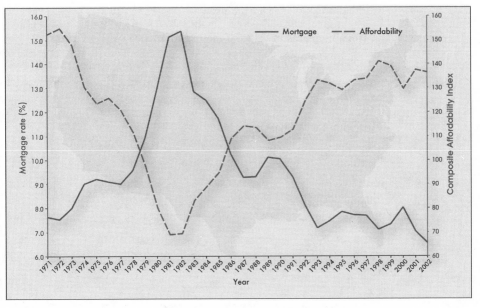

11.1. U.S. mortgage rates and affordability index, 1971–2002.

local rather than the national housing market. In 2002 the median sales price varied from $309,650 in Los Angeles to $146,369 in Loudon County, Virginia, and $97,400 in Fayetteville, North Carolina. Table 11.3 shows the variation in the median sales prices of existing one-family homes in selected metro areas of the U.S. They range from $475,900 in San Francisco to $136,500 in Wilmington, Delaware. The difference is not just between cities with expanding and contracting economies. Atlanta, one of the fastest-growing metro areas of the past twenty years, has relatively low median house prices. This marked variation has major consequences for those groups on low incomes or for ones at nationally set wage levels. It is much better to be lower income in Wilmington than San Francisco since your dollars will buy you more housing.

Table 11.4 presents data from a study by the Center for Housing Policy that identified families in housing crisis, defined as being unable to afford decent housing unless they spend more than half of their income. The study focused attention on working families earning more than the minimum income to 120 percent of the median income in their metro area. It was found that 76 percent of these moderate-income families spend more than half of their income on housing costs, while the rest live in substandard housing.[5]

TABLE 11.3

Housing prices in selected metropolitan areas in 2001

Metro area	Median sales price of one-family homes ($)
Anaheim–Santa Ana, California	355,600
Atlanta	138,800
Baltimore	158,200
Los Angeles	241,400
Miami	162,700
New York	258,200
Providence	158,000
San Francisco	475,900
Wilmington, Delaware	136,500

Note: See http://www.realtor.org/research.nsf/pages/HousingInx.

TABLE 11.4

Housing affordability in 2001

Metro area	Families in housing crisis	% of all working families
San Jose	45,278	27
San Francisco	49,609	26
Oakland	63,953	22
Tampa	56,206	21
Boston	88,573	20
Washington, D.C.	90,280	16
Baltimore	44,628	13
New York	513,649	12
Los Angeles	401,402	9

Notes: See M. Stegman, R. Quericia, and G. W. McCarthy, *Housing America's Working Families.* For a more recent follow-up study, see B. J. Lipman, *Something's Gotta Give: Working Families and the Cost of Housing.*

The increase in, and expensive, house prices in certain metro areas raise real problems of housing affordability. The squeeze affects even higher-income households who have to divert a significant part of household incomes to pay rising housing costs. There is often the paradox of where there are jobs, there are few affordable houses, and where there are affordable houses, there are often fewer jobs. In some parts of the country local municipalities have responded to the problem of housing affordability in a range of creative ways. Montgomery County in Maryland, a rapidly growing suburb in the south of the state close to Washington, D.C., introduced a set-aside policy. In larger developments 12 percent of new units were set aside at affordable prices, with a ten-year rule so that housing will remain in the affordable price range for some time. Between 1973 and 2000 more than eleven thousand units were set aside. In other parts of the region, especially in the Virginia counties, developers often resist the set-aside initiatives and fight them in the courts. Even more radical solutions include new forms of public housing such as third-sector housing involving housing cooperatives and housing associations. The main barrier to more creative solutions is the lack of government encouragement.

Encouraging owner-occupation is the government's main and often only housing policy. The extension of owner-occupation to lower-income groups is not without its problems. Unaffordable down payments, high interest rates, and an inability to pay housing costs such as maintenance, repair, and property taxes often make owner-occupation difficult for low-income households to reap substantial benefits. Various government programs back zero-down-payment mortgages and attempt, without much success, to reform the subprime lending market. Lower-income households are forced through lack of any alternative into owner-occupation and often into a precarious financial position.[6]

Externalities affect house prices. Positive externalities, such as a good school district, and negative externalities, such as the siting of a trash incinerator, affect local house prices very dramatically. The recognition of externalities is behind many households' locational choices as they seek to maximize the positive and minimize the negative. Houses in good school districts sell at a premium for households with children.

The importance of housing wealth formation explains much of the substance of community protest groups. With increasing owner-occupation there are more people with a financial stake in maintaining and improving positive externalities in their neighborhood. Actions that disrupt the possible increase in housing values are resisted. Thus, the so-called NIMBY ("not-in-my-backyard") type of protest is in part a financial response to a fear of the loss of house value. On top of the psychic and emotional value that comes from inhabiting a particular property, there is also a hard core of material interests that shape the character and substance of local political activity.

There are owner-occupiers and owner-occupiers. The more affluent can resist outside pressures that impinge upon their property values. There are even racial differences. Michael Shapiro argues that part of the wealth gap between whites and blacks is that black homes have not grown in value, as they are often locked into segregated areas with poor schools. Whites, on average, inherit more from their parents than blacks do, and differences in inherited housing wealth continue to play a part in past and contemporary inequalities.[7]

Public Housing

As with so many other federal policies, housing policy benefits the wealthier more than the poor. Tax relief and capital-gains relief packages used to stimulate owner-occupation disproportionately help the middle- and upper-income households rather than the very poor. Those individuals at the bottom end of the income scale find it difficult to enter owner-occupation, and when they do it is in the form of "shaky palaces" rather than "money machines." In many other social democracies, housing for the less wealthy was and still is provided by public housing. However, public housing in the U.S. plays a relatively insignificant part in the national housing picture.

The Housing Act of 1937 created subsidies for local public-housing agencies to provide low-rent accommodations, effectively introducing public housing. The 1949 Housing Act, under Title III, outlined ambitious plans for 810,000 units over the next six years, but by 1953 only 156,000 units had been constructed. Public housing received little official support or much local enthusiasm. Unlike in western Europe, where public housing was an important part of government housing policy in the third quarter of the twentieth century, in the U.S. it failed to achieve legitimacy as little more than warehousing for the very poor. The association of public-housing programs with the construction of high-rise modernist blocks reinforced the negative imagery. Public housing also became associated with minority households and minority neighborhoods. In Chicago the Housing Authority built 16,000 units between 1951 and 1968, most of them tower blocks in predominantly black areas. The Robert Taylor Homes project begun in 1960 and finished in 1962 consisted of twenty-eight identical sixteen-story blocks; it was one of the largest public-housing projects in the world at the time. Separated from white neighborhoods by the fourteen-lane Dan Ryan Expressway, a local newspaper quickly dubbed it a "seventy million dollar ghetto." In Chicago between 1955 and 1966 the council approved fifty-one public housing projects, forty-nine of them built in the black areas of the South, West, and near North Sides.

There are still 1.3 million households living in public-housing units managed by more than three thousand public-housing agencies. Most public-housing tenants are very poor with an average income of less than ten thousand dollars, more than half are elderly or disabled, and 40 percent consist of single adults with children. U.S. public housing is a warehousing program for the marginal and marginalized, available only to households that earn less than 50 percent of the median area income. The housing is often of poor quality and deteriorating. More than 100,000 of the 1.4 million units are officially classified as "seriously deteriorating." Under the latest program, Hope VI, more than 78,000 units will be demolished and 150,000 people will lose their homes.

Since the 1960s very little new public housing has been constructed. Housing provision for the poor has shifted from housing construction to rent subsidization. In 1968 the Housing and Urban Development Act introduced a rent-subsidy program, which in 1974 was developed further, under the commonly used name of Section 8. Under Section 8 the federal government provides money to public-housing agencies to help low-income households obtain housing. By 2000 1.4 million households were receiving $6,667 million in federal subsidies that ranged from approximately $3,000 per recipient in West Virginia to $7,744 in the District of Columbia. Under Section 8 a rent subsidy is available to make up the difference between 30 percent of a household's income and a fair market rent. For example, households that make $2,000 per month could rent property at $900, with $600 coming from their own income and $300 in the form of a subsidy. In some cities many landlords have come to specialize in meeting the steady government subsidization of Section 8 households.

Eligibility for public housing is restricted to households with less than 50 percent of the area's median income. However, only about 25 percent of eligible households receive rent subsidies. Although the U.S. housing market plays an important part in the creation and embodiment of a substantial middle class, it has been less successful in meeting the needs of low-income households. More than 7 million households pay in excess of 50 percent of their income toward housing, and 28 million households are burdened by housing costs that are barely affordable.

Homelessness

Though everyone has housing needs, not everyone can exercise housing demand. The U.S. housing system does well in providing the majority of households with relatively good housing. It is less successful in providing good housing for the lower-income groups. The almost complete reliance on the market means that the housing system responds more to housing demand rather than housing needs. The most obvious failure in any housing system is the extent of its homelessness. In the U.S. as elsewhere, accurate figures are difficult to obtain. The more reliable estimates suggest that between 2.3 million and 3.5 million people are currently homeless in the U.S. Approximately 1 percent of the U.S. population experiences homelessness at least once during any one-year period. A survey of the homeless by the U.S. Conference of Mayors in 2003 suggested an upturn in the homeless numbers of more than 10 percent over the past several years.

The causes of homelessness cluster around two main sets of reasons. There are the economic factors of lack of affordable housing, low income, and unemployment. There are also the social and personal tragedies of mental illness, substance abuse, domestic violence, and recent imprisonment. Homelessness is a tragedy that is at the very heart of multiple deprivation and economic collapse. A report from the Urban Institute by Martha Burt and Laudon Aaron, published in 2002, noted at least one bright spot in an otherwise dreary story. Since the late 1980s there has been a growth in the number of homeless services around the country, such as soup kitchens, meal distributions, and networks of support. From 1988 to 1996 the number of beds in sheltered accommodations grew from 275,000 to

608,000—not enough to take up all the housing needs but still a vast improvement. It occurred in a time of sustained economic growth. The question remains: will future downturns in the economy diminish the ability of local municipalities to meet the recurring crisis of homelessness?

Producing Housing

House building is an important sector of the U.S. economy. In 2000 the residential-construction sector employed almost 781,000 people, with an annual payroll of $25,519 million and a total value of $374,457,000,000, constituting 45 percent of all new construction. The construction of single-family homes in separate lots dominates residential construction. The industry is an important bellwether of the U.S. national economy. House building rises and falls in line with economic growth and confidence.

House building is a speculative enterprise in that most builders build before they have a specific customer. Speculative building of this kind is very dependent on external sources of financing, both to fund the production process, since expenditures are made before sales are made and profits realized, and to lubricate the financing of house purchasers. The industry is thus crucially dependent on interest rates. Very rapid increases in interest rates can make house buyers reconsider their purchases and put fiscal crunches on builders with overextended credit lines. Government fiscal policies affect house building. When the economy is in recession, reducing interest rates encourages the building and purchase of new homes, increasing aggregate demand in the economy. When the economy is growing too fast, with the threat of inflation, raising interests rates deflates housing demand, thus reducing aggregate demand and inflationary pressures.

New housing is just one part of the overall housing stock. Housing is a durable good that lasts a long time. The average life of a dwelling may be more than fifty years. Older housing is thus an important part of the total housing stock. In some cities the housing stock of a particular style or vintage becomes associated with the identity of the city. The residences of the French Quarter of New Orleans, the art nouveau bungalows of Pasadena, the high-density houses of Georgetown in Washington, D.C., or the Frank Lloyd Wright houses of suburban Oak Park in Chicago are just a few examples of distinctive housing associated with specific places.

The housing stock can be considered as a pipeline. At one end, recent housing construction adds to the stock, while at the other, demolitions and change in use reduce the stock. In the urban U.S. the most dominant change in the housing stock has been suburban construction of single-family dwellings. Since 1969 the yearly number of new privately owned housing units completed averages around 1.5 million, ranging from just over 2.1 million in 1973 to 1 million in 1982. This changes reflects general economic conditions, with recessions reducing, and growth spurts increasing, the number of completions. The vast majority—more than 85 percent—of these new houses are built in the suburban areas of metropolitan regions. Waves of new housing form the extending range of the suburban frontier. In the nineteenth century the settlers went west; since the 1950s they have made the great trek toward the suburbs. The new frontier is ever larger houses on the edge of the metropolis. The average square footage of a house in 1980 was 1,595; by 2001 it had increased to 2,103. The new larger homes are also better equipped; in 1980 only 63 percent of new homes had central air-conditioning, and only 25 percent had more than 2.5 bathrooms; by 2001 the comparable figures had increased to 86 percent and 56 percent, respectively. New houses are bigger, fancier, and take up more lot size. A wave of new large houses in expansive lots has turned farms into suburbs and fields into neighborhoods.[8]

Demolitions and abandonment are also significant. We have already touched upon the large-scale demolition of housing in the wake of the urban-renewal schemes of the late 1940s and 1950s. Since the 1970s the number of demolitions has tailed off. The federal bulldozer no longer creates as much havoc as it used to. However, in many large cities there has been a pattern of housing abandonment and demolition in inner-city neighborhoods. In Detroit, for example, there were 529,012 housing units in 1970, but by 2000 the number had fallen to 375,096. Between 1990 and 2000 alone the city demolished 34,931 housing units. It was by far the largest housing demolition loss of any city in the U.S. St. Louis and Philadelphia came in second and third, with figures of 18,565 and 12,941, respectively. This process is not the demolition of physically unfit, "slum" housing. In most cases it is the end result of the abandonment of physically sound properties. Houses are devalued to such an extent that doing repairs becomes a losing proposition. When repair costs are greater than possible resale value, abandonment is an economically rational act. As more houses are boarded up, they send a message of decay and decline. And so the process works like a contagious blight across the property market. As houses lie vacant, they become crack houses, sites of illegal activities, vandalized. Long-term vacant lots bring down the value of remaining houses and make it more difficult to maintain property values. A domino effect is created, as one abandoned property brings down the remaining value of the existing houses, thus making it more rational to abandon than to repair the remaining properties. Abandonment is an insidious blight that devalues neighborhoods.

Abandoned houses become breeding grounds for rats and cockroaches, fungus and mold. There is an epidemic of juvenile asthma in inner-city neighborhoods caused in part by the effects on children's health of living close to the abandoned housing that is a breeding ground for disease and germs. The extra days lost from school due to respiratory problems further educationally disadvantage these children and form just one strand in a binding web of social deprivation.

The demolition figures for individual cities are deceptive, as they highlight cities that have a more aggressive demolition policy. The City of Baltimore demolished only 3,229 units in the 1990s. This number was much less than the top three cities in this category, but this figure reflects a lack of demolition, not a low level of abandonment. The city has a limited budget for demolition, much of it reserved for immediate public-health or public-safety issues. Certain inner-city neighborhoods in Baltimore have a postapocalyptic character, as boarded-up dwellings proliferate in the more distressed communities. The number of vacant and abandoned dwellings is almost 40,000 in a city with a housing stock of 300,000.

At one end of the housing stock is the suburban frontier of large "Mc-Mansions" on impressive lots; at the other are the boarded-up units, vacant lots, and social despair of blighted neighborhoods. The precise mix of Mc-Mansions and blight varies with the relative economic health of the metropolitan region. Housing abandonment is a major problem in selected neighborhoods of the urban U.S., a problem concentrated in the older Rust Belt cities and all cities with an older housing stock and substantial job loss.

As housing ages it changes hands. If there is a substantial change in the social status of the successive residents, then the housing may be said to filter down or up the social hierarchy. Throughout inner-city America there has been a steady filtering down of much of the housing stock over the past fifty years, as the more affluent people move out to the suburbs. Some elite city communities sustain their exclusivity, such as Roland Park in Baltimore. Beacon Hill in Boston is another example of an old inner-city neighborhood that has retained its higher-income residents. The charm and cachet of a Beacon Hill address offset its lack of parking. Such neighborhoods are rare in the metropolitan U.S., where a restless quality of change and transformation is the rule rather than stability and endurance.

There has been a substantial change in the social and racial character of many inner-city neighborhoods. Although the dominant process is of older housing stock filtering down the social scale, there are some examples of the reverse process of gentrification. A strict definition of gentrification is the replacement of lower-income households inhabiting the housing stock with higher-income households. The term also refers to the movement into city neighborhoods of higher-income households, whether through their replacement of lower-income households or in the form of movement into custom-designed buildings. It has both a positive and a negative connotation. Many developers and downtown elites eager to lure higher-income households into the city to provide a stronger tax base and a population with higher disposable incomes promote the positive aspects. Gentrification is trumpeted as a revival of the city, bringing life back into the city. The advocates of the poor and lower-income individuals who see gentrification as a form of class warfare over space consider the process in a negative light.

Not all cities experience gentrification. The typical gentrifying city is large so that an inner-city location cuts down on substantial commuting time and costs and has a significant amount of high-waged service jobs in the central city. For many small, formerly industrial cities gentrification is rare or negligible, but in such cities as New York, Philadelphia, and San Francisco the preconditions are met. Gentrifiers tend to be younger people, often in single-person or nonchild households. People without children of school age are not affected by the perceived poor quality of public education in city school districts.

New York is home to a number of gentrifying projects. One is Harlem, home to many poor African Americans. However, major construction projects such as Towers on the Park, which opened in 1988, and individual households buying up brownstone dwellings have led to a distinct form of gentrification along the western corridor of central Harlem. More recently, Harlem was made a federal empowerment zone in 1994. Two Democrats introduced the federal empowerment zone legislation in 1994: Bill Bradley, a senator from New Jersey, and Charlie Rangel, the congressman from Harlem. The legislation targeted inner-city communities for tax credits, federal and state monies. The aim was to encourage private investment back into neighborhoods. Six areas were initially selected in Atlanta, Baltimore, Chicago, Detroit, Philadelphia, and New York. The Upper Manhattan empowerment zone comprising Harlem did in fact lead to increased investment. A large indoor mall opened in 2000 with chains such as Disney, Old Navy, and HMV that have previously ignored Harlem. The mall received a federal loan of $11.2 million. While retail choice has improved for many Harlemites, there has been an upward drift on house prices; brownstones can now sell for $500,000, and apartments without rent control are hiking up rents. The cost of renting commercial property is also increasing. Lower-income households and small-business owners are feeling the squeeze as Harlem gentrifies.

Just across the Hudson River from Lower Manhattan sits the small, formerly working-class city of Hoboken, just a quick ferry ride across from New York City's financial district. The process of gentrification began around 1980. Controls that maintained the presence of lower-income households such as tenant protection and rent control became more lax. The housing stock was effectively emptied of lower-income residents in favor of the higher-income households. And what was long a working-class town became a yuppie suburb of Manhattan. As the bull market of the 1990s expanded the amount and remuneration of financial services workers in Manhattan, the process of gentrification lapped even farther out into such places as Newark and New Brunswick.

In Philadelphia gentrification began in the early 1960s in the Society Hill area of the city, just south of the Independence Mall. A combination of state, private business, and public-private enterprises implemented the building of new high-rise apartments, Society Hill Towers, and the restoration of the older housing stock, much of it federal style. The result was the making of personal fortunes by developers, significant gains to select owner-occupiers and landlords, and the transformation of an entire area of the city. The process also involved the displacement of lower-income households pushed aside by the gentrification.

A similar set of processes took place on the other side of the country. The increased employment opportunities in San Francisco from the early 1990s generated an extraordinarily tight housing market. The Mission District, close to the downtown, was particularly vulnerable to gentrification, as it had a relatively cheap housing stock. The area of working-class families and recent Latino immigrants quickly transformed, as housing values, rents, and evictions all increased. Whereas the average rent of a two-bedroom apartment increased 6 percent in the city as a whole from 1997 to 1999, the comparative figure for the Mission District was 26 percent. Annual eviction notices in the city effectively doubled, from around fifteen hundred in the late 1980s and early 1990s to almost three thousand by 1998. And although the Mission District held only 9 percent of the city's rental units, it had 16 percent of the city's evictions.

Broad cycles of gentrification coincide with the cycles of the market, especially the rise and fall of business services that require downtown locations. The recession of the early 1990s saw limited gentrification in selected cities, but the economic upturn of the late 1990s saw another cycle of gentrification in such neighborhoods as the Lower East Side in New York City and West Town in Chicago. A buoyant market, the rapid growth in downtown business services and employment, and demographic trends that led to more single-person and two-person childless households fueled the process. Gentrification occurs in some smaller cities. One example that embodies many of the conflicting elements in the process of gentrification is contained in the story of one neighborhood in Columbus, Ohio.[9]

The Olde Towne East District, adjacent to downtown Columbus, was like many late-nineteenth- and early-twentieth-century residential areas. Built close to the city, it contained both high-income and middle-income residents in a housing stock that contained some large dwellings. Post–World War II suburbanization drew off the wealthier residents, and then a mixture of urban renewal and highway construction ripped the heart out of the neighborhood. Originally a stable residential area throughout most of the early twentieth century, by the 1960s the dwelling stock was in decline and most of the residents were low-income African Americans living in rented accommodation. This pattern was typical for much of the inner-city U.S., as downtown residential areas became racialized and stigmatized as the housing stock deteriorated. However, being so close to the downtown and with some substantial housing remaining, the area soon attracted the attention of white gay men seeking to buy and improve housing. In many cities gentrification has been associated with the coming out of a gay community. Single-person or nonchild households are often less concerned with the nature of the school districts. Inner-city neighborhoods of relatively sound housing and good accessibility provide an opportunity to invest both resources and sweat equity. In the Olde Towne East District the struggle between the white, male, gay newcomers and the longer-term residents—mainly low-income African Americans—took a particular form, as the new residents sought to designate the area as historic. For the longer-term low-income residents it was a financial penalty, as they were often unable to afford the costs of meeting historic-preservation codes. The property-cost increases forced out many of the low-income renters. The recent history of this area encapsulates a number of different cleavages—race, class, income, and sexual orientation—as two marginalized communities fought a turf war over the price and meaning of the residential space.

Gentrification is also part of a more fundamental rewriting of urban space, as it is often associated with the more aggressive policing of urban space. Mayor Rudy Giuliani's New York, before 9/11, for example, was marked by an attack on the homeless and the marginal and a policing of a new urban order to suit a more gentrified city freed from the politics of the street and the voices of those citizens on the margins and increasingly marginalized. The term *marginalized* is appropriate. It involves an active shove to the periphery, a self-conscious distancing and removal from both public space and public discourse. In selected neighborhoods around the nation, the gentrified city embodies all these active political moments into a compelling sociospatial urban transformation.

12

Politics and the City

"Informal Arrangements . . . Formal Workings"

THE U.S. CITY is a vibrant political arena within a national system of federal and state involvement and a wider global context of capital flows. In the past fifty years the broad story of this arena has been one of reductions in federal and state aid, metropolitan fragmentation of local governments with the consequent fiscal crisis of many central cities, the politics of growth in many suburban areas, and the shift from a managerial to an entrepreneurial city.

Levels of Government

The U.S. has a federal system with three distinct levels of government: federal, state, and local. The federal government is primarily responsible for national defense and foreign policy, while individual states are responsible for the provision of much of the physical and social infrastructure such as road maintenance, education, and police. There is both tension and cooperation among the three levels. The federal government wants to maintain ultimate power yet pass on responsibility to the other two. States want more fiscal autonomy from the federal government but federal help during recessions; in relations with local governments, they want to keep control and pass on responsibility. Local governments are often responsible for implementing policies laid down by the federal and state governments, but often lack the necessary fiscal basis to do so. Local governments are "creatures of the states," to use the words of Justice John F. Dillon, an Iowa

Supreme Court justice who ruled in 1868 that localities can exercise only powers that have been explicitly granted by the state. Although the relationship of local government to states varies, it remains an unequal one, with the state dominating.

The three levels of government work out various compromises and deals in order to pursue their shared goals and differing objectives. Tensions increase as cities become more different from the rest of the country in terms of racial mix and political attitudes, with more conservative state legislatures and more right-leaning federal governments often in implicit and explicit opposition to the more left-leaning cities.

One broad trend is the rise of the "new federalism." From the New Deal to the 1970s there was an enormous increase in local government spending with a significant increase in the intergovernmental transfer of resources. Much of it was in the form of grant-in-aid targeted at specific national programs. Federal dollars flowed into states and localities. The new federalism, first introduced by the Nixon administration in 1974 and codified during the Reagan administration with the 1981 Omnibus Budget Reconciliation Act, involved the devolution of power from the federal government to the states and a corresponding shift from directed, grant-in-aid funding to block grants that ostensibly gave the state more power to spend without federal strings attached. The new federalism, in principle, was intended to make government smaller, more efficient in delivering services, and more responsive to local variation in needs. In reality, the new federalism involved the shifting of responsibilities from the federal government to the state and from the state to local governments without the corresponding increase in expenditure capabilities. From 1980 to 1999 the percentage of federal funding of state and local government revenue declined from 18.3 to 15.0.

The majority of local government revenue comes from states. In 1999, for example, out of total revenues of $952,330 million, only $31,687 million came from federal government and $295,892 million came from the states. By the late 1990s state aid to local governments was only around 32 percent of total state spending, the lowest proportion since statistics were collected in 1957. To meet these deficits local governments increased taxes. Since 1985 there has been a sharper increase in local taxes than state or federal taxes.

Along with the decline of federal funding came the greater discretion of local governments and states. A study of the community-block-grant implementation between 1975 and 1981 in Milwaukee and Baltimore showed that although the federal aim was to help low-income households, city administrations in both cities gave higher priority to stimulating economic growth and expanding mayoral patronage than to improving low-income housing. Federal policy was co-opted at the local level for more parochial and partisan interests.[1]

Let us also consider the example of one of the largest overhauls to the social-welfare legislation. In 1996 a new act was signed into law, the Personal Responsibility and Work Opportunity Reconciliation Act. It was a central piece of the Clinton administration's welfare reform. Under this legislation the federal government replaced open-ended matching grants for general assistance and aid to families with dependent children with much more flexible block grants to states. In many states this responsibility devolved to local governments to set the level of benefits and entry requirements for the assistance programs. Although this legislation gave greater local autonomy in setting benefit levels, it also introduced such wide variation that the concept of equal protection under the law was compromised.

Each of the different levels of government is responsible for generating revenue and spending money. The federal government derives most of its income from personal income taxes and spends most of the money on transfer payments—especially social security—and national defense. States derive the bulk of their revenue from general taxes, with sales taxes and individual income taxes accounting for two-thirds of the tax revenue, and federal transfers accounting for the remainder. They spend much of the money on public welfare and education. Local governments derive most of their revenue from state grants and taxes, with property taxes providing more than one-quarter of all revenue, and spend most on education.

The federal government has the most power to set the fiscal agenda. There was a steady increase in the level of federal income tax from 1945 to 1980. Since then the ascendant Republican Right has achieved success with the rhetoric and policies of "no new taxes" and "tax reductions." Federal politicians, listening to their constituents, consequently define the fiscal reality as one of limiting tax increases. This national political reality of an effective capping of federal income tax, while maintaining high government spending, exerts extra fiscal pressure on the other two levels of government.

A fiscal crisis of the state occurs when expenditures outrun revenue. Borrowing may bridge the gap, but the different levels of government have varying creditworthiness. The federal government can borrow on the world market and use the power and prestige of national economic strength to secure creditors' good favor. Local governments, by contrast, are much more hampered in their ability to raise revenue. The general story of the past fifty years has been, with variations and loops in the basic tale, the endemic fiscal crisis of central-city governments.

The fiscal crisis of central cities is caused by the erosion of the tax base because of the outflow of jobs and people and the decline of state and federal transfers. Economic downturns reinforce these negative trends. The most impacted cities are the older Frost Belt cities that have seen a substantial loss of population and economic dynamism. The least-affected cities are the ones with increasing population and economic vitality. Again, the contrast between cities such as San Jose and Schenectady comes to mind. Metropolitan fragmentation magnifies the problems because it segregates out the declining and expanding parts of the metropolis into separate municipal jurisdictions. There is a pronounced central city-suburban fiscal-disparity problem as the metropolitan cores experience the cost of decline while the benefits of growth are shared among suburban areas. Though some cities have maintained a solid tax base and credit rating, many of the older, less economically buoyant cities have experienced an ongoing fiscal crisis. There is more recent evidence that the fiscal crisis is now also affecting the inner ring of suburban municipalities.[2]

This urban fiscal crisis fluctuates in line with general economic and political conditions. From the 1950s though the 1960s and into the early 1970s city government revenues grew from local sources and federal and state aid. An expanding economy was the tide that raised all government revenues, but by the mid-1970s a sluggish economy led to a crisis, as expenditures went beyond revenue. The case of New York City vividly demonstrates the character of a severe urban fiscal crisis.

From the 1930s to the mid-1970s New York City's government had an ambitious social agenda, reflected in public-health, education, and social-services spending that increased between 4 percent and 5 percent every year from 1945 to 1975. However, in the same time period, the tax base was weakened by the outmigration of people and jobs to the suburbs. Municipal revenues declined because of the erosion of the tax base, and by the early 1970s city politicians borrowed heavily in order to hold the line on tax increases and maintaining services and the jobs of city workers. The city was deep in debt, and after a six-month period from October 1974 to March 1975 when the banks sold city securities, the city was unable to borrow any more money. A fiscal crisis was declared, budgeting was taken out of the hands of locally elected officials, and almost forty thousand workers were laid off. There was a freeze of the city's budget and a state takeover of city finances. President Ford refused federal assistance. One of the more famous newspaper headlines on the front page of the October 30, 1975, *New York Daily News* read in block capital letters, "FORD TO CITY: DROP DEAD." The city avoided bankruptcy, but in paying off the debt it reduced other expenditures. By 1977 more than 20 percent of city spending went toward servicing short-term debt, workers were sacked, and services were reduced. The immediate cuts were directed at social services, public hospitals, and education.

The fiscal crisis of New York City marks a turning point in urban politics. From 1945 to 1975 city governments, if they had the political will, could and did pursue more redistribution policies by spending money on welfare, public health, and education. After 1975 the fiscal realities precluded such ambitious social spending. The tax base declined in most cities, and the reliance on raising money meant a greater reliance on obtaining and keeping a strong credit rating. Since most cities now need to borrow money, their credit rating determines the ease and cost of borrowing money (table 12.1). Credit ratings are based not only on the basic financial health of a city's finances but also on the policies they are pursuing. Pursue policies that are considered too radical by the credit agencies, and a city's credit rating drops. Credit-rating agencies are much more stringent in rating cities after the New York City fiscal crisis, which they failed to predict. All the major credit-rating agencies gave the city a good rating right up until the crisis was made public. Subsequently, the agencies have looked at all cities with a much more critical eye, and today the generally conservative opinion of credit agencies structures the policies of cities more than the needs, demands, or political will of their citizens.

TABLE 12.1

Credit rating of selected cities, 2001

City	Standard and Poor's bond rating
New York	A
Los Angeles	AA
Chicago	A+
Houston	AA-
Philadelphia	BBB
Phoenix	AA+
San Diego	AA
Dallas	AAA
San Antonio	AA+
Detroit	A-

Since the "DROP DEAD" headline, New York City's fiscal base has stabilized. The Koch administration (1977–1989) spent a considerable amount of effort winning back investor confidence by pursuing fiscally conservative policies. The progressive hiatus of David Dinkins, who was mayor from 1989 to 1993, saw a short-lived return to more liberal policies that were in turn undercut by a major recession. Under the Giuliani administration from 1993 to 2001 emphasis returned to public safety, education, tax cuts, and economic growth. An economic upturn solved some of the problems, and the long boom of the 1990s, especially in the financial-services sector, raised city revenues. However, the economic downturn of the early 2000s raises again the specter of an urban fiscal crisis, and not only in New York City. According to a 2003 survey of 328 cities by the National League of Cities, U.S. cities were once again in a fiscal crunch. The survey noted that the largest negative impacts on their budgets were increased costs of city workers' health and pension benefits, reductions in state aids, downturns in the local economy, and rising infrastructure needs. Cities were responding by increasing fees for services, reducing city employment, and cutting back on services.

Forms of Urban Government

There are a variety of forms of urban government. Within any large metropolis there will be at least three: counties, special districts, and municipalities. In twenty-one states there are also townships. This pattern is the predominant form of local government in New England, where originally decisions were made by a gathering of all adult males. In most places a more representative form of government now exists, with the electorate voting for candidates for public office and the governing body, probably the most immediate and direct form of local urban government in the U.S.

Counties form the basic unit of local government in the U.S. There are just over three thousand counties in the country, and their functions vary by population density. Counties are the administrative arm of state government at the local level. Urban counties provide a wide range of services including police, sewerage, education, and social welfare. As urban growth spreads out across the landscape, counties in metropolitan areas now comprise a growing proportion of the metropolitan population. Take the case of the Baltimore-Washington corridor (fig. 12.1). In 1950 the population of the two cities and nine counties that made up this area was 3.5 million, with almost half living in the two cities of Baltimore and Washington.

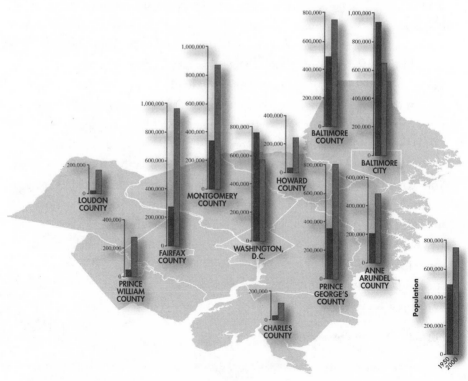

12.1. Baltimore-Washington area population, 1950 and 2000.

By 2000 the population had increased to almost 6 million, with only 20 percent in the two cities. And in the four counties of Baltimore, Montgomery, Prince George's, and Fairfax the population is greater than the population in either of the two cities. More of the metropolitan population now lives under county governments rather than city governments.

Special districts come in all different types, including school districts, fire service districts, library districts, and even mosquito-abatement districts.

Municipalities are the form of government in most U.S. cities. Their charters of incorporation lay out their powers that typically include such general services as public health, police, fire, education, public works, and planning. There are three different types of municipal government, reflecting stages of political change. Under the oldest, the mayor-council form of governance, the municipality is divided into wards or districts represented by elected councillors constituting a council that is the main decision-making body, with the elected mayor as the chief executive. Under a strong mayoral system the mayor wields enormous executive power by directly appointing the heads of the different departments such as fire and police. Under a weak mayoral system council committees run municipal departments. Even under the weak mayoral system, however, mayors are very important political players. The mayor-council form of government was the most important form of city government in the cities of the East and Midwest in the nineteenth and early twentieth centuries. This period was a time of mass immigration into the U.S., with many different ethnic groups pouring into the central cities. Political socialization was often through political parties, which controlled the votes. With the demand for municipal services and the power of the organized votes came the rise of so-called machine politics and the boss system. Through their control of voting mobilization, political-party bosses used their power to effectively run city governments. The bosses dispensed jobs and contracts and controlled elections. They channeled municipal services and jobs to certain groups who in turn voted for the party machine. The system enriched the bosses, socialized generations of recent immigrants, and limited the power of working-class votes. Machine politics exacerbated ethnic rivalries and promoted control and manipulation rather than democratic discussion. It was a profoundly conservative force that did not challenge the capitalist order or political system. It left as its legacy a system of political patronage and opportunities for political corruption that exist to this day. The mayor-council form of government is found in 50 percent of all municipalities, operates in 80 percent of cities of more than a half-million population, and is the predominant form of city government in the large cities of the Northeast and Midwest.

Whereas the rich could and did move outside the city to avoid the "rabble-ruled" cities, the middle-class business interests especially in the recently established cities often fought the boss system. The reform movement began in the last third of the nineteenth century as a response to the worst excesses of machine politics. Reformists sought a new form of city government, with nonpartisan councillors elected at large rather than representing specific districts, to minimize the concentrated power of ethnic minorities under the control of a political boss. Under the commission form of municipal government first proposed in 1900, citizens vote in a nonpartisan citywide election for a three- to seven-member commission that fixes tax rates, determines budgets, and makes policies. This form of government persists in 10 percent of municipalities and is most common in the newer cities of the West.

The council-manager form of municipal government was first proposed in 1911: it involves citywide, nonpartisan elections for a three- to nine-member council that sets general policy and hires a manger to administer city government. This type was the preferred norm for the early reformers, many of whom represented business interests eager to overturn the more populist boss politics. Under this system, people could continue to run their private business affairs and still influence general policy in the city, while a full-time manager assumed the day-to-day administration. This form of government occurs in 40 percent of all municipalities and predominates among medium-size suburban cities, especially in the West.

Under both reformist models emphasis is placed more on nonpartisan politics rather than party politics, citywide constituencies rather than concentrated ethnic enclaves, and the administrative discourse of rationality and efficiency rather than patronage and social justice.

Types of Urban Government

While the formal arrangements of government are important, there are informal arrangements of power that dictate the outcomes of government deliberation. We can summarize the issue by asking a fundamental question, who rules the city? There have been a variety of answers. In an early study of Atlanta, published in 1953, Floyd Hunter essentially asked the influential citizens who the power brokers were. A number of names kept appearing; the most prominent was Robert Woodruff, the Coca-Cola magnate. Hunter's analysis pointed to the dominant role played by a self-conscious business elite.[3]

Robert Dahl challenged this elitist position in his answer to the question posed in the title of his 1961 book, *Who Governs?* His analysis of New Haven, Connecticut, provided a more pluralist answer. In his examination of urban redevelopment, education, and party nominations, he discovered the involvement of a rich variety of different individuals and pressure. There was no tight group of names involved in everything; however, on closer inspection his work did show that despite the plurality of different individuals and separate organizations, the dominant voice was of middle- and upper-income residents and business interests.

What is clear is that business interests play an important role in shaping urban policies, oftentimes directly through the interlocking personal and business connections between the business elite and the political elite. Even where there is a more formal separation between businesspeople and politicians, business interests shape the boundaries and nature of local political debate. A study of urban renewal in Oakland, for example, discovered business interests promoted urban renewal and that the issues of the destruction of low-income housing and black displacement were never even raised as items for discussion. Matthew Crenson showed how air pollution was simply not an issue in many U.S. cities in the 1960s. Large companies disputed the scientific findings and successfully linked air pollution in many people's minds with economic growth and job creation. Power resides not only in the control of the formal levers of power but also in the ability to promote, to isolate, or to marginalize certain topics and interests for political debate. A more subtle understanding of local political power involves not only the analysis of issues and decisions but also what the nonissues and nondecisions are. Power resides in the creation of the political agenda as well as in formal political decision making. An "urban-growth machine" formed by the leading players in U.S. cities whose agenda is stimulating public and private investment to foster economic growth while limiting the social-welfare functions of the local area exerts subtle and sometimes not-so-subtle political direction. Realtors, banks, corporate chairs, and the organized power of chambers of commerce make up the heart of the urban-growth machine that works to define the city's overriding political concerns.[4]

Successful politics is the "art of the deal," the compromise that works. Sometimes business interests have to work with new political realities. Clarence Stone, drawing on his analysis of the governing of Atlanta from 1946 to 1988, identifies what he calls "urban regimes" that he defines as the "informal arrangements that surround and complement the formal workings of governmental authority." Urban regimes consist of informal governing coalitions that make decisions and get things done in a city. The two primary sets of actors are political power brokers and business interests. There has been some change in each set. In many of the large central cities the power brokers now represent African Americans and Hispanics as well as whites. Business interests now number multinational companies as much as simply local business interests. According to Stone, Atlanta now has a complex, durable urban regime that includes the downtown business elite and the black middle class. Business interests managed to incorporate the black elite, who in turn believed that they gained from the deal.[5]

A variety of urban regimes have been identified, but they tend to be variants of three broad general types: central city, suburban, and inner suburban. Central-city regimes, as in Atlanta, consist of alliances of business interests with the power brokers of the formal political machines. Urban-growth issues are elided with issues of social inclusiveness, and the progrowth lobby is less tempered by the need to maintain and extend political support across a coalition of varied political interests. In the suburban regimes the population is united by a shared agenda of keeping taxes low and protecting property values. The local regimes exist to maintain the status quo and often work to keep out lower-income and racially different groups. County governments with suburban regimes tend to minimize the notion of politics as a basis for discussion about compromises between differing interests and instead focus attention on nonpolitical issues of administrative decision making. Growth interests, especially for real estate agents, builders, and land developers, are often given political priority. Issues of rationality and efficiency trump concerns of equity or social justice.

TABLE 12.2

Population change in the Baltimore-Washington corridor

	Population 1950	Population 2000
Cities		
Baltimore	939,024	651,154
Washington, D.C.	763,956	572,059
Counties in Maryland		
Baltimore	492,428	754,292
Howard	36,152	247,842
Montgomery	340,928	873,341
Anne Arundel	206,634	489,656
Prince George's	357,395	801,515
Charles	32,572	120,546
Counties in Virginia		
Loudon	24,549	169,599
Fairfax	275,002	969,749
Prince William	50,164	280,812

Occasionally, some real politics emerges, and there are cases of antigrowth or no-growth backlashes. One example is Loudon County, Virginia, one of the fastest-growing counties in the country (table 12.2; see also fig. 12.1). The county increased its population from around 70,000 in 1985 to 235,000 in 2003. During that time just over 300 people were moving into the county every single week. The rate of growth was rapid enough to cause such high levels of traffic congestion and pressure on local schools and services that a slow-growth backlash emerged. In 1999 eight county supervisors were elected on a slow-growth platform, and the newly elected board of supervisors consequently cut the number of new houses planned for the county by 80,000. This strategy did not please the local development industry, which successfully bankrolled a number of candidates for the 2003 election. The new progrowth board soon created a new plan for the county that, although cutting educational spending by 5 percent, overturned the previous slow-growth estimates, reversed legislation that would allow localities to charge developers fees to offset school construction, revised plans to build new housing, rescheduled historic-preservation plans, extended water and sewer lines to aid further development, and created fast tracks for businesses seeking county approval. Although slow- or no-growth coalitions may occur, in the world of local county politics developers' dollars can go a huge distance in influencing opinion and political outcomes. A county in neighboring Maryland, Prince George's, also experienced fast growth. By 2004 some county council members proposed legislation to prohibit new construction in areas with adequate police and fire protection. One developer so angered by this turn of local political events helped to finance a campaign to add two at-large members to the council who would in effect be more prodevelopment. By late 2004 the FBI was investigating allegations of corruption and bribery involving Prince George's County councillors and developers.

The political regimes of inner suburbs undergoing decline have yet to be studied in great depth. However, as many inner suburbs begin to share the same economic fate of many central cities, we may be witnessing the dawn of a new form of suburban regime shaped by the facts of economic contraction and population decline.

The Decline of the Keynesian–New Deal City and the Rise of the Entrepreneurial City

The Keynesian–New Deal city is named, in part, after the English economist John Maynard Keynes (1883–1946) who argued that government had a major role to play in stimulating effective demand in the economy. While Keynes was mapping out the theory of an activist government in capitalist societies, Franklin Roosevelt's New Deal was putting it into practice. Faced with massive unemployment, Roosevelt's administration began in 1933 to use government spending to get the economy working at higher capacity, soak up unemployment, and secure social stability. The Keynesian–New Deal city lasted from the 1930s to the 1980s.

The period from 1933 through the 1980s marks the high point of the Keynesian–New Deal city when there was a consensus between capital and labor on the role of government. Government spending stimulated demand so that unemployment would be limited and controlled. The social consequences of business downturns were softened through government spending on programs that ensured that the majority of the population had access to relatively affordable health, housing, education, and social welfare. In the U.S. business interests held a stronger hand in comparison to northwest Europe, where organized labor was relatively stronger and social-welfare programs were not so curtailed by the greater resistance to taxes and to the role of government in general. Military spending sustained the U.S.'s global reach but restricted social-welfare spending. On both sides of the North Atlantic, however, the economic muscle of organized labor impacted the deal by forcing concessions out of business and government. Life in the Keynesian–New Deal city took away the rough edges of a capitalist economy.

From the 1980s the Keynesian–New Deal city began to disappear. There were many factors at work that have been widely documented: the persistence of stagflation that seemed to disrupt the balancing act of government spending that minimized unemployment while avoiding inflation and a growing resistance to government taxation as programs were funded by deepening and widening the income-tax and local property-tax base. However, what especially underlay the seismic shift was the declining power of organized labor. The loss of manufacturing jobs and the consequent decline in the size and importance of organized labor meant that business interests strengthened. Beginning in the 1980s a new metanarrative took over that limited government spending (especially on welfare programs), reduced social subsidies, freed up markets, globalized economies, and imposed limits on tax increases, all resulting in a massive redirection of government spending and a dramatic reorientation in the nature of the city.

The entrepreneurial city replaced the Keynesian–New Deal city. As the federal government reduces social spending and the tax base declines in many formerly buoyant industrial cities, city authorities are more concerned with generating money than spending. And even the spending tends toward creating a more fertile business climate. This shift involves specific strategies such as looking at the development opportunities of plots of publicly owned land and creating public-private partnerships in which business and local governments pursue joint developments. Concerns about improving the competitiveness of local businesses and attracting footloose capital dominate the urban debate. To a certain extent the debate is pitched at the level of general welfare, a variation of the trickle-down theory, which justifies large developments in terms of job creation and positive tax benefits. What we may call the TINA factor—"there is no alternative"—reinforces the arguments. At the end of a long period of Keynesian–New Deal dominance, it appears as if the center-Right now has a seemingly more coherent policy and a more muscular commitment to informing and shifting public opinion.

The shift from the Keynesian–New Deal city to the entrepreneurial city also involves a shift in political culture resulting in a less caring city. People as residents and citizens are reconstituted into people as workers and consumers. Being poor is less a condition and more of a moral failing. To be economically marginal in the entrepreneurial city is to be at best a social cipher, at worst a social threat.

The decline in communal public spaces and the rise of commodified, semipublic, semiprivate spaces, such as malls, distance those individuals less able to consume and buy. General urban public spaces became more segmented into income groups, and the marginal disappear as citizens and reappear as threats. And the more people hide behind gated communities, live in segregated suburbs, and patronize socially segmented sites, the more urban public space becomes less a site of regular interaction and more of a scary encounter. The higher the walls go up, the less the feeling of safety and security. As middle- and upper-income groups retreat from urban public space, the more it becomes a place of danger to be disciplined, policed, controlled, and avoided.

The End of Urban Politics?

Given the severe fiscal constraints on many of the nation's largest cities, it is legitimate to ask these questions: Has real politics, the politics of debating different alternative strategies, been abolished? Has the overwhelming power of financial power and the relentless logic of competition for scarce resources put cities in the nonpolitics of restricted political choices? Mark Gottdiener's provocatively entitled 1987 book *The Decline of Urban Politics* argues that cities, hemmed in by the power of banks and financial institutions and federal and state failure to provide the necessary revenue, have seen the eclipse of the polity.

There are some countervailing trends to this bleak view. Lynne Weikart, for example, followed expenditure policies in New York City since the mid-1970s fiscal crisis. Examining the policies of Koch, Dinkins, and Giuliani, she found that although the mayors' amount of money to spend was restricted by outside forces, they had some measure of autonomy in what to spend it on. Koch increased the number of city employees, Dinkins increased the amount of spending on social services, while Giuliani reduced social services and health services and spent more on law and order. The results of this careful study reveal two things. First, the external fiscal reality primarily and fundamentally shapes urban politics. The credit-rating agencies play a huge role in threatening negative ratings if taxes are raised or more money is borrowed, and they are particularly critical of more liberal mayors such as Dinkins. Second, the mayors did have some measure of relative autonomy in affecting policies. There was an urban politics at work but one severely shaped by external forces. The need to concentrate on economic development and supporting business interests squatted so forcefully on the agenda of city government that everything else was elbowed to the periphery.[6]

The shift in urban government toward a more entrepreneurial posture is nowhere more evident than in the use of eminent domain. Eminent domain is the condemnation of private land by public authority. It was traditionally used to help the construction of railways, roads, and schools. Underpinning it was a sense that government could appropriate private land for the public good. The definition of "public good," however, became more elastic during the time period we are examining. A radical shift was made with the *Berman v. Parker* Supreme Court ruling in 1954 that we have already touched on in Chapter 2. A large swath of southwestern Washington, D.C., a predominantly black, middle- and low-income residential area, was slated for renewal. The plaintiff was Sam Berman, executor of the estate of Max Morris, a department store owner in a relatively prosperous commercial part of the area. Berman argued that the family should be allowed to continue the business. The Supreme Court ruled against him, stating that the entire area needed "redesigning." The renewal plans went ahead, with dismal results. The area became a concrete wasteland lacking vitality, an example of the sterility of many urban-renewal schemes. Seizing land for schemes that promoted private economic gain became possible, feasible, and routine. Municipalities regularly used eminent domain for economic development; land, especially land, in low-income and minority areas was condemned and then sold to private developers who made money by building more upscale developments. The authorities used their constitutional power to ensure private gain on the assumption that the tax base was increased and some jobs were created. Fast-forward to 2005, and another court ruling again ruled in favor of the practice. By the early 2000s the economy of New London, Connecticut, like many former manufacturing towns and cities, had declined. The tax base was shrinking, and people and jobs were leaving. The city created a development corporation that produced a plan for a construction of a resort hotel, a conference center, almost 100 new luxury residences, offices, and retail space. The city approved the plan in 2000; it involved the compulsory purchase of 115 lots in the low-income neighborhood of Fort Trumbull. Fifteen of the owners refused to sell and took their case to court. The case is named after Susette Kelo, one of the property owners. It eventually wound up in the Supreme Court. The city argued that the process was legitimate because it promoted economic opportunities for people in the city. The plaintiffs' attorney argued that the city's actions violated the Fifth Amendment, which limits government condemnation of property to public use, because the proposed economic development did not qualify as public use. Taking land from one group of people and giving it to another just to generate taxes was not a public use. On June 23, 2005, in a five-to-four decision, the Supreme Court ruled in favor of the city. In one way the ruling reaffirmed what had become standard practice—urban authorities condemning private land, especially the property of lower-income minority residents, and reselling it to private redevelopers who made substantial gains all in the name of economic development. However, the ruling was so controversial that a backlash was created. In a dissenting opinion Justice Sandra Day O'Connor noted that "the beneficiaries are likely to be those citizens with disproportionate influence and power in the political process, including large corporation and development firms." Justice Clarence Thomas also noted that "losses will fall disproportionately on poor communities." One group, Freestar Media, LLC, proposed development of a piece of property in New Hampshire that just happened to belong to one of the majority-decision judges, David Souter. Their plan included a Lost Liberty Hotel with a Just Desserts Cafe. In a rare case of bipartisan politics, both Democrats and Republicans, responding to the public outcry in the wake of the decision, sought to reign in the power of municipalities to condemn houses. While the *Kelo v. New London* ruling reaffirms what had become standard practice, it may also signal the beginning of a change.[7]

A real urban politics does continue to exist, but it is heavily constrained by fiscal realities and economic pressures. In the late 1990s the City of Toledo, Ohio, for example, gave DaimlerChrysler exemption from property taxes and moved eighty-three households and sixteen businesses so that the company could expand. This arrangement is a typical example of the incentives cities offer to companies and corporations. And as each city offers incentives, the results are more generous tax breaks and fiscal incentives, a growing public subsidy of private interests. Cities have to compete, but the more they compete, the less the prize is worth. The political discourse of the city is now less about the social welfare of citizens and more about the competitiveness of local business, less a place of residence and more a site of business.

PART FOUR

The Emergent Metropolis

13

Reimagining the City

"Place Wars"

CITIES ARE NOT ONLY PLACES of work and residence but places for creative imagination as well. The "imagineering" of cities has long been an important feature of civic life in America. In the early years cities had to be marketed to foreign investors and migrants from overseas. The eighteenth and nineteenth centuries are full of examples of cities representing themselves as sites of profitable investment and suitable destination points for ambitious and hardworking immigrants. On the rolling western frontier, cities sold themselves as land-development opportunities with the coming of the railway. After the Civil War urban boosterism in the South was targeted at northern investors. Atlanta has had one of the most sustained urban campaigns, stretching from the early "Forward Atlanta" aimed at northern industrialists to the more global coverage associated with hosting the Olympic Games. The very names of some U.S. cities still conjure up images of mythical renewal (Phoenix) and classical splendor (Syracuse).

In recent years, however, there is a renewed concern with representing cities in the wake of the changing economic geography of capitalism. Throughout much of the nineteenth century and most of the twentieth there was a relatively crude division of labor; manufacturing production was undertaken in the industrial cities of the capitalist-core economies. In the past thirty years technological developments, leading to the deskilling of labor and the decreasing size of transport costs, allowed manufacturing production to be undertaken around the world. Labor costs determine location more now than the need to be close to markets or pools of skilled labor. The net effect is the relocation of manufacturing, a global shift that has seen the decline of older manufacturing cities in the capitalist-core economies and the growth of cities in the newly industrializing countries. New footloose industries have also emerged, especially in the high-tech sectors. These brain-driven, knowledge industries have a high degree of locational flexibility. Service and command functions can also locate away from the previously dominant cities, owing to changes such as e-mail, video conferencing, and cheaper telephone and fax rates.

In the world of hypermobile capital and global competition between places, world cities no longer have a monopoly of command-and-control functions. Industrial cities in the developed world have to compete with places around the world, and all cities compete for the benefits of the postindustrial economy. The term *place wars* has been used to describe this competition.[1]

It is in this highly competitive and zero-sum game that city marketing campaigns occur. Images portrayed by cities tend to be developed by the city's marketing consultancy contracted by the chamber of commerce, economic development associations, visitors bureau, and the nexus of organizations that link local business elites with political regimes. Each city selects and authorizes particularly favorable images. The main objectives of this kind of marketing are raising the competitive profile of the city and attracting inward investment. The targets are business firms, industrial plants, corporate and divisional headquarters, investment capital, sports teams, tourists, conventioneers, and also residents. Today's cities are commodified, packaged, advertised, and marketed much as any other product in a capitalist society.

Although much is made of city advertising, it is important to place it in a broader context. Advertising by all cities in the U.S. amounts to only one-tenth of the advertising budget of Miller Lite and only one-twentieth of Burger King's. However, city advertising can afford to be smaller because it is targeted at the business press, the opinion makers and business leaders. Favored outlets include the *Wall Street Journal, Business Week, Fortune, Forbes, New York Post, Newsweek, Time,* and the *New York Times.* The effects of this expenditure are impossible to evaluate, but cities continue to spend money on advertising in part because they think it might work and in part because other cities are doing it. In the deregulated global economic context of contemporary place wars, all cities need to be noticed.

Many cities advertise themselves in major business or travel journals. A colleague and I collected thirty-four cities' advertisements from the following periodicals, *Advertising Age, Business Week, Financial World, Forbes, Fortune, Historic Preservation, National Geographic Traveler,* and *New Choices for Retirement Living,* for the period 1994–1995. Some of these ads are major texts; the page count for advertising supplements for Boston, Kansas City, Milwaukee, Philadelphia, and Rochester regularly exceeded twenty pages. Two things, the slogans and the dominant images, signified each city.[2]

As an eye-catching device, the slogan is one of the simplest and most effective means to implant ideas and to aid in name recognition. A list of city slogans is given in table 13.1, where two categories are shown: the first group reflects the business sell and the second group the more tourist-oriented slogans. The slogans come in all types, from Rochester's emphasis on its photocopying and photographic industrial base to San Jose's simple geographic exclamation, and they range in understanding from Philadelphia's clever cinematic reference to Omaha's strange message.

Table 13.2 lists a set of common images or standard repertoires. Cities marshal a long list of good incentives and images in their ads that revolve around the broad themes of economic benefits and quality of life. Cities trumpet their probusiness political climate, ideal workforce, high-technology industries and research institutes, solid infrastructure, and healthy local economy. They also emphasize quality of life, including healthy green environments and cultural and recreational facilities.

Most advertisements use an impressive listing of (inter)nationally known companies based in local areas. It is one rhetorical device through which advertisers seek to give credibility to their discourse by referring to their previous successes. The quotations from independent surveys on the city are also one of the popular features in the ads. For example, Kansas City boasts of its number-one-ranking workforce in the U.S. by *Fortune* based on skills and availability; Fairfax County mentions that in the previous year *City and State* proclaimed the county the best financially managed county in the nation. A popular device is the testimonial of senior executives of local companies who express their satisfaction with the city.

TABLE 13.1

City slogans

City	Business slogan
Atlanta	Strategically located for global business
Baltimore	More service, more choices
Boston	Progress through partnership; America's working city
Chicago	At the heart of everything
Dallas	The city of choice for business
Fairfax	The 21st century's first destination
Findlay, Ohio	Hot spot for business development
Jacksonville	The expansion city on Florida's First Coast
Kansas City, Missouri	America's smart city
Los Angeles	Capital of the future; Together we're the best
Memphis	America's distribution center; The new gateway of the world
Miami	The birth of new Miami
Milwaukee	The city that works for your business
New York	The business city that never sleeps
Norfolk	Where business is a pleasure
Oak Ridge, Tennessee	When it comes to technology . . . Oak Ridge means business!
Philadelphia	The real Philadelphia story; All roads lead to Philadelphia
Phoenix	Moving business in the right direction; The best of the best
Pittsburgh	America's future city; A model of postindustrial economic renaissance
Rochester, New York	The world's image center
San Jose	Capital of Silicon Valley
Troy, Ohio	A great location for your company

(continued on facing page)

Photography is one of the major elements in the advertisements. The pictures capture images of great natural beauty, postmodern architecture, high-tech equipment, gorgeous night scenes of downtown, rich historical and recreational places, festivals, and photos of governors and chief executive officers (CEOs) of major local companies.

There are many common features in the designs because of the similarity in the projected images and also because of the preferences of the dominant advertising agencies specializing in place marketing, such as Leslie

TABLE 13.1 (*cont.*)

City slogans

City	Tourist slogan
Atlantic City	America's favorite playground
Battlement Mesa, Colorado	Where every day is picture-perfect
Denver	A cultural and environment adventure
Fisher Island, Florida	Unlike any community in the world
Hampton, Virginia	From sea to the stars
Lexington, Kentucky	The gateway; What's not far away
Lincoln City, Oregon	Here, the sights see you too
Louisville, Kentucky	Your kind of place
Nashville	Music City
Omaha	Wild creatures loose in city
Orlando	Sun and fun; You never outgrow it
Salisbury, North Carolina	Where the past is still present
San Antonio	Something to remember
Santa Fe	Where traditions live on
Saratoga, New York	Discover the magic!
St. Augustine	Your place in history

Singer Design, responsible for the majority of city advertisements printed in *Forbes*. Despite the similarities, however, there are also examples of efforts to distinguish a city from others. Advertisers create specific symbols or metaphors: Boston's local research institutes with impeccable reputations, Chicago as a world-class financial center, Fairfax's and Oak Ridge's high-tech capabilities, Memphis's distribution advantages, Rochester as a world image center, Atlantic City's year-round entertainment, Nashville's music, Jacksonville's and Orlando's professional sports teams, and St. Augustine's historic heritage. They each claim that its particular individual advantage is globally or nationally recognized.

The two principal themes in the imaginary cities of the journal advertisements are the city as a place for profitable business and the city as a good place to live. There are also subthemes of the cosmopolitan city, the green city, the fun city, the culture city, the pluralist city, and the postindustrial city that all condense complex imagery into simple slogans, easily un-

TABLE 13.2

Major repertoires in city advertisements

Category	Content
Probusiness political climate (public/private partnership)	Business-assistance programs
	Sound fiscal policies
	Industry-specific taxes and incentives
Ideal workforce	Young, educated, skilled, hardworking labor force
	Concentrations of educational institutions
	Sound work ethic
	Successful labor/management relations
High-technology (the advent of the twenty-first century)	High-tech industry/university partnership
	Concentration of high-tech industries
Solid infrastructure	Transportation (highway, international airport)
	Telecommunications (fiber optics network)
	Local gas and electricity
	Economic stability or fast economic growth
Healthy local economy	Upswing trend in job creation
	Higher proportion of future's industries
Central location	Central time zone
	Proximity to large markets (population)
	Border cities or coastal cities
High quality of life	Affluent natural amenities (beach, lake, mountain, clean air, and so on)
	Mild weather (sun, warm climate)
	Health services (world-class hospitals)
	Low cost of living; wide range of housing options
	Friendliness
Distinct lifestyle advantages	High quality of cultural and recreational activities (museum, opera, symphony orchestra, theater, art center, festivals, fairs, professional sports teams, golf courses)
	Historical heritage

derstood images, and accessible selling points. There are specific urban reimaginings built around specific strategies for certain city types; they include wannabe world cities, industrial-city makeovers, cities for new business, and capitalizing culture.

World Cities and Wannabe World Cities

There are three truly command cities of global capitalism: London, New York, and Tokyo. In the case of New York, a series of campaigns have been mounted to secure the city's position as the country's world city. From the hugely successful earlier slogan of "I love New York" to the more recent "The business city that never sleeps" campaign, the city has sought to promote a positive image. There are cities that have some command functions but want more. I will refer to them as "wannabe" world cities. In the U.S. they include Atlanta, Chicago, and Los Angeles. As one slogan for Atlanta optimistically noted, Atlanta is "claiming its international destiny." In some cases, there is a conscious attempt to attract formerly big-city functions such as banking. Charlotte, North Carolina, is now one of the largest banking centers in the United States. The wannabe world cities compete for world spectacles. A good, though not infallible, guide to wannabes is to note those U.S. cities that have either hosted or applied to host the Summer Olympic Games (table 13.3). Olympic Games offer the opportunity to be the site of a global spectacle and achieve international name recognition and also provide a giant urban redevelopment opportunity.

Wannabe world cities are concerned with ensuring the most effective international image. It is essential to have all the attributes of a world city; they include an international airport, signature buildings of big-name architects (for example, Michael Graves, Arata Isozaki, Philip Johnson, I. M. Pei, John Portman, Richard Rogers, Aldo Rossi, or James Stirling), impressive buildings, and cultural complexes with art galleries and symphony halls. Combining these elements is a useful strategy: it pays to hire a famous architect to design a cultural complex, as in Richard Meier's Getty Center and Frank Gehry's Disney concert hall, both in Los Angeles, or Atlanta's High Art Museum, also designed by Meier. Wannabe cities are cities of spectacle, cities of intense urban redevelopment, and cities with a powerful growth rhetoric.

Wannabe cities have an edgy insecurity about their role and position in

TABLE 13.3

Host and candidate cities for the Summer Olympic Games

Year	Host city	U.S. candidate cities
1964	Tokyo	Detroit
1968	Mexico City	Detroit
1972	Munich	Detroit
1976	Montreal	Los Angeles
1980	Moscow	Los Angeles
1984	Los Angeles	Los Angeles
1988	Seoul	—
1992	Barcelona	—
1996	Atlanta	Atlanta
2000	Sydney	—
2004	Athens	—
2008	Beijing	—
2012	London	New York

the world that gives tremendous power and energy to their cultural boost-erism. The desperate scramble for big-name architects, art galleries, and cultural events is a fascinating part of the "place wars" in the United States among cities aiming for the top of the urban hierarchy. The struggle is never-ending, as events can have a negative impact on even the most care-fully constructed image. Witness the case of Los Angeles. After several years of bad press in the early 1990s, spawned by earthquakes, riots and uprisings, mudflows, fires, and scenes of police brutality that resounded around the world, the city established the public-private Los Angeles Mar-keting Partnership, which subsequently launched a five-year media blitz aimed at presenting a more positive image of the city, images to counter the popular conception of the city as a dystopia sliding into anarchy and de-struction. In 1995 $4.5 million was spent on billboards and advertisements initially targeted at the Greater Los Angeles district in order to raise local spirits, generate civic pride, and dominate the discourse on what the city is about. The emphasis of the campaign was on the city as a place to do busi-ness, with such slogans as "Los Angeles is the no. 1 port of entry in the country," "It exceeds New York," and "L.A. has a bigger economy than

South Korea and South Korea is booming." The advertising firm hired to oversee the campaign was Davis Ball and Colobatto, whose previous successful campaigns included the rejuvenation of the sales of eggs despite their reputation for high cholesterol.

Look, No More Factories!

Industrial cities in the developed world have a difficult time in an era of world competition and the global shift of industry toward much lower-cost centers. To be seen as industrial is to be associated with the old, the polluted, and the out-of-date. A persistent strand of urban (re)presentations has been the reconstruction of the image of the industrial city. Cities such as Syracuse, Pittsburgh, and Milwaukee have all been (re)presented by a more attractive package that emphasizes the new rather than the old, fun rather than work, the fashionable postmodern rather than the merely modern.

The industrial town of Gary, Indiana, embarked on an expensive program to change the image of the city through various promotions, including hosting the Miss U.S.A. pageant in 2001 and building a new baseball stadium, and plans are afoot to build a National Civil Rights Hall of Fame. The success of Cleveland's Rock and Roll Hall of Fame has been widely followed by other cities seeking urban-development schemes that help to promote a new postindustrial image.

Emblematic of these shifts in meaning was the change in the logo of Syracuse. This city of more than a half-million people in New York State had an industrial history originally based in salt production and later in a range of chemical- and metal-based economies. It was a typical Frost Belt industrial city, with an official seal that celebrated its industrial base with images of factories and salt fields. In 1972 the mayor of the city organized a design competition to replace the one hundred–year-old seal. There was community resistance, and it was only in 1986 that another mayor was able to introduce a new city logo. This logo represents a clean lake and an urban skyline with not a factory chimney to be seen.

Reimagining the industrial city involves the physical reconstruction of the city. Baltimore's Harbor Place and Pittsburgh's downtown developments are good examples. The process of deindustrialization sometimes allows opportunities for urban redevelopment, as factories are abandoned and new geographies of production and circulation leave old docks and railway lines economically redundant. The urban redevelopments are schemes to make money but are also attempts at reimagining the city in the form of postmodern architecture and postindustrial economics.

The representations of an industrial city also involve an internal debate as well as the manipulation of external images. Industrial cities have a culture, an emphasis on manual work, a collective sense of meaning and significance tied to the city's industrial and manufacturing base. Industry not only provides a means of living but also creates a context for individual and collective identities. Deindustrialization destroys this meaning, and representations of a postindustrial city challenge and undermine these identities. Image makeovers are also struggles about which image will dominate.

An important part of this internal debate is the renegotiation with the physical environment. Old-fashioned industry was very polluting; waste was dumped on the ground and in the rivers and lakes. There was an attitude and orientation to the physical environment that stressed work. The environment was merely a backdrop, a context, and a refuse bin for industry. Reimagining the industrial city involves restructuring the social-environmental relationship. In the case of Syracuse, its lake was represented in the new logo as pristine and suitable for recreation despite the ugly reality that the lake still held toxic waste.

The internal debate involves the creation of new agendas and the suppression of old ones. In 1988 John Norquist was elected mayor of Milwaukee. The old image of the city was as the beer capital of the nation, an industrial city, and a place with a rich socialist tradition. Deindustrialization in the 1970s and 1980s had destroyed the old job base of the city, challenged the collective identity of the city, and left a vacuum for new representations. Mayor Norquist led an aggressive campaign to (re)present and restructure the city. He trashed the city's welfare tradition and created a probusiness climate by offering competitive, that is, low, utility rates and tax rates, initiating a series of lakefront festivals, and promoting public-private downtown construction schemes, including a new convention center. Norquist became a symbol of urban reimaginings and was both quoted and feted in the national media.

In the current economic climate many local politicians have to present a probusiness image for their cities. However, they also have to get elected. Whereas business has the finances, the people have the votes. The reimaginings of the city thus have a curious mix of probusiness sentiments with shadings of wider social concerns. The varying forms of urban reimaginings embody differences in community identity, local political culture, and the rhetorics that are most likely to carry the day in particular cities.

The City for New Business

The probusiness message is a standard theme in the reimagining and selling of cities. The hypermobility of capital and the intense, growing competition between cities reinforce the age-old basic booster message that this city is the city to do good business. Urban promotion in the United States is most often a private-sector activity, the local chambers of commerce being particularly active, either on their own or as the dominant partners in joint public-private initiatives. Thus, urban representation in the United States more totally reflects the needs of business. Let us consider the example of Memphis.

The primary advantage of Memphis is location. Located on the Mississippi, in the central time zone, and close to roads and railroads, the city is a major distribution center. It is the hub for two airlines, the center for more than two hundred trucking companies, and since 1973 the location of the private mail-distribution company Federal Express. Despite this geographical advantage, however, the old image was of a hick town, the city of Elvis. In 1981 the Memphis Chamber of Commerce employed the ad agency Walker and Associates to launch a campaign that stressed the city's locational advantages. The campaign involved advertisements in the business press, direct mail to Fortune 500 companies, and a slogan, "Memphis: America's distribution center," that was used in the ads and as a bumper sticker on the trucks of all local trucking companies. The campaign was all the more successful because of the growth of Federal Express, which employed almost 20,000 people in Memphis by the early 1990s. The company also introduced Memphis-based pricing so that companies in Memphis receive better mail rates.

From 1985 to 1995 103,000 new jobs were created in the Memphis region. According to the chamber of commerce, 60 percent of these jobs were directly attributable to the marketing campaign. However, precisely how many businesses relocated because of the campaign and how many came simply because of the cheaper distribution rates is impossible to ascertain with any degree of certainty. However, it is certain that the campaign was successful in drawing attention to the new locational advantages of the city in a time of increased home shopping.

Capitalizing Culture

A three-state evolution in city marketing has been noted. The first generation, *smokestack chasing*, is concerned with attracting manufacturing jobs through attracting companies with subsidies and the promise of low operating costs and higher profits from existing or alternative sites. The poaching of factories from other cities was, and in some (especially southern) states still is, a major element of local job promotion. Urban representation centers on low operating costs and availability of subsidies. The second generation, *target marketing*, involves the attraction of manufacturing and service jobs in target industries currently enjoyable profitable growth. There are still attempts at luring plants from other locations, but the promotion also includes improving the physical infrastructure, vocational training, and stressing good public-private cooperation. Representation continues to mention low operating costs but includes the suitability of the local community for target industries and the more general notion of a good quality of life. The third generation, *product development*, contains the objectives of the first two stages but includes emphasis on the "jobs of the future" and a representation that includes global competitiveness, human and intellectual resources, as well as low operating costs and a good quality of life. With each successive stage the message becomes more sophisticated, and urban representation has to include matters of culture and wider issues of quality of life.[3]

Art shows and galleries, opera halls, museums, festivals, and symphony halls are a now vital part in the reimagining of cities. They intimate world-city status, a city that can attract and retain the executive classes and skilled workers of the high-tech industries of the present and the future. The cultural attributes are also a source of revenue in their own right. Culture is now big business. In 1995 the Art Institute of Chicago held a very successful exhibition of Claude Monet's paintings. The exhibition ran from July 22 to November 26 and generated $389 million in economic benefit to the city and a $5 million profit for the Art Institute. Cultural strategies—and they can be defined as attempts to identify, mobilize, market, and commodify a city's cultural assets—are now major elements in urban regeneration and the stimulation of a city's economy.

Urban cultural-capital promotion includes more than just so-called high culture. Popular culture in a variety of guises is also important. Cities now represent themselves as fun places, places where the good life is increasingly defined as not only lucrative employment but also ample time for leisure. The marketing of the city as a center for play has been tied to dining, shopping, nightclubbing, and outdoor pursuits. A number of sub-themes can be noted: *The historic feel* emphasizes the historic connections of the city or particular city neighborhoods; sometimes whole districts are historicized with "antique signs," "authentic" landmark sites, and guided historical narratives in the form of marked routes, maps, and brochures. In this merchandising of history, urban makeovers present a positive image of the city by highlighting its historical depth. *The festival package* emphasizes frivolity, resorts and spas, sporting events, and shopping. Miami and New Orleans use this package to sell themselves in the popular press. *The green-and-clean theme* situates the city in a postindustrial world with clean air, good beaches, easy access to the "natural" world, and active recreation such as sailing, fishing, and swimming. San Francisco, San Diego, Seattle, and Portland work this theme into their urban representation. *The package of pluralism* highlights the rich ethnic mix that leads to a varied urban experience, including specialized shopping centers, ethnic restaurants, and ethnic carnivals. New York, Los Angeles, Chicago, and San Francisco sell this theme. These four themes are not mutually exclusive, and an individual city may use elements of all of them in its representation.

There is one item of popular culture that is particularly desirable to many American cities. A professional sports team is a powerful image-generating machine for a city, and many cities expend considerable efforts toward building a new sports stadium with the intent of attracting a professional sports team that would provide them with big-city status, a vital and youthful image, and a possible vehicle for economic development. Professional sports in the United States, particularly basketball (National Basketball Association or NBA), football (National Football League or NFL), baseball (Major League Baseball or MLB), and, of slightly lesser importance, ice hockey (National Hockey League or NHL), is big business. Cities want the sport franchises for the money they directly generate and for the image they represent. To have an NBA, NFL, MLB, or NHL team is to play in the big leagues, to have your city's name mentioned in the extensive sports coverage that saturates the mass media. A successful sports team is considered great public relations for the city, ready-made and constant name recognition. One city even built its reimagining around professional sports. Indianapolis initiated a new public relations exercise and economic-development strategy in 1982 aimed at improving its image. More than $1 million was spent over four years. As a central part of the representation of the city, Indianapolis lured the NFL's Colts from Baltimore in 1983 to begin the 1984 season as the Indianapolis Colts. Professional sports teams provide revenue, taxes, a possible source of civic pride, and name recognition in the national and world media. The slogan of Jacksonville, "The expansion city of Florida's First Coast," is more meaningful when you realize that the city was awarded an NFL expansion team. Having obtained an NFL team, the city used the fact in its promotional advertising. Jacksonville extended its connection to the NFL by hosting the Super Bowl in 2005. As the vice president of the city's chamber of commerce noted, "After this week, everyone is going to know where we are, and you'd like to think some of them might even want come back." The mayor hoped "it will be parlayed into economic opportunity. It's an extraordinary chance for us to develop more business for a city that already has a low tax burden and a great quality of life." The immediate economic impact on the city is in the region of $300 million, but positive effects may also unfold in the next two to five years. The chamber of commerce official noted, "Many of the people who come to this game are corporate movers and shakers. The next time their company looks at where they're going to put a new office or a new manufacturing facility, they'll think about us."[4]

The very attractiveness of sports franchises for cities gives the owners leverage, as cities compete with one another in order to keep their teams, lure existing franchises, or snag expansion teams. In recent years owners have moved their teams in order to get better stadia with higher-revenue-generating facilities, sweetheart deals, and tax breaks. Despite the relocations, some teams retain their former names with only the city named changed. Thus, the name of the Utah Jazz from Salt Lake City is only understandable when you know that this NBA team relocated from New Orleans in 1980, and the Los Angeles Lakers originally were the Minneapolis Lakers. Teams negotiate for better arrangements with the threat of moving if their demands are not met. Culture can be capitalized, but do not be surprised if your cultural capital threatens to move to another city.

Light and Shadow

Every bright light casts a shadow. The flip side of the sunny portrayal of the city is the dark side that has to be contained, controlled, or ignored. This other discourse works through silence, as some issues and groups are never mentioned; through negative imagery, in which some groups and issues are presented as dangerous, beyond the confines of a civil debate; and in specific debates, where some groups are blamed for urban decline. From the early 1960s to the mid-1970s race was a recurring motif in the discourse of decline. The background, of course, was the so-called race riots in the 1960s, when President Richard M. Nixon evoked the image of cities "enveloped in smoke and flame." At the heart of the perceived urban problem was a large black population concentrated in ghettos. The rhetoric of the discourse was repeated in such apocalyptic phrases as "urban crisis," "city as wilderness," and "urban society on the verge of collapse." The secretary of the Department of Housing and Urban Development, George Romney, speaking in 1972, noted that "the whole social web that makes living possible [in the cities] is breaking down into a veritable jungle." Even Democratic senator Robert Kennedy remarked, "We confront an urban wilderness more formidable and resistant in some ways more frightening than the wilderness faced by the Pilgrims or the pioneers."[5] Cities were less the promised land and more the American nightmare. And the id of the urban imagination was the black presence. By the 1990s the vocabulary had changed; the terms *underclass, ghetto, welfare,* and a host of others were in vogue, sometimes deeply coded, often not. The problem was laid at the door of the inner-city blacks, who in this discourse of blame were a cause of crime, urban decay, moral collapse, and the decline of the city.

A second and related theme is the issue of social control. The business elites in the United States have long had a distrust of participatory democracy. However, the emphasis in urban-booster rhetoric is not so much on excluding the "public" as encouraging private-public partnerships. In effect, these partnerships disfranchise the general urban population and allow debates to go behind closed doors in a cozy corporate compromise. The marginal groups remain marginal, and the ones at the center continue to define the terms, set priorities, and allocate both resources to ensure success and blame to account for failure.

A third theme is the foreclosing of alternatives, often attempted by linguistic usage. The use of such terms as *the bottom line, fiscal realities,* and the *new urban realism* are all phrases that seek not so much to identify fiscal constraints as to close off an alternative discourse about other fiscal priorities and different spending choices. The constant use of biological analogies in urban boosterism—for instance, employing the notion of a heart in need of revitalization when describing the city center—not only dramatizes the endeavor but also presents it as the work of a wise doctor tending a sick patient. Who could possibly argue with such an image?

All discourses have their silences. In the new representations, more is said about the city as a place for business, a place for work, and attractive to the senior executives and the governing class of the business community, and much less is said about the city as a place of democratic participation or as a place where all citizens can lead dignified and creative lives. The dominant representations play down equality, social justice, and an inclusive definition of the good city. The place wars have reinforced the business boosters. Representations of the city are not politically neutral; neither are they devoid of social implications. There is a struggle for the meaning of cities. There is a need for an alternative representation, for urban imagineers who can represent the just, fair city. In such an economically competitive atmosphere it is all too easy to succumb to the dominant rhetoric. But the attempt should be made if we are not to lose the image of the city as a just, fair, and decent place to live for all of its citizens.

14

Civic Engagement in the City

"Civic Spirit"

A GROUP OF RELIGIOUS LEADERS had a meeting in Boston to discuss the problems besetting society. They identified a decline in family values, too many lawsuits, too much sex and drugs, and the lack of what they called "civic spirit." Nothing unusual about the conclusions, except that the meeting took place in 1679.

A Recurring National Obsession

There is a recurring obsession with the promise and practice of a "more perfect union" in the political discourse of the U.S. Perhaps because of its foundation in the sovereignty of individual rights, there have been recurring fears that the Republic is little more than a fragile collection that can too easily splinter into diverse individuals and groups unable to create the civic spirit recognizable to those New England clerics more than three hundred years ago. This fear has been expressed in different ways, from the wariness over religious and ethnic ties that could militate against national citizenship to a more recent anxiety that an active citizenry is being replaced by a passive set of atomistic individuals. Worries of separate ethnic identity or individual selfishness trumping the requirements of a collective civic community have been the anxious underside to the active creation of U.S. citizenship.

In recent years a number of commentaries have expressed a pronounced fear that civic disengagement is increasing. The dominant image they present is a society in which civic ties are broken by rampant individualism. A good example is the report titled *A Nation of Spectators*, published in 1998 by a nonpartisan group that called itself the National Commission on Civic Renewal. The report claims to show increasing civic disengagement in the contemporary U.S. To prove this point they created an index of civic health: a high index suggests a healthy, engaged society; a lower index indicates a weakening society. The graph from 1960 to the 1990s shows a precarious decline of sixteen points—clearly, a cause for concern. The report notes "troubling evidence of civic decline" and "civic disengagement from the civic realm."[1]

Let us look at this index in some detail. The National Commission on Civic Renewal looked at declining voter turnout as a bad thing—a mark of decline. An alternative interpretation seems equally plausible. People exercise choice by not voting. We may not agree with the choice, but we should respect it. Freedom and democracy are also about making the choice to not get involved. A withdrawal from the formal political system, not voting is an antipolitics that refuses to give legitimacy to a system in which money buys votes. The commission did not look at this broader issue of political power.

Another variable chosen as an indicator of civic health is trust in government. The report notes that confidence in the federal government fell from 76 percent of the sampled population believing in the government to do the right thing in 1964 to only 40 percent in 1994. This component counts for 10 percent of the weight of the index. Again, however, an alternative view is plausible. To not trust government can be a sign of political maturity. After innumerable examples of government failure and malfeasance, it seems not only legitimate but also prudent not to trust the government. What surprises me is how many still trust government, given so much of the evidence to the contrary.

Even the indicators that more accurately refer to civic engagement seem unclear. Membership in groups, even according to the commission's own data, reveals a steady pattern, with more than 80 percent belonging to a local group or attending a religious service in both 1975 and 1994. This pattern is reinforced by the work of A. M. Guest and S. K. Wierzbicki who used data from the General Social Survey from 1974 to 1996. Their analysis revealed very little evidence of declining social ties in the neighborhood. The idea of "community lost" is more often proclaimed than demonstrated.[2]

One indicator identified by the commission's report clearly demonstrates civic disengagement. The figures on active participation in groups did show a decline from 13 percent to 8 percent over the period 1975 to 1995. And although the low values exaggerate small changes, I feel there is something to note here. There are many counters to the pulls of community and civic purpose. The increasing workload borne by many citizens aligns with the increasing importance of corporate as opposed to civic identity. The work sphere occupies more of our efforts and time. When our employers rather than our government are responsible for health benefits and other vital collective goods and services, it is easy to see how a civic disengagement is both possible and to a certain extent unavoidable. The partial withdrawal from civic life is perhaps a consequence of increasing workloads, a shift from civic to corporate identity, and new domestic burdens that create a time bind of longer hours for work and domestic reproduction and less time available for civic matters. However, some of the decline in civic engagement may also reflect a replacement of volunteers by paid employees. When fewer people volunteer to be teacher assistants but more people are paid for the same tasks, then the decline in volunteerism is little more than a reorganization of how tasks are performed. Yet the commission does not unpack the causes, consequences, and alternative interpretations of these data. Rather, it assumes that we are a nation of spectators. Like the New England clerics, the citizenry is lambasted for a decline of civic virtue. And like the earlier criticisms, the image of a crumbling civic society, especially when presented in a comparison with a golden age of dense and active civic ties, is a nostalgic creation that tells us more about current angst than past realities. This golden-age picture ignores the effective disfranchisement of a significant minority of our population that was never extended the full benefits of active citizenship. In this simplistic model, the 1960s was the golden age of civic engagement. Yet this period is when large numbers of ethnic and racial minorities were effectively disfranchised.

A more sophisticated and nuanced discussion of civic engagement is available in Robert D. Putnam's *Bowling Alone: The Collapse and Revival of American Community*. Putnam documents a process of disengagement from 1970, as formal membership in all sorts of civic organizations declined between 10 and 20 percent. Using rough guesstimates he suggests that suburbanization and sprawl account for about 10 percent of the civic disengagement. This disengagement is very important because it leads to a collapse of social networks and a consequent decline in social capital that has marked effects. Where social capital is lacking, the effects of unemployment, economic disadvantage, and family breakdown are much worse. Social capital is disproportionately important in poor neighborhoods because there are fewer individual resources.

The ideas of social capital have been taken up in the urban literature. One influential contributor is the sociologist William Julius Wilson. In *The Truly Disadvantaged* he argues that job loss in the inner city, especially in the wake of mechanization, suburbanization of jobs, and overseas relocation of manufacturing, was a prime cause of urban poverty. In a later book, *When Work Disappears: The World of the New Urban Poor,* he concentrates on the role of culture, or what some term *social capital.* He argues that the loss of work undermines important values and leads to a decline in local institutions and adequate levels of social organization. Families not organized around work are at a distinct disadvantage; the culture of work is necessary to establish good behavior.

I find Wilson's work interesting because it moves from an economistic understanding of inner-city decline to a broader account that includes cultural factors. He is aware of the structural economic conditions behind poverty yet also sensitive to cultural factors and especially the destructive effects of the loss of work and the outmigration of work-oriented families in poor neighborhoods. He avoids the easy prescription of blaming the poor for their troubles but also does not ignore the behavioral foundation to collective economic performance. In response to the key question of how poor neighborhoods can be turned around, his answers avoid the easy palliatives of blaming the poor or blaming the economy.

Individual behavior is shaped and informed by neighborhood norms. Political scientists have known this fact for some time; the neighborhood effect has been identified in countless studies of voting patterns and attitudinal surveys. The connections between the neighborhood effect and social capital need to be interwoven with debates about improving not only civic spirit but also civic economic health. Household behavior and attitudes reflect the community values of the neighborhood. Our neighbors influence our view of the world and how to act in it. In neighborhoods that lack a work ethic and solid family values, then, individual households will find it easier to pursue feckless behavior. The role of social capital in shaping neighborhood fortunes is an important topic that deserves much deeper investigation.

An Active Citizenry?

Underlying Putnam's discussion is the notion that citizenship is not simply a passive category, but a site of active involvement and engagement. This idea has a long history, part of the republican ideal that liberty is associated with active forms of self-government. A number of writers such as Michael Sandel call for a revival of this civic tradition. In contrast, others such as Michael Schudson argue that in the contemporary world the notion of an actively involved citizenry is unrealistic. The pressures of too much information and too little time are brute facts of present-day reality. The good citizen needs to monitor rather than be actively involved.[3]

The criticism of (a lack of) civil society is a common refrain in the history of this country, with a constant distance between the promise and the reality. And this distance is a point of criticism, as much in the twenty-first as the seventeenth centuries, a creative criticism providing the impulse to an emancipatory project. However, there is also a Puritan flagellation of the citizenry. The strident insistence on civic engagement can deflect a critical gaze from concerns such as business engagement, investor responsibility, political reform, and social justice.

For many, civil society and an engaged citizenry are the new panaceas. They seem to offer a cheap solution in an era of distrust in government and a withdrawal from the welfare state. But if we use the Hegelian definition of civil society as the nongovernment public realm, we have to be careful because civil society contains the sad and the mad as well as the good and the just. Civil society contains the Michigan Militia as well as bowling leagues, the Ku Klux Klan as well as soccer moms. And Nazi Germany was an active civic society with multiple forms of civic engagement. To make the obvious, though often uncommon, remark, there is civic engagement and civic engagement. Not all of it is necessarily for the good.

Multiple Civics and Many Forms of Engagement

The term *civic engagement* needs some further elaboration, as there are a variety of civics and a multitude of engagements. Two extremes on the continuum of civics are, on one hand, national citizenship and, on the other, local community membership. As citizens of the national community we have a set of rights and obligations. At the other extreme is the more local community. This loose term may coincide with political forms of jurisdiction or may even be as small as the local neighborhood. This local sense of attachment can sometimes be reinforced and at other times undermined by forms of political representation. The term *local community* will mean many different things, from "the people living around me" to "my city." Between the local and the national there are a variety of claims to our loyalty, from the state to the region to the city.

There are also different forms of engagement, from the formal participation in voting to the more informal associations such as Rotary and neighborhood associations and from the purely symbolic such as witnessing a Fourth of July celebration to the more participatory such as running your neighborhood-association meeting.

A distinction has also been drawn between vertical and horizontal engagements. Vertical engagement crosses class and geographic boundaries, whereas horizontal forms of engagement rarely involve interaction outside of a narrow community. Engagements can span the dimensions of formal and informal, spectating and participating, local and national. There are often crosscutting connections. For example, with reference to the local-national dimension, some associations such as the Rotary Club both are actively involved in the local community and draw upon the local community for membership and involvement yet collectively operate in the national and international arenas. Though generally drawing upon a restricted social base for their membership, a form of horizontal association, their engagement can also be more vertical. Rotary Clubs are important local civic associations, yet collectively they are active global citizens in their campaign to eradicate polio around the world. The very local and the very global, the steeply vertical and the widely horizontal combined. Other groups, such as the American Association of Retired People, may have a national organization without much local representation. We can imagine a categorization of associations that span local, national, and global in different combinations.

I have taken some time to distinguish different forms of civic engagement in order to situate the specific form examined in this chapter: civic engagement of the vertical kind at the metropolitan level. I want to explore the connection between this form of civic engagement and the social organization of space.

The Social Organization of Space

A model of relatively small-scale communities underlies many of the debates on civic engagement and civic society. But, as we have shown earlier, more people in the U.S. now live in large metropolitan areas. The opportunities for civic engagement that covers an entire metropolitan community are made more difficult. The civic writers discuss community-wide associations as if we lived in small, dense places, rather than the sprawling metropolitan areas that most Americans inhabit.

Effective citywide engagement is made more difficult in the U.S. because of metropolitan fragmentation. The steady suburbanization of the population has been a selective process, with middle-income whites moving out from the central cores. The process of gentrification, though of local importance in some cities, has done little to reverse this trend. The typical U.S. city is a balkanized arrangement of numerous municipal governments and various school districts.

The most effective forms of meaningful vertical civic engagement are more likely to be the ones that encompass the whole metropolis rather than segregated suburbs. Yet civic engagement at the metropolitan level is undercut by the social organization of urban space in the U.S.

It is difficult to gauge the precise effects of segmentation and privatization of space on the civic spirit. But as citizens are bracketed out into differing experiences of urban living, it is difficult to see how these trends could be improving civic life, as traditionally defined. The pervading sense of fear of the other in the U.S. may, in part, be attributed to the fact that as we become cordoned off into the separate spaces of life experiences, we meet others only through the stereotypes and fantasies of the media. When we lose the shared spaces that allow seeing the other in person, we lose an essential element of a truly civic society.

Nostalgia for a time when community was stronger is long-standing. The depiction of the past as golden age is a constant thread running through cultural commentary in the U.S. In this arcadian vision, community was stronger in the past, and civic disengagement in the present is a cause for concern. People have been seeing a loss of civic sensibilities throughout the life of the Republic.

I have argued that the functioning unit in the contemporary U.S. is the metropolis. Debates on civic engagement need to address this wider community. In the past the balkanized city allowed different groups to exist and in some cases prosper. But in today's society the fragmented metropolis maintains social inequality and does not allow a full-ranging civic interaction and discussion to take place. Although metropolitan government is an unlikely candidate for mass support, policies on revenue sharing are clearly in order. And it need not be an either-or proposition. The small-scale nature of much local government can be combined with metropolitan-wide revenue-sharing and civic discussions.

Today, just as much as in 1679, we realize that there is a civic spirit to be cultivated in metropolitan areas, an urgent need for shared spaces that connect the individual and the collective, public and private, society and comity, the collectivist impulse and the democratic spirit, private affluence and public squalor, civic obligations and individual needs, public duties and private actions. The early Puritans wanted to build a city upon a hill. We still need to build that city.

15

Emerging Trends

AT THE HEART of the urban experience in the U.S. is a ceaseless restlessness and constant changeability. Dynamism is the one constant of the urban U.S. A comparison of the urban U.S. in 1950 and in the present shows how the nation has become more urban, more suburban, and more metropolitan. A closer look reveals how central cities have declined, new forms of suburbanization have spread, some old established cities have declined, and new urban centers have developed, especially in the South and West.

A nighttime satellite image of the mainland territory of the U.S. in 1950, if such a thing were possible, would show cities as distinct points of light. There would be a heavy concentration in the Northeast, some along the Pacific coast, and a scattering throughout the interior, with a concentration around the Great Lakes. There would be as much rural darkness as urban brightness. Fast-forward to today, and a satellite from the same position shows that the light has spread outward from the old centers, new centers especially in the South and West have developed from the darkness, and, though there are still some areas of shadow in certain western states, the nation is now more fully bathed in light. Formerly distinct points of light meld into a dispersed constellation of brightness, as fifty years of urban growth and suburban spread now brighten the dim rural areas and unlit wilderness.

The Evolving Urban System

Cities are individual entities, but they are also part of a national arrangement of urban places. The U.S. urban system has exhibited enormous change and constant transformation, as new cities arise while some old es-

1950		1970		1990		2000	
Rank	MSA Name	Rank	MSA Name	Rank	MSA Name	Rank	MSA Name
1	New York - Northeastern NJ	1	New York, NY	1	New York, NY (CMSA)	1	New York, NY (CMSA)
2	Chicago, IL	2	Los Angeles - Long Beach, CA	2	Los Angeles, CA (CMSA)	2	Los Angeles, CA (CMSA)
3	Los Angeles, CA	3	Chicago, IL	3	Chicago, IL (CMSA)	3	Chicago, IL (CMSA)
4	Philadelphia, PA	4	Philadelphia, PA	4	Washington, DC (CMSA)	4	Washington, DC (CMSA)
5	Detroit, MI	5	Detroit, MI	5	San Francisco - Oakland, CA (CMSA)	5	San Francisco - Oakland, CA (CMSA)
6	Boston, MA	6	San Francisco, CA	6	Philadelphia, PA (CMSA)	6	Philadelphia, PA (CMSA)
7	San Francisco - Oakland, CA	7	Washington, D.C.	7	Boston, MA (CMSA)	7	Boston, MA (CMSA)
8	Pittsburgh, PA	8	Boston, MA	8	Detroit, MI (CMSA)	8	Detroit, MI (CMSA)
9	St. Louis, MO	9	Pittsburgh, PA	9	Dallas, TX (CMSA)	9	Dallas, TX (CMSA)
10	Cleveland, OH	10	St. Louis, MO	10	Houston, TX (CMSA)	10	Houston, TX (CMSA)
11	Washington, D.C.	11	Baltimore, MD	11	**Miami, FL (CMSA)**	11	Atlanta, GA (MSA)
12	Baltimore, MD	12	Cleveland, OH	12	Seattle, WA (CMSA)	12	Miami, FL (CMSA)
13	Minneapolis - St. Paul, MN	13	Houston, TX	13	Atlanta, GA (MSA)	13	Seattle, WA (CMSA)
14	Buffalo, NY	14	**Newark, NJ**	14	Cleveland, OH (CMSA)	14	Phoenix - Mesa, AZ (MSA)
15	Cincinnati, OH	15	Minneapolis - St. Paul, MN	15	Minneapolis - St. Paul, MN (MSA)	15	Minneapolis - St. Paul, MN (MSA)
16	Milwaukee, WI	16	**Dallas, TX**	16	**San Diego, CA**	16	Cleveland, OH (CMSA)
17	Kansas City, MO	17	Seattle, WA	17	St. Louis, MO	17	San Diego, CA
18	Houston, TX	18	**Anaheim, CA**	18	Pittsburgh, (MSA)	18	St. Louis, MO
19	Providence, RI	19	Milwaukee, WI	19	**San Juan, PR (CMSA)**	19	**Denver, CO (CMSA)**
20	Seattle, WA	20	**Atlanta, GA**	20	**Phoenix - Mesa, AZ (MSA)**	20	San Juan, PR (CMSA)

- Source: US Census

- Bold denotes New to the Top Twenty

15.1. Twenty largest cities in the U.S. by population, 1950–2000.

tablished ones shrivel. Figure 15.1 lists the twenty largest cities in the U.S. from 1950 through 2000. Two things stand out. There is stability in the hierarchy, as certain major cities maintain their relative size. New York, Los Angeles, Chicago, and Philadelphia remain in the top five, and New York remains atop the urban hierarchy over the entire fifty years. But there is also change, as some cities appear and disappear from the top twenty. There is a definite pattern to this reshuffling. Cities that enter the list include the Sun Belt cities of Dallas, San Antonio, San Diego, Memphis, Phoenix, San Jose, Jacksonville, and Austin as well as growing cities in the Midwest such as Indianapolis and Columbus, Ohio. Cities that drop from the top twenty include the Frost Belt or Rust Belt cities of Pittsburgh, Buffalo, Cincinnati, Cleveland, the interior cities of Kansas, and Minneapolis and the shrinking-population cities of New Orleans and Washington, D.C. The relative position of individual cities such as Houston, which moved from fourteenth in population in 1950 to fourth in 2000, and Baltimore, which moved from sixth to seventeenth, tell us much about the changing economic geography of the U.S. Phoenix exhibited an extraordinary trajectory, moving from ninety-ninth in 1950 to ninth in 2000.

Figure 15.2 tells a similar story for metropolitan regions. The giant urban regions of New York, Los Angeles, and Chicago retain their dominance. New metro areas push onto the list from the Sun Belt and West such as Atlanta, Miami, San Diego, and Denver. City regions that drop off the list include such Rust Belt metro areas as Buffalo, Cincinnati, Milwaukee, and Pittsburgh. Others such as Newark and Anaheim that appear in 1970

1950		1970		1990		2000	
Rank	MSA Name	Rank	MSA Name	Rank	MSA Name	Rank	MSA Name
1	New York - Northeastern NJ	1	New York, NY	1	New York, NY (CMSA)	1	New York, NY (CMSA)
2	Chicago, IL	2	Los Angeles - Long Beach, CA	2	Los Angeles, CA (CMSA)	2	Los Angeles, CA (CMSA)
3	Los Angeles, CA	3	Chicago, IL	3	Chicago, IL (CMSA)	3	Chicago, IL (CMSA)
4	Philadelphia, PA	4	Philadelphia, PA	4	Washington, DC (CMSA)	4	Washington, DC (CMSA)
5	Detroit, MI	5	Detroit, MI	5	San Francisco - Oakland, CA (CMSA)	5	San Francisco - Oakland, CA (CMSA)
6	Boston, MA	6	San Francisco, CA	6	Philadelphia, PA (CMSA)	6	Philadelphia, PA (CMSA)
7	San Francisco - Oakland, CA	7	Washington, D.C.	7	Boston, MA (CMSA)	7	Boston, MA (CMSA)
8	Pittsburgh, PA	8	Boston, MA	8	Detroit, MI (CMSA)	8	Detroit, MI (CMSA)
9	St. Louis, MO	9	Pittsburgh, PA	9	Dallas, TX (CMSA)	9	Dallas, TX (CMSA)
10	Cleveland, OH	10	St. Louis, MO	10	Houston, TX (CMSA)	10	Houston, TX (CMSA)
11	Washington, D.C.	11	Baltimore, MD	11	**Miami, FL (CMSA)**	11	Atlanta, GA (MSA)
12	Baltimore, MD	12	Cleveland, OH	12	Seattle, WA (CMSA)	12	Miami, FL (CMSA)
13	Minneapolis - St. Paul, MN	13	Houston, TX	13	Atlanta, GA (MSA)	13	Seattle, WA (CMSA)
14	Buffalo, NY	14	**Newark, NJ**	14	Cleveland, OH (CMSA)	14	Phoenix - Mesa, AZ (MSA)
15	Cincinnati, OH	15	Minneapolis - St. Paul, MN	15	Minneapolis - St. Paul, MN (MSA)	15	Minneapolis - St. Paul, MN (MSA)
16	Milwaukee, WI	16	**Dallas, TX**	16	**San Diego, CA**	16	Cleveland, OH (CMSA)
17	Kansas City, MO	17	Seattle, WA	17	St. Louis, MO	17	San Diego, CA
18	Houston, TX	18	**Anaheim, CA**	18	Pittsburgh, (MSA)	18	St. Louis, MO
19	Providence, RI	19	Milwaukee, WI	19	**San Juan, PR (CMSA)**	19	**Denver, CO (CMSA)**
20	Seattle, WA	20	**Atlanta, GA**	20	**Phoenix - Mesa, AZ (MSA)**	20	San Juan, PR (CMSA)

- Source: US Census   - Bold denotes New to the Top Twenty

15.2. Twenty largest metropolitan areas in the U.S. by population, 1950–2000.

have coalesced into the giant urban regions of consolidated metropolitan statistical areas.

A variety of urban hierarchies can be identified other than just through population figures. If we rank cities in relation to command-and-control functions such as headquarters of multinational companies, then New York and Chicago stand out, followed by San Francisco, Detroit, and Los Angeles. Change the exact measure, and the hierarchy varies. In terms of economic dominance New York is at the pinnacle, surrounded by the inner core of Chicago, Los Angeles, and San Francisco. The next tier includes such as cities as Boston and Philadelphia. However, if we consider other factors, then slightly different patterns emerge. Richard Florida ranks cities according to a creativity index based on the number of people in the "thinking" professions, numbers of high tech-workers, number of patents per capita, and the percentage of college-educated and number of artistically orientated people. The resultant rank order was San Francisco, Austin, San Diego and Boston (tied), Seattle, Raleigh-Durham–Chapel Hill, Houston, Washington-Baltimore, New York, Dallas and Minneapolis–St. Paul (tied).[1]

U.S. cities fall into a myriad of hierarchies depending on what is under discussion. These rankings are more than just academic differences. There are the business rankings of best places to do business. Increasingly, cities are ranked by quality-of-life criteria. Recent titles in this genre include "Fifty Best Small Southern Towns," "America's Best One Hundred Places to Retire," and "Fifty Fabulous Places to Raise a Family." *Places Rated Almanac,* published every four years, rates places on nine factors: cost of living, employment prospects, education, crime, the arts, health care, recreation, transportation, and climate. Not to be outdone, *Cities Ranked and Rated* uses fifty categories, including most days of sunshine, best air and water quality, and shortest commutes. With greater vocational flexibility for business and households and the growing retired population whose locational choices are less guided by employment opportunities, these rankings become important guides to corporate and individual locational decision making.

Urban systems are networks as well as hierarchies. People, money, goods, and ideas flow through the U.S. network of cities. We have seen the emergence of three dominant physical networks: the interstate-road system that now links most cities, airport links that connect all the major cities, and the emerging Internet that connects cities along the information highway. Over the years each network has been pivotal to the growth and development of cities. The interstate and airline networks reinforce the position of some cities. The Internet's impact is more complex. A popular idea is that the Internet allows people and companies to escape from the tyranny of distance and the need for agglomeration. Cities, it is often argued, are less relevant when people can connect through the World Wide Web. In this "end-of-geography" thesis, large cities are relics of the predigital age. In reality, there is a metropolitan bias to Internet activity. Anthony Townsend argues that the need for face-to-face contact in association with the new telecommunications systems is creating a hierarchy of networked cities. He mapped the infrastructural links between cities as well as the geography of domain names. Alongside the established global cities of New York, Los Angeles, and Chicago, he identified a new network of highly connected cities including San Francisco and Washington, D.C., in the top tier, a second tier including Dallas and Boston, and a third tier that includes Miami and Denver. Most revealing was the existent of information "black holes" that include Detroit, Philadelphia, Cleveland, and St. Louis (table 15.1). The longer-term future of these cities is in jeopardy if the information highway bypasses them.[2]

U.S. cities are also part of a global network of cities. Although there has been much anecdotal debate about what constitutes a global city, there has been little empirical work. I have referred to this lack as the "dirty little secret" of world-cities research. Indeed, the debate has been clouded by

TABLE 15.1

Internet measures of networked cities

Metro area	Number of domains per 1,000 population	Backbone capacity (mbps)
Level 1		
San Francisco-San Jose	15.9	28,297
Washington, D.C.	10.7	28,370
Level 2		
Dallas	9.7	25,343
Houston	9.0	11,522
Atlanta	9.7	23,861
Boston	10.9	8,001
Seattle	12.4	7,288
Level 3		
Miami	11.9	4,478
Minneapolis	11.0	1,545
San Diego	12.1	2,160
Phoenix	11.1	6,701
Denver	11.5	8,674
Las Vegas	11.1	4,791
Black holes		
Detroit	4.9	2,245
Philadelphia	6.9	4,280
Cleveland	4.2	6,201
St. Louis	5.7	10,342

Notes: mbps = megabits per second. See Anthony Townsend, "The Internet and the Rise of the New Network Cities, 1969–1999."

boosters, academic as well as business interests, who make claims for the global status of "their" city. The Los Angeles School of Urban Research is one of the more obvious examples of a body of work whose main goal, it sometimes appears, is less to analyze the city than to trumpet its global primacy.

A discussion of network flows in the global-urban hierarchy would be incomplete without mentioning the work of the Globalization and World Cities (GAWC) researchers who have constructed an invaluable data inventory that identifies a global-city network through the distribution of advanced producer services. GAWC generated a data matrix of 316 cities and 100 firms in accountancy, advertising, banking and insurance, law, and management consultancy. They identified firms with at least 15 identifiable separate offices. They identified connectivity between the 316 cities. The ones that had at least one-fifth of the connectivity of the most connected city, which was London, were identified as global cities. A total of 123 world cities were identified. The GAWC data provide us with one of the most sophisticated world-city networks produced to date. The data for U.S. cities reveal a number of trends. New York City emerges as one of the dominant global cities, sharing with London a pivotal position on the global network. In terms of global connectivity there are distinct tiers:

New York

Chicago and Los Angeles

San Francisco

Atlanta, Miami, and Washington, D.C.

Dallas and Houston

Miami is interesting because both the GAWC data and airline-connectivity data generated by Short and Kim clearly reveal that the city is the "capital" of Latin America, its high global connectivity a result of its gateway function for Central and South Americas. Miami is as much a Latin as a North American city.[3]

The GAWC data have also identified command-and-control centers in the global-urban network. Table 15.2 provides a summary and shows the identity of U.S. cities in the different levels of the hierarchy of dominance. Again, the data show New York is the most globally connected and dominant city in the network.[4]

Satellite images would not be able to pick up on more subtle changes in the character of the urban U.S. since 1950. The view from space does not give us a picture of urban ground truth. Ed Soja has identified six processes of transformation: regional-city formation, the development of the post-Fordist city, the rise of the world city, the creation of the dual city of polarized communities, the carceral city of closely controlled urban spaces including prisons and gated communities, and the simulacrum city of hyperreality production and consumption.[5] I have touched on these themes throughout this book. Let me end with three metatrends that have

TABLE 15.2

U.S. cities and the global urban network

Network position	U.S. cities	Other cities
Dominant	New York	London
Major	Chicago, Miami	Hong Kong, Paris, Tokyo, Frankfurt, and others
Medium	Los Angeles	Amsterdam, Sydney, and others
Minor	Atlanta, Boston, Detroit, Indianapolis, San Francisco, Washington, D.C.	Lyons, Melbourne, Taipei, Munich, and others

Note: See P. J. Taylor, *World City Network*, 89.

emerged over the past half century with growing momentum and impact: privatization, globalization, and polarization. Together they constitute some of the more dominant forces shaping the character of the urban U.S. at the beginning of the twenty-first century.

Privatization

The Newport on the Levee shopping center in Cincinnati has a published code of conduct: "All youths under 16 years of age," notes the document in rule no. 3, "after 8 PM must be under the supervision and control of a parent or guardian." In other shopping centers the curfew is as early as 6 PM, and in some cases as late as 9:30 PM. Some also restrict the congregation of minors in groups of more than four. In 1996 the nation's largest mall, the Mall of America in Minneapolis, stipulated that "teenagers of 15 and under must be accompanied by an adult after 6 PM on Friday and Saturday nights."[6]

The story of the policing of the malls is a complicated one, but at its heart is the trend that more and more "public space," the space that we use for the reproduction of civil society, is becoming much less public. Shopping takes place in malls, recreation in entertainment complexes. The streets are being abandoned as places for wide and deep social interaction. More and more of our social activity is done in privatized space masquerading as public space. Although they may appear public, they are not.

They are policed, monitored, controlled. Many people like to go to them for this very reason: they give an aura of security and safety. The culture of fear that so permeates the U.S. fastens onto the dangers of public spaces, and the result is an urban agoraphobia, especially for the children of the suburbs who have grown up in the privatized worlds of private automobiles and homogenous residential areas. Urban public space now appears as more dangerous, populated by the other, the different, the dangerous.

There is a need for the control of public space. Having rules of silence in libraries, for example, is a good thing; otherwise, we would all have to listen to other people's conversations and cell phones. Unprotected public space simply leaves more room for the ill-mannered and the unregulated behavior of social bullies. What is at issue is not the need for the policing of public, and by policing I mean an agreed-upon set of rules and conventions, but what type of policing. This debate, which is never easy or settled, has been abandoned, as more of the space outside the home is privatized. We have given up the complicated task of creating flexible rules for how we conduct ourselves in public spaces and handed the task over to corporate interests to devise rules. We should not be surprised when these rules meet their needs rather than truly public interests.

There has been a loss of democratic public control of public space. The privatization of the U.S. city is evident in a number of ways: public streets replaced by private malls, the rise of gated communities (now numbering almost two million people), and the development of "bunker architecture" in our public and private buildings. For example, there has been a decade-old building boom in the downtown U.S. of prisons and detention centers.

There has always been a tension in U.S. cities between private and public. For a society founded on the protection of individual rights, the public space of cities and city living have always been problematic. In the interests of safety and social order, more of our "public space" is controlled, policed, and monitored. The introduction of surveillance cameras, closed-circuit televisions, and eyes in the sky have all led to a more profound policing of our public spaces. A renewed call for this authoritarian public space exploits 9/11 for its justification. As more of our public space is barricaded and bollarded, controlled and surveyed, more of our social activity takes place in privatized public spaces such as malls. But the mall wants consumers, not citizens; shoppers, not flaneurs. Much of the joy of the sheer randomness, weirdness, and unpredictability of the urban experience has disappeared, replaced with arid exercises in scripted dramas and controlled, commodified experiences.

On average, people aged twelve to nineteen in the U.S. spend 3.5 hours each week in a mall. They are policed and controlled in order to make customers feel safe and to keep them coming back and spending more money. The temples of consumerism have become the agoras of the contemporary U.S., places where the public comes. But it is not public space. There is agoraphobia in the contemporary U.S. that makes the privatization of public space as much a consumer demand as a corporate conspiracy.

As truly public space declines, corporate space asserts itself, from the branding of new sports stadia to the more overt creation of special zones. Turner Field is the home of the Atlanta Braves baseball team. It has been designed to look like an old-style ballpark, a nostalgic re-creation with a contemporary corporate twist. Corporate slogans surround the grounds; Coca-Cola has part of the upper deck, where giant Coke bottles dominate the skyline. There is a club level, now called the Lexus Level, that houses the corporate suites. In the Lexus Level, in contrast to the other levels, there is air-conditioning, carpeted floors, and full buffet service. Sponsored visitors pass by the latest luxury car models on their way to their full-service suites. Right beside Turner Field, the most accessible parking spots are reserved exclusively for owners of Lexus vehicles at the widely publicized Lexus Lot. The stadium re-creates a community ritual in the shared space of the stadium, but patrons have very different experiences in the segmented spaces of ticket holders. The bleachers and the corporate suites are the segmented spaces of an unequal society where the same event is experienced very differently. The stadium, like the city, is fragmented. The corporatization of the space is palpable. The privatization of urban public space on closer inspection involves the decline of genuine public space and the corporatization of choice locations and prime sites.

Globalization

Table 15.2 highlights the more globally connected U.S. cities. However, globalizing trends profoundly affect all of urban America, especially economic globalization. The U.S. is deeply enmeshed in global production and worldwide trade. Long transnational production chains link producers and consumers around the world. The most obvious effects are the deindustrialization of urban economies in the wake of the global shift of manufactured jobs to a small range of countries, previously Japan and Korea and now China and Vietnam. The knock-on effects include the destruction of those urban economies based on manufacturing, the decline of organized labor, pressures on the middle class, and downward pressure on the wages and conditions of many workers, especially the ones in sectors more susceptible to global shift. From the early 1970s this change affected mostly the manufacturing sectors. In more recent years there has been a significant increase in the global shift in service employment. A new round of economic globalization, made possible by changes on technology, is sending a range of service employment overseas from the U.S. to the developing world. Back offices in Bangalore, India, now process home loans for U.S. mortgage companies, while many insurance claims made in the U.S. are routinely processed in offices situated in New Delhi. The economics are simple. Software designers in the U.S. cost seven thousand dollars a month, whereas experienced designers in India cost only one thousand dollars a month. U.S. companies now routinely outsource work previously done only at home. In the 1970s and 1980s engineers would come to the U.S. and Europe; now the jobs come to them.

There are some who have done well out of economic globalization. The past twenty years have seen a significant increase in the wealth of the global elite: owners of international companies, transnational executives, globalizing bureaucrats, globalizing politicians, and professionals. These groups are the main beneficiaries of the rise of global capitalism: they are the asset-rich and knowledge-rich individuals who obtain their power and influence from their pivotal roles in owning and managing the global economy. And although they may live in the same cities as the rest of us, they inhabit a very different world.

There also has been a profound cultural globalization throughout most of the world in the past fifty years. The U.S. is the foremost producer of global culture yet has remained remarkably parochial and introspective. The most visible sign of cultural globalization in U.S. cities is the immigration wave that began in the 1960s to reach levels not seen since the previous era of mass immigration in the early twentieth century. Immigrants from Latin America and Asia profoundly transform the very fabric of the nation as well as the nature of city neighborhoods. U.S. cities are now much more ethnically and racially varied than they were in 1950. The diasporic networks play an important role in economic globalization, as family and country ties become important channels of international commerce: trade in technology with China and remittances to El Salvador are just some of the ways that the new immigrant groups link the U.S. economy to the wider world. Compared to much of the rest of the world, this mass immigration has proved to be relatively untroublesome.

The U.S.'s role in the world of political globalization is most evident in the rise of the military-industrial complex, which was harnessed from 1945 to 1989 in the cold war against the Soviet Union and its allies. The U.S. rise to globalism was built on the transformation of urban economies into engines of military production. As the country became a world power, selected urban economies benefited enormously. The peace dividend after the fall of communism had little time to develop before 9/11 inaugurated a renewed commitment to national security. As the world's only hyperpower, the military-industrial complex continues to have a life of its own, now morphing into a scientific-military-industrial-security complex. And the connection between the Pentagon and urban growth continues to develop. But 9/11 also brought new changes. New forms of surveillance and control were introduced, the barricading and bollarding of cities continues apace, both reflecting and reinforcing fear of urban public space. The U.S.'s role in the wider world continues to affect its cities and citizens.

Polarization

From 1950 to the mid-1970s a dominant force was the emergence of a mass middle class, employed in well-paying jobs and housed in owner-occupied suburbs. The strength of the U.S. economy and the broadly liberal social legislation, such as the G.I. Bill and FHA mortgages, helped many people into the middle class while also creating a reasonable safety net for those individuals at the bottom. The situation was not perfect. Racial issues continued to cast a stain on the foundational claim of universal democratic principles, and there were still persistent pockets of poverty in poor, rural areas and inner-city neighborhoods. But, in general, the first twenty-five years after the ending World War II witnessed the widest sharing of the national wealth in the history of the Republic. Since then, wealth and income are ever more unevenly distributed.

The income gap has widened. The percentage of households earning close to the median income has fallen over three decades. The percentage of households with incomes between $35,000 and $49,999 has fallen from 22.3 percent in 1967 to 15 percent in 2003. Increases in average income have been greatest for the richest. The richest fifth saw an increase of 75.6 percent in their household income from 1967 to 2003, whereas those households in the bottom three-fifths saw little more than 30 percent. In 1975 the chief executive officer in a private company made, on average, $500,000, or the equivalent of 36 families earning the U.S. median income. By 1995 the average CEO made $5.25 million (in constant dollars), or the equivalent of 133 families earning the U.S. median income.

The data shown in table 15.3 tell the story. The rich got a larger share of national wealth, while the rest were squeezed. The richest fifth increased their share to almost one-half, whereas the share of the remaining four-fifths declined from 56.3 percent to 50.3 percent.

At the bottom, the effects of globalization reduced a significant amount of good-paying jobs for the relatively low skilled. In the 1950s and even into the 1960s white males leaving high school without graduating could still secure a good-paying job in a factory earning the equivalent of seventeen dollars an hour today. Those jobs have gone. The jobless rate is highest among the people with the least education. In January 2004 those individuals with no high school diploma had an unemployment rate of 8.8 percent; for those with a bachelor's degree or higher, the rate was only 2.9 percent. The wages of less educated, lower-skilled workers have stagnated

TABLE 15.3

Share of national wealth, 1967 and 2003

	1967	2003
Richest fifth households	43.8	49.8
Second fifth households	24.2	23.4
Third fifth households	17.3	14.8
Fourth fifth households	10.8	8.7
Poorest fifth households	4.0	3.4

in the past twenty years. Income growth is skewed toward the employees with higher skill levels. Lower-end jobs no longer support a middle-class lifestyle.

The middle class has thinned, as income distributions have polarized. There was an increase from 18 percent to 22.5 percent of those individuals earning less than half of the median income from 1969 to 2002, while the ones earning double the median income increased in the same period, from 10.8 percent to 16.8 percent. The middle class has been squeezed. There has been an increasing number of bankruptcies and foreclosures in the past twenty-five years. The average middle-class family can no longer buy a house without putting at least two people to work. Even two incomes in a household does not guarantee financial security.

Many factors worsen the position of the middle- and lower-income households. Economic restructuring, which created easier access to imports and a deindustrialization of manufacturing jobs, has taken away many of the solid seventeen-dollar-an-hour jobs for the semiskilled and unskilled. The consequent decline of unions, especially in the private sector, weakens labor's power to maintain high incomes. Large immigrant flows, especially of unskilled and low-skilled workers, reduce the bargaining power of labor. The shift in the tax load from corporations to individuals creates an increased fiscal burden that along with the massive increase in health and college-education costs places a heavy weight on middle-income families. Middle-class status and lifestyle elude the average wageworker, and many are falling from middle-class status. Katherine S. Newman describes this process as "falling from grace," as those workers losing well-paying jobs see their dreams of middle-class comfort disappearing.[7]

Since the Reagan administration, wealth accumulation has been biased toward the already wealthy. One of the nation's most acute political observers, Kevin Phillips, was one of the first to note, in his 1990 book *The Politics of Rich and Poor,* that middle-class incomes were stagnant. He predicted some form of populist reaction. However, the long boom of the 1990s papered over many of the inequalities. The rising tide of economic activity meant rising incomes and a decline in unemployment, with labor shortages in some of the more highly skilled sectors. Life was not getting easier, as more people in households had to work longer and harder just to

maintain lifestyles in the wake of increasing health, education, and housing costs. The pace of work increased as part of the overall speeding up of
people's lives. People were more highly geared, overextended, and just
plain exhausted by the pace of keeping up.

Meanwhile, the rich got richer. It was the New Gilded Age. The *New
Yorker* even used this title in a compilation of articles written in the 1990s
about the 1990s. It was the time of Bill Gates and Donald Trump, conspicuous consumption, and a renewed sense of entitlement by the rich. The emphasis, as in the previous age, was on accumulation and display. There
were some interesting differences. Consumption patterns echoed some of
the counterculture of the 1960s, as the wealthy undertook conscientious
consumption that showed not only how rich but also how cultured they
were. David Brooks identifies them as BOBOS, bourgeois bohemians, who
thought nothing of spending fifteen thousand dollars on a sleek fridge or
an industrial-strength cooking range. It was the age of luxury fever.[8]

Some of the excesses of the 1990s exuberance faltered by the end of the
century as the "dot.com" craze ended and corporate scandals revealed just
how greedy and crooked much of corporate America had become. However, even those executives not crooked were making literally hundreds of
million of dollars on stock options. The sheer disparity with the strains and
anxieties of average middle-class life is mind-numbing. Whereas the vast
majority are harassed by mounting health costs, college-education fee increases for their children, and growing economic uncertainty, for a tiny minority there is another world of private jets, multimillion-dollar salaries,
golden parachutes, and million-dollar stock options.

There has always been inequality in the U.S. And inequality on its own
is not necessarily something to always decry. When some people work
harder than others or are more talented or gifted, then differential rewards
may be a good thing; it may encourage harder work and excellence. But
rising inequality in the contemporary U.S. is not necessarily connected
with work and effort. Generous stock options are paid to executives even
as their companies falter and workers are let go. Wealth and riches seem
unconnected to performance and results. The riches go most often to the
connected rather than the meritocratic. Those individuals lucky enough to
have rich parents have an increased probability of getting rich. Wealth accumulation is less the operation of a truly free market and more the result

of crony capitalism. It is not a capitalist economy rewarding the best and the brightest but economic and political oligopolies feathering their own nests. Meanwhile, the nonwealthy are having a harder time getting by. The decks are stacked against them, as wealth disparities feed into educational attainment that affects employment opportunities. It is a vicious circle for the majority and a benign cycle for the wealthy. What is particularly disturbing is the declining level of social mobility in the U.S. People are spending longer in lower-income brackets, and social-mobility rates in the U.S. are now less than most countries in western Europe. Whereas 44 percent of poor people in the Netherlands left poverty within a year, the figure in the U.S. is 17 percent for whites and 8 percent for blacks.[9]

A recent series of articles in the *New York Times* brought discussions of the class divisions in U.S. society to a wider audience. In the overview article Janny Scott and David Leonhardt showed the pervasive importance of class. Class mobility is much less than previously thought, and although some class lines are blurring—the ranks of the elite are widening, and the tight connection between race and class is disappearing—class lines are hardening, as economic success is still largely a function of family background. Wealthier households can provide a cluster of privileges to their children that poorer households cannot. The greater reliance on the private market as opposed to more egalitarian public services reinforces the trend. Inequality is increasing, and it is feeding into wider disparities in educational attainment, income, and life chances.[10]

The nature of the metropolitan U.S., with central cities politically cordoned off from suburbs and different groups partitioned into different urban spaces, reinforces inequality. A 2004 report from the Brookings Institution reveals that one-fourth of all households in the bottom income quintile now live in the one hundred largest cities. There has been a declining proportion of households with high incomes. Cities now contain more of the poor and less of the rich. And the public policies that promote small government are in effect reinforcing the inequities by minimizing the taxation of the wealthy and reinforcing disparities that filter into health outcomes, educational-attainment levels, and employment prospects. The increasing income inequality is spatially reinforced by the segregation of income groups, as the wealthy spatially segregate themselves into gated communities and exclusive suburbs.[11]

There is a segmentation of urban space. As metaphor we can think of the sports stadia. New stadia are being built around the country with luxury boxes. The spectators are now divided into separate spaces with differing conditions, similar to the separation of people into very different municipalities in the metropolitan region. The decline in communal public spaces and the rise of commodified, semipublic-semiprivate spaces, such as malls, distance those individuals less able to consume and buy. General urban public spaces are more segmented by income groups, and the marginal disappear as citizens and reappear as a threat. And the more people hide behind gated communities, live in segregated suburbs, and patronize socially segmented sites, the city becomes less of a site of regular interaction and more of a scary encounter. The higher the walls go up, the less the feeling of safety and security. As middle- and upper-income groups retreat from the urban scene, the more the city becomes a place of danger to be disciplined, policed, controlled, and avoided.

The city is a public achievement, and the story of the U.S. city is one of constant hopes, dreams, and aspirations uneasily melding with the starker realities of privatization, globalization, and polarization. The city is the space where the constant alluring prospect of improvement and the equally constant practice of brute economic power and differential political strength play out in a ceaseless drama of innocence and experience. The prospect of a city of alabaster, undimmed by human tears, continues to beckon.

Appendix

Notes

Guide to Further Reading

Works Cited

Index

The Cities of New York State

THERE HAVE BEEN SMALL permanent settlements in New York State since precolonial times. Some of the Native American villages housed almost five hundred people, and the long houses of the Iroquois were large enough for European commentators to describe them as castles. The name lives on in one settlement in central New York, Oneida Castle. But towns and cities as we now use the terms emerged most fully in the colonial period.

The Rise of Cities

Cities played a vital role in colonial New York. They were important command and trading centers. The largest of them were vital nodes in a global trading system. Early Dutch settlements clustered around the Hudson, close to the ocean. New Amsterdam was established on the tip of Manhattan in 1626 as a trading post and fort, and, farther up the river, Fort Orange (now Albany) was a strategic location in the fur trade. Both places were military outposts as well as collection centers for sending raw materials back to Europe.

Dutch rule was relatively short. By 1664 New Netherlands had become an English colony, and New Amsterdam became New York. The Dutch presence lives on in the landscape. Names such as the Bronx, Brooklyn (Breuckelen), Hoboken, and Yonkers are an enduring Dutch legacy.

In 1664, when the English took control of the colony, the population of the newly named town of New York was only around eight thousand. During the English colonial period most towns in New York remained relatively small. They were trading centers, market centers, and military outposts that stretched up the Hudson and lower Mohawk valleys. They exported raw materials such as furs and timber and agricultural products and imported the manufactured goods from the imperial center. They were part of an expanding commercial and military order, focal points in the commodification of the land and the dispossession of the Native Americans. They were lively places, with a hubbub of European voices, predominantly English and Scots, some French, commingling with the dialects of local tribes as well as the slaves' cadences from Africa. New York City was even more heterogeneous. Dutch and English, white and black, Jew and Christian were if not quite fusing together then at least negotiating a shared space and a common mercantile purpose.

After the Revolution, the lands of the powerful Iroquois were taken over in central and western New York. The entire Mohawk Valley, central and western New York, was opened up for settlement, and we see the early beginnings of such cities as Syracuse, Rochester, and Buffalo.

The Canal

A major engine on the urban-growth machine was the Erie Canal. Authorized in 1817, it was opened in 1825. The canal effectively linked New York City with the Mohawk Valley, central and western New York, and the western interior of the Great Lakes region. The canal collapsed space and time. Freight rates between Buffalo and New York City fell from one hundred dollars a ton to ten dollars a ton. Raw materials could flow down to New York City, while manufactured goods and immigrants could move westward. All along the route of the canal town growth was stimulated and enhanced, as settlers, immigrants, and trade passed through the locks. Between 1825 and 1835 the population of Albany, Lockport, Syracuse, Troy, and Utica doubled, and Rochester tripled. Buffalo had a population of only fifteen hundred in 1812, but by 1835 it had increased to twenty thousand. New York City now had a continental hinterland and was propelled into world-city status. The canal stimulated agricultural production and urban growth all along its route and laid the foundation for urban settlement. The southern-tier counties of New York, without the benefit of the canal, never achieved the same levels of urbanization as the counties along the Erie Canal. Later, the railways tended to reinforce the urban spine first laid down by the canal.

Industrial Cities

In the last three-quarters of the nineteenth century the growth of cities was intimately linked to the growth of industry. Manufacturing had previously been a small-scale activity. Sawmills and the forges were widely dispersed through the settlements of the state. Throughout the rest of the century and well into the twentieth century, urban growth in the state was intimately associated with industrial expansion. Cities grew, as New York State became an industrial powerhouse.

Many factors were at work in the Industrial Revolution. There were the transport improvements. The canals and then the railways allowed heavier goods to be transported. Technological advances allowed anthracite rather than charcoal to be used by forges and furnaces. A national market was generating a larger demand for goods. Large-scale immigration created a large pool of cheap labor. New York State became one of the centers of the industrial transformation that involved larger manufacturing plants located in towns and cities. By 1890 the state had become the most populous, with a population of 6 million. The bulk of the population growth occurred in the expanding industrial cities. Take the case of Buffalo, which had originally grown as one more city along the canal. By 1900 it had become a center for iron and steel manufacturing. The metal-base industries were the backbone to the growth of the city from 75,000 in 1855 to around 300,000 by the end of the century. The city of Rome developed as a brass and copper center, with copper mills, canning factories, and cable and wire manufacturers and by 1920 became the sixth-largest city in the state, with a population of 26,341. Manufacturing was very specialized, and individual cities became associated with specific industries: shirt making in Troy, paper making in Glens Falls, carpet making in Amsterdam, knitwear in Utica, glove making in Gloversville, furniture making in Johnstown, and electrical goods in Schenectady.

New York State was and is one of the most urbanized states in the Union. As early as 1900 almost three-quarters of the population lived in urban places, defined in the census as having a population of more than 2,500.

The cities became the arena for both big capital and organized labor. The industrial cities of New York State witnessed the birth and growth of organized labor, often in the crucible of severe capital-labor conflict. The history of these industrial cities is marked by cycles of compromise and conflict between the two in line with the booms and slumps of the capitalist economy.

Half the urban population in 1855 was foreign born. Immigrants into nineteenth-century New York tended to end up in the towns and cities more than as agricultural settlers. With a huge demand for industrial labor, and with more of the agricultural land already long settled, the city was the main destination point for immigrants.

Immigrants flowed into the industrial cities in waves—first the Irish and Germans and then the Italians. Later, African Americans would come up from the South and people from Asia and Latin America. The cities became the destination for both overseas and internal migration. Attracted by jobs and economic opportunities, the immigrants would bring their cultures and group ties with them. Separate ethnic neighborhoods emerged. New-style politics developed; the patrician class had to compete with the political power of the organized ethnics. Machine politics soon dominated the cities, and there emerged the Democratic control of the bigger cities compared to the more conservative Republican rural areas.

Cities were not just producing goods but also creating a civic culture: trade associations, business groups, labor organizations, political parties, and civic reformers. In the shared space and common experience of the city, civic cultures developed and thrived. The labor movement, for example, was shaped by the shared experience of industrial workers trying to improve wages and conditions. Urban reformers were appalled at the inefficiencies and corruption of machine politics.

Postindustrial Cities

Industrial and urban growth continued into the twentieth century. The city of Buffalo, for example, grew from seventy-five thousand in 1855 to almost three million in 1930. The Depression saw a marked decline, but later war production and the immediate postwar expansion saw new spurts in industrial and urban growth. But since the 1950s there has been a marked decline in manufacturing employment in New York State. There are a number of reasons behind the decline. The industries have become more efficient and need less labor. Some industries have closed; gloves are no longer made in Gloversville. Others have moved to cheaper labor areas in the Sun Belt or offshore. The net effect has been for industrial jobs to shrink and with it the fortunes of many of the predominantly industrial cities. The peak population of both Schenectady and Utica was in 1930. Buffalo, Rochester, and Syracuse all saw their peak population in 1950. Some of the subsequent decline is owing to suburbanization, but much of it is a function of the decline of the manufacturing base.

The central cities of Albany, Buffalo, Syracuse, and Rochester, for example, have declined since 1950, but the suburban rings have continued to increase. The core populations have not only shrunk in size but changed as well. The population in the core of the older industrial cities has become a concentration of lower-income and especially lower-income minority groups. The loss of their tax base and the hemorrhaging of high-paying jobs and tax-paying factories have compromised the fiscal health of the cities. The industrial cities of New York State exhibit the problems of other cities in the so-called Rust Belt: a shrinking manufacturing base, concentrated urban poverty, and declining city tax base.

The recent economic history of all cities in New York has been a shift from manufacturing to services. The central cities in particular are becoming less manufacturing areas and more service centers. Offices and stores are replacing factories and mills. The deindustrialization of the cities has meant a loss of high-paying secure jobs and a transformation of urban space as the older industrial areas fall vacant. In some cases this change has provided an opportunity for creative reuse and adaptation. The construction of a downtown baseball stadium in Buffalo and the use of an old warehouse section of Syracuse, Armory Square, are part of a larger nationwide trend to retheme the central city toward entertainment and cultural attractions.

New York City

New York City has been the largest city in the United States for more than two hundred years. In the very first census of the Republic, in 1790, New York was the biggest city, with a population of 33,131. The next-largest city was Philadelphia, with 28,522. The city has never lost its prime position and since that first census has reinforced its national prominence. Since 1850 it has consistently been between two to three times the size of the next-largest city, even as that position was filled by different cities;

Philadelphia in 1850, Chicago in 1900, Los Angeles in 2000. New York City has stood at the peak of the urban hierarchy over the entire life of the Republic, whereas the fate of other New York State cities has taken a different path. In 1900 New York City was the first ranked city, Buffalo was the eighth largest, Rochester was twenty-fourth, Syracuse thirtieth, and Albany fortieth. By 1990, while New York City was still number one, Buffalo had fallen to fiftieth, Rochester to sixty-sixth, and Albany and Syracuse had dropped from the list of one hundred largest cities.

The city is the center of the largest metropolitan region in the country, which in 2000 had a population of just over 21 million and extended over four states: Connecticut, New Jersey, New York, and Pennsylvania. New York owes its prominence to its strong and varied economic base. It has been a trading center since first established by the Dutch, and it has never lost its sense of business hustle and search for commercial opportunity. It is a major manufacturing center, the epicenter of financial transactions, and the home to major corporations. Even such specialized trades as book publishing and the diamond wholesale business do much of their business in the city. Wall Street is synonymous with the business world, Madison Avenue with the world of advertising. It is a world city with global connections. It is the home of the United Nations. When terrorists wanted to strike at the heart of America they flew jets into the World Trade Center in downtown Manhattan.

New York City is the most global city in the United States. Its economic transactions and population links cover the globe. It is as much a world city as an American city. Of its five boroughs, only one of them is in the continental United States; the other four in a metaphor for the city as a whole float between the United States and the rest of the world. There are tremendous disparities in wealth. From the socialite set who appear at charity events at the Metropolitan, live on Park Avenue, and summer in the Hamptons to those individuals packed in four to a room in Chinatown. The city contains the very wealthy and the very poor, the powerful and the weak, the CEOs of major corporations and illegal aliens working as seamstresses in clothing sweatshops.

The city has been the single biggest destination point of immigrants in to the U.S. More than 12 million immigrants passed though Ellis Island between 1892 and 1954, many of them remaining in the region. The name of some of the city's neighborhoods tell their own story: Chinatown, Harlem, Little Italy, Spanish Harlem. Since the 1965 Immigration and Nationality Act, immigration levels have reached and surpassed the levels reached when Ellis Island was processing immigrants. At least 10 percent of immigrants to the U.S. are arriving in New York City, an average of more than 100,000 a year. One in three New York City residents was born outside the United States. The city continues to act as a magnet for foreign immigrants and internal migrants. The pull of the city, like its image, its business transactions, and its social ties, extends around the world.

Notes

1. The Rise of Metropolitan America

1. The U.S. Census Web site (http://www.census.gov) is an indispensable first source of information and data. It can be a bit overwhelming at first glance. There are links to state and county "quick facts" as well as other simple statistics on such topics as income and poverty under the subcategories of "People." For the user researching metropolitan regions (referred to by the Census Bureau as metropolitan statistical areas or MSAs), following the link to American FactFinder will be more useful. From there, access the Fact Sheets to find community profiles, or follow the link to Data Sets to access more specific data from the 2000 U.S. Census. If you are having trouble finding what you are looking for, try the "Search" function. Click on the "Search" link on the Web site and enter the appropriate key words.

2. Urban Renewal: "We Must Start All Over Again from the Ground Up"

1. Catherine Bauer, "House and Cities," 79–80.

2. A full discussion of the discourse of urban decline is available in Robert A. Beauregard's *Voices of Decline: The Postwar Fate of U.S. Cities*.

3. The case arose from an urban-renewal project in Washington, D.C.'s Southwest neighborhood. The area contained many small businesses and homes for African Americans. Sam Berman was the executor of an estate that contained a small department store in the area. When the store was condemned under eminent domain by the public agency responsible for the project, he took the issue to court. It ended up in the Supreme Court that ruled in favor of the public agency and the subsequent urban renewal that demolished the homes and business and replaced them with offices and residential and hotel complexes. For years afterward Southwest had that dismal, antiseptic feeling of poor architecture and even worse urban design that marked so many of the urban-renewal schemes. Lacking restaurants, shopping, and entertainment the area was a sterile, barren, monotonous district. Since the early 2000s there are signs of revival, almost fifty years after the Supreme Court ruled in favor of its destruction.

4. Thomas J. Sugrue, *The Origins of the Urban Crisis*, 55. Sugrue's careful analysis of De-

troit suggests that concentrated racialized poverty owes its roots to the urban policies pursued in the 1940s and 1950s.

5. See Chester Hartman, "The Housing of Relocated Families."

6. Herbert Gans, *The Urban Villagers*, 315.

7. Raymond A. Mohl, "Planned Destruction: The Interstates and Central City Housing," 227.

3. Stimulating Suburbs, Starving Cities: "I Should Prefer to See the Ash Heaps"

1. Quoted in R. M. Fogelson, *Downtown: Its Rise and Fall*, 375.

2. Catherine Bauer, "The Dreary Deadlock of Public Housing," 141.

3. I have drawn heavily on Alexander von Hoffman, "Why They Built Pruitt-Igoe."

4. Robert Moses Versus Jane Jacobs: "Hack Your Way with a Meat Ax"

1. The definitive biography is Robert Caro, *The Power Broker*.

2. Marshall Berman, *All That Is Solid Melts into Air: The Experience of Modernity*, 295.

3. Jane Jacobs, *The Death and Life of Great American Cities*, 371.

5. Downtown: "The Heart That Pumps the Blood of Commerce"

1. In *Urban Fortunes: The Political Economy of Place*, urban scholars John Logan and Harvey Molotch use the term *urban growth machine* to refer to urban business interests and their success in dominating the civic agenda with stimulating economic growth and urban renewal rather than issues of redistribution of benefits or social equity.

2. Sam Walton with John Huey, *Sam Walton: Made in America*, 46.

3. Roger Noll quoted in Sally Jenkins, "Is the District Being Sold a Bill of Goods?" *Washington Post*, September 20, 2004, D11.

4. J. Ritter, "Americans Discover Charms of Living near Mass Transit," *USA Today*, November 18, 2004, 6D.

5. See W. Neill, "Lipstick on the Gorilla: The Failure of Image-Led Planning in Coleman Young's Detroit."

6. Lorlane Hoyt, "Business Improvement Districts: Untold Stories and Substantiated Impacts." For a range of opinions on the BID debate, see Heather MacDonald, "Why Business Improvement Districts Work," http://www.manhattan-institute.org/html/cb_4.htm; Jerry Mitchell, "Business Improvement Districts and the 'New' Revitalization of Downtown"; and William K. Tabb, "Privatization and Urban Issues."

6. Creating a Suburban Society: "A Landscape of Scary Places"

1. Plans for a national highway system had been in the air since the 1930s. Under President Eisenhower the plans were extended, implemented, and generously funded. Eisenhower's military experience led him to conclude that an interstate-highway system, similar to Germany's high-speed autobahns, would enhance troop mobilization and rapid population

evacuation in the event of war. The highway program is formally entitled the Dwight D. Eisenhower National System of Interstate and Defense Highways.

2. J. Persky and H. Kurban, "Do Federal Funds Better Support Cities or Suburbs?"

3. For conflicting interpretations, see Peter Calthorpe, *The Next American Metropolis: Ecology, Community, and the American Dream;* and Robert Venturi, D. S. Brown, and S. Izenour, *Learning from Las Vegas.* At her inauguration in 1998 as governor of New Jersey, Christine Todd Whitman said, "Sprawl eats up our open space. It creates traffic jams that boggle the mind and pollute the air. Sprawl makes us feel downright claustrophobic about the future."

4. From the charter of New Urbanism: "Neighborhoods should be compact, pedestrian-friendly, and mixed use. . . . Many activities of daily living should occur within walking distance, allowing independence to those who do not drive, especially the elderly and the young. Interconnected networks of streets should be designed to encourage walking, reduce the number of and length of automobile trips and conserve energy. Within neighborhoods a broad range of housing types and price levels can bring people of diverse races and incomes into daily interaction, strengthening the personal and civic bonds essential to an authentic community" (http://www.cnu.org/charter.html, November 9, 1999).

5. See Douglas Frantz and Catherine Collins, *Celebration USA;* and Andrew Ross, *The Celebration Chronicles.*

6. For a range of opinion, see Larry R. Ford, "Lynch Revisited: New Urbanism and Theories of Good City Form"; Alex Krieger, "Whose Urbanism?"; and Emily Talen, "Sense of Community and Neighborhood Form: An Assessment of the Social Doctrine of New Urbanism."

7. See Joel Garreau, *Edge Cities: Life on the New Frontier.*

8. Lewis Mumford, *The City in History: Its Origins, Its Transformations, and Its Prospects,* 486

9. James Howard Kunstler, *The Geography of Nowhere,* 273. See also Timothy Beatley and Kristy Manning, *The Ecology of Place;* and Richard Moe and Carter Wilkie, *Changing Places: Rebuilding Community in the Age of Sprawl.*

10. See Robert D. Putnam, *Bowling Alone: The Collapse and Revival of American Community.*

11. See Juliet F. Gainsborough, *Fenced Off: The Suburbanization of American Politics.*

12. See Gregory Giroux, "A Line in the Suburban Sand," http://governing.com/articles/6cqburbs.htm, posted June 27, 2005.

7. New Suburban Realities: "Trouble in Paradise"

1. See M. Baldassare, *Trouble in Paradise: The Suburban Transformation of America.* Among the many scholarly studies of suburban diversity, see B. M. Berger, *Working Class Suburb: A Study of Auto Workers in Suburbia;* W. M. Dobriner, *Class in Suburbia;* W. H. Hudnut III, *Halfway to Everywhere: A Portrait of America's First-Tier Suburbs;* B. Katz and R. E. Lang, eds., *Redefining Urban and Suburban America: Evidence from Census 2000;* and J. J. Palen, *The Suburbs.*

2. See W. H. Frey, "Melting Pot Suburbs: A Study of Suburban Diversity."

3. W. H. Lucy and D. L. Phillips, *Confronting Suburban Decline: Strategic Planning for Met-*

ropolitan Renewal; T. Swanstrom, C. Casey, R. Flack, and P. Drier, *Pulling Apart: Economic Segregation among Suburbs and Central Cities in Major Metropolitan Areas.*

8. Metropolitan Fragmentation: "Obsolescent Structure of Urban Government"

1. See D. Gordon, "Capitalist Development and the History of American Cities."

2. See P. M. Joassart-Marcelli, J. A. Musso, and J. R. Wolch, "Fiscal Consequences of Concentrated Poverty in a Metropolitan Region."

3. Daniel Patrick Moynihan, "Toward a National Urban Policy," 4.

9. Urban Economies: "All That Is Solid Melts into Air"

1. See Philip Fisher, *Still the New World: American Literature in a Culture of Creative Destruction.* We have become so used to this constant change that we assume lack of change is the same as stagnation and death. Places that do not change, people that do not grow, developments that do not take place are seen not as signs of stability but as marks of failure.

2. See F. F. Piven and R. A. Cloward, *The Breaking of the American Social Compact.*

3. See William Julius Wilson, *When Work Disappears: The World of the New Urban Poor.*

4. Piven and Cloward, *Breaking the Social Compact,* 145.

5. John Goss, "The 'Magic of the Mall': An Analysis of the Form, Function, and Meaning in the Contemporary Retail Built Environment," 40.

6. See Lizabeth Cohen, *A Consumers' Republic: The Politics of Mass Consumption in Postwar America.*

7. See Malcom Gladwell, "The Science of Shopping."

10. Race and Ethnicity: "E Pluribus Unum"

1. The term *Hispanic* was adopted by the federal Ad Hoc Committee on Racial and Ethnic Definition. It was coined in 1965 and first used in the census forms in 1980. The debate behind the designation is outlined in Darryl Fears, "The Roots of Hispanic," *Washington Post,* October 15, 2003, A21.

2. Since the mid-1990s there has been a marked migration of blacks to southern cities, especially Atlanta, followed by Dallas, Charlotte, and Orlando. See William H. Frey, *The New Great Migration.*

3. A report by the Harvard Civil Rights Project suggests even further resegregation: http://www.civilrightsproject.harvard.edu/research/deseg/deseg05.php.

4. Michael Dobbs, "Schools and Lives Are Still Separate," *Washington Post,* May 17, 2004, A1, A6.

5. See David Fasenfest, Jason Booza, and Kurt Metzger, *Living Together: A New Look at Racial and Ethnic Integration in Metropolitan Neighborhoods, 1990–2000.*

6. Henry Louis Gates Jr., "The Black Leadership Myth," *New Yorker,* October 24, 1994, 7–8.

11. Housing and the City: "Shaky Palaces"

1. See U.S. Department of Housing and Urban Development, "Discrimination in Metropolitan Housing Markets," http://www.huduser.org/publications/hsgfin/hds.html; A. H.

Munnell, G. M. B. Tootell, L. E. Brown, and J. McEneaney, "Mortgage Lending in Boston: Interpreting the HMDA Data"; and M. A. Turner and F. Skidmore, eds., *Mortgage Lending Discrimination: A Review of Existing Evidence.*

2. See A. E. Hillier, "Spatial Analysis of Historical Redlining: A Methodological Exploration."

3. The Community Reinvestment Act was created in response to widespread criticism of bank lending policies. It was designed to make banks lend money in areas from which they receive deposits. The law had few enforcement powers, and no lending levels were stipulated. However, some community groups have used the act to force banks in local areas to lend more money. In 1990 all banks had to disclose their CRA rating, a measure of the extent to which they were meeting the requirements.

4. See Matthew Edel, Elliott D. Scalar, and Daniel Luria, *Shaky Palaces: Homeownership and Social Mobility in Boston's Suburbanization.*

5. Haya El Nasser, "Affordable-Housing Shortage Overtaking Working Families," *USA Today,* June 2, 2000, 3A.

6. U.S. Department of Housing and Urban Development, "The Sustainability of Homeownership," http://www.huduser.org/publications/affhsg/homeownsustainability .html.

7. See Michel M. Shapiro, *The Hidden Cost of Being African American.*

8. Valuable information on the U.S. housing stock and housing markets is contained in the American Housing Survey (AHS) conducted by the U.S. Bureau of the Census for the Department of Housing and Urban Development. The AHS collects data on the nation's housing, including apartments, single-family homes, mobile homes, vacant housing units, household characteristics, income, housing and neighborhood quality, housing costs, equipment and fuels, size of housing unit, and recent movers. National data are collected in odd-numbered years, and data for each of forty-seven selected metropolitan areas are collected currently about every six years. The national sample covers an average of fifty-five thousand housing units. Each metropolitan-area sample covers forty-one hundred or more housing units. The AHS returns to the same housing units year after year to gather data; therefore, this survey is ideal for analyzing the flow of households through housing. Another useful source, also produced by the Department of Housing and Urban Development, is the quarterly *U.S. Housing Market Conditions Report,* which provides a range of housing data as well as profiles of local housing markets across the nation.

9. I have drawn extensively on a television documentary, the transcript of which is available at http://www.pbs.org/pov/pov2003/flagwars/special_taleco.html.

12. Politics and the City: "Informal Arrangements . . . Formal Workings"

1. See K. K. Wong and P. E. Peterson, "Urban Response to Federal Program Flexibility: Politics of Community Block Grants."

2. See R. Hendrick, "Assessing and Measuring the Fiscal Health of Local Governments: Focus on Chicago Suburban Municipalities."

3. See Floyd Hunter, *Community Power Structure.*

4. E. Hayes, *Power Structure and Urban Policy: Who Rules in Oakland?* M. Crenson, *The Un-politics of Air Pollution;* Logan and Molotch, *Urban Fortunes.* See also A. Jonas and D. Wilson, eds., *The Urban Growth Machine.*

5. Clarence Stone, *Regime Politics: Governing Atlanta, 1946–1988,* 3.

6. See Lynne Weikart, "Follow the Money: Mayoral Choice and Expenditure Policy."

7. The context for the *Berman v. Parker* decision is available in Charlotte Allen, "A Wreck of a Plan: Look at How Renewal Ruined SW," *Washington Post,* July 17, 2005, B1. *Kelo v. New London* is examined at http://en.wikipedia.org/wiki/Kelo_v_New_London. Reactions to the ruling are discussed in Kenneth Harney, "Eminent Domain Ruling Has Strong Repercussions," *Washington Post,* July 23, 2005, F1, F10.

13. Reimagining the City: "Place Wars"

1. See D. Haider, "Place Wars: New Realities of the 1990s."

2. J. R. Short and Y. Kim, "Urban Crises/Urban Representations: Selling the City in Difficult Times."

3. See J. T. Bailey, *Marketing Cities in the 1980s and Beyond.*

4. Leonard Shapiro, "Jacksonville Gets Super-Sized," *Washington Post,* January 31, 2005, D1, D7.

5. Beauregard, *Voices of Decline,* 201.

14. Civic Engagement in the City: "Civic Spirit"

1. National Commission on Civic Renewal, *A Nation of Spectators,* 3.

2. See A. M. Guest and S. K. Wierzbicki, "Social Ties at the Neighborhood Level."

3. See M. J. Sandel, *Democracy's Discontent;* and M. Schudson, *The Good Citizen: A History of American Civic Life.*

15. Emerging Trends

1. Richard Florida, *The Rise of the Creative Class.*

2. Anthony Townsend, "The Internet and the Rise of the New Network Cities, 1969–1999."

3. The GAWC Web site is a very useful source of information and ideas from researchers around the world: http://www.lboro.ac.uk/gawc/. See also J. R. Short and Y. Kim, *Globalization and the City.*

4. See P. J. Taylor, *World City Network.*

5. E. Soja, *Postmetropolis.*

6. Associated Press, "For Many Teens a Night at the Mall Requires an Escort," *Baltimore Sun,* September 19, 2004, 3A.

7. Katherine S. Newman, *Falling from Grace: The Experience of Downward Mobility in the American Middle-Class.*

8. David Brooks, *BOBOS in Paradise: The New Upper Class and How They Got There.*

9. See Aarin Bernstein, "Is America Becoming More of a Class Society?"

10. The eleven-part series appeared in 2005 and is available at http://www
.nytimes.com/indexes/2005/05/15/national/class/. Janny Scott and David Leonhardt's
book of the series, titled *Class Matters,* was published by Times Books in 2005.

11. Alan Berube and Thacher Tiffany, *The Shape of the Curve: Household Income Distributions in US Cities, 1979–1999.*

Guide to Further Reading

THIS LIST IS NOT a comprehensive guide. I have selected only a small sample of classic and recent work from the vast literature on the metropolitan U.S.

1. The Rise of Metropolitan America

Abbott, C. *The Metropolitan Frontier: Cities in the Modern American West.* Tucson: Univ. of Arizona Press, 1993.

Bernard, R. M., ed. *Snowbelt Cities: Metropolitan Politics in the Northeast and Midwest since World War II.* Bloomington: Indiana Univ. Press, 1990.

Bernard, R. M., and B. R. Rice, eds. *Sunbelt Cities: Politics and Growth since World War II.* Austin: Univ. of Texas Press, 1983.

Biles, R., ed. *The Human Tradition in Urban America.* Wilmington, Del.: SR Books, 2002.

Fox, K. *Metropolitan America: Urban Life and Urban Policy in the United States.* Jackson: Univ. Press of Mississippi, 1986.

Hirsch, A. R., and R. A. Mohl, eds. *Urban Policy in Twentieth-Century America.* New Brunswick: Rutgers Univ. Press, 1993.

Miller, Z. L., and P. M. Melvin. *The Urbanization of Modern America.* San Diego: Harcourt Brace Jovanovich, 1987.

Mohl, R. A. *Searching for the Sunbelt: Historical Perspectives on a Region.* Knoxville: Univ. of Tennessee Press, 1990.

Mollenkopf, J., and K. Emerson, eds. *Rethinking the Urban Agenda.* New York: Century Foundation Press, 2001.

Mumford, Lewis. *The City in History: Its Origins, Its Transformations, and Its Prospects.* New York: Harvest Books, 1968.

2. Urban Renewal: "We Must Start All Over Again from the Ground Up"

Anderson, M. *The Federal Bulldozer.* New York: McGraw-Hill, 1967.

Beauregard, Robert A. *Voices of Decline: The Postwar Fate of U.S. Cities.* 2d ed. Malden, Mass.: Blackwell, 2003.

Berman, Marshall. *All That Is Solid Melts into Air.* New York: Simon and Schuster, 1982.

Gans, H. *People and Plans.* New York: Basic Books, 1968.

Gittell, R. J. *Renewing Cities.* Princeton: Princeton Univ. Press, 1992.

Jacobs, Jane. *The Death and Life of Great American Cities.* New York: Random House, 1961.

Keating, W. D., and N. Krumholz, eds. *Rebuilding Urban Neighborhoods.* Thousand Oaks, Calif.: Sage, 1999.

Mohl, R. A. "Planned Destruction: The Interstates and Central City Housing." In *From Tenements to the Taylor Homes,* edited by J. F. Bauman, R. Biles, and K. M. Szylvian. University Park: Pennsylvania State Univ. Press, 2000.

———. "Race and Space in the Modern City: Interstate 95 and the Black Community in Miami." In *Urban Policy in Twentieth-Century America,* edited by A. R. Hirsch and R. A. Mohl. New Brunswick: Rutgers Univ. Press, 1993.

Sugrue, Thomas J. *The Origins of the Urban Crisis.* Princeton: Princeton Univ. Press, 1996.

Teaford, J. C. *The Rough Road to Renaissance: Urban Revitalization in America, 1940–1985.* Baltimore: Johns Hopkins Univ. Press, 1990.

Wilson, J. Q., ed. *Urban Renewal: The Record and the Controversy.* Cambridge: MIT Press, 1967.

3. Stimulating Suburbs, Starving Cities: "I Should Prefer to See the Ash Heaps"

Baxandall, R. F., and E. Ewen. *Picture Windows: How the Suburbs Happened.* New York: Basic Books, 2000.

Gans, H. J. *The Levittowners: Ways of Life and Politics in a New Suburban Community.* New York: Random House, 1967.

Hanchett, T. W. "The Other 'Subsidized' Housing: Federal Aid to Suburbanization, 1940–1960." In *From Tenements to the Taylor Homes,* edited by J. F. Bauman, R. Biles, and K. M. Szylvian. University Park: Pennsylvania State Univ. Press, 2000.

Hayden, D. *Building Suburbia: Green Fields and Urban Growth, 1820–2000.* New York: Pantheon Books, 2003.

Jackson, K. T. *Crabgrass Frontier: The Suburbanization of the United States.* Oxford: Oxford Univ. Press, 1985.

Katz, M. B. "With or Without Jim Crow: Black Residential Segregation in the United States." In *Urban Policy in Twentieth-Century America,* edited by A. R. Hirsch and R. A. Mohl. New Brunswick: Rutgers Univ. Press, 1993.

Kelly, B. M. *Expanding the American Dream: Building and Rebuilding Levittown.* Albany: SUNY Press, 1993.

Thomas, J. M., and M. Ritzdork, eds. *Urban Planning and the African American Community: In the Shadows.* Thousand Oaks, Calif.: Sage, 1997.

4. Robert Moses Versus Jane Jacobs: "Hack Your Way with a Meat Ax"

Caro, Robert A. *The Power Broker: Robert Moses and the Fall of New York.* New York: Vintage Books, 1975.

Jacobs, Jane. *The Death and Life of Great American Cities.* 1961. Reprint. New York: Modern Library, 1993.

———. *The Economy of Cities.* New York: Random House, 1969.

Phillips, P. C., ed. *City Speculations.* Queens, N.Y.: Queens Museum of Art, 1996.

Rodgers, C. *Robert Moses, Builder for Democracy.* New York: Henry Holt, 1952.

Schwartz, J. *The New York Approach: Robert Moses, Urban Liberals, and Redevelopment of the Inner City.* Columbus: Ohio State Univ. Press, 1993.

Seely, B. L. *Building the American Highway System: Engineers as Policy Makers.* Philadelphia: Temple Univ. Press, 1987.

5. Downtown: "The Heart That Pumps the Blood of Commerce"

Baim, D. V. *The Sports Stadium as a Municipal Investment.* Westport, Conn.: Greenwood Press, 1994.

Bedford, H. F. *Trouble Downtown: The Local Context of Twentieth-Century America.* New York: Harcourt Brace Jovanovich, 1978.

Danielson, M. N. *Home Team: Professional Sports and the American Metropolis.* Princeton: Princeton Univ. Press, 1997.

Fogelson, R. M. *Downtown: Its Rise and Fall.* New Haven: Yale Univ. Press, 2001.

Ford, L. R. *America's New Downtowns: Revitalization or Reinvention?* Baltimore: Johns Hopkins Univ. Press, 2003.

Graham, B. J. *A Geography of Heritage: Power, Culture, and Economy.* London: Oxford Univ. Press, 2000.

Jonas, A., and D. Wilson, eds. *The Urban Growth Machine.* Albany: SUNY Press, 1999.

Noll, R. G., and A. Zimbalist. *Sports, Jobs, and Taxes: The Economic Impact of Sports Teams and Stadiums.* Washington, D.C.: Brookings Institution Press, 1997.

Project for Public Spaces. *Managing Downtown Public Spaces.* Washington, D.C.: Planners Press, 1984.

Warrion, M. E. *The Living City: Baltimore's Charles Center and Inner Harbor Development*. Baltimore: Maryland Historical Society, 2002.

6. Creating a Suburban Society: "A Landscape of Scary Places"

Baldassare, M. *Trouble in Paradise: The Suburban Transformation of America*. New York: Columbia Univ. Press, 1986.

Calthorpe, Peter. *The Regional City: New Urbanism and the End of Sprawl*. Washington, D.C.: Island Press, 2001.

Corbin Sies, M. "North American Suburbs, 1880–1950." *Journal of Urban History* 27, no. 3 (2001): 313–46.

Duany, A., E. Plater-Zyberk, and J. Speck. *Suburban Nation: The Rise of Sprawl and Decline of the American Dream*. New York: North Point Press, 2001.

Fishman, R. *Bourgeois Utopias: The Rise and Fall of Suburbia*. New York: Basic Books, 1987.

Gainsborough, Juliet F. *Fenced Off: The Suburbanization of American Politics*. Washington, D.C.: Georgetown Univ. Press, 2001.

Garreau, Joel. *Edge Cities: Life on the New Frontier*. New York: Doubleday, 1991.

Garvin, A. *The American City: What Works, What Doesn't*. New York: McGraw-Hill Professional, 2002.

Gillham, O. *The Limitless City: A Primer on the Urban Sprawl Debate*. Washington, D.C.: Island Press, 2001.

Katz, D. *Home Fires: An Intimate Portrait of One Middle Class Family in Postwar America*. New York: Aaron Asher Books, 1992.

Lang, R. E., and S. Talbott. *Edgeless Cities: Exploring the Elusive Metropolis*. Brookings Metro Series. Washington, D.C.: Brookings Institution Press, 2003.

Marshall, A. *How Cities Work: Suburbs, Sprawl, and the Roads Not Taken*. Austin: Univ. of Texas Press, 2001.

Scott, T. *The United States of Suburbia: How the Suburbs Took Control of America and What They Plan to Do with It*. Amherst, Mass.: Prometheus Books, 1998.

Suarez, R. *The Old Neighborhood: What We Lost in the Great Suburban Migration, 1969–1999*. New York: Free Press, 1999.

7. New Suburban Realities: "Trouble in Paradise"

Baldassare, M. *Trouble in Paradise: The Suburban Transformation of America*. New York: Columbia Univ. Press, 1986.

Berger, B. M. *Working Class Suburb: A Study of Auto Workers in Suburbia*. Berkeley and Los Angeles: Univ. of California Press, 1968.

Cervero, R. *American Suburban Centers: The Land-Use Transportation Link*. Boston: Unwin Hyman, 1989.

Dobriner, W. M. *Class in Suburbia.* Englewood Cliffs, N.J.: Prentice-Hall, 1963.

Downs, A. *New Visions for Metropolitan America.* Washington, D.C.: Brookings Institution Press, 1994.

Hudnut, W. H., III. *Halfway to Everywhere: A Portrait of America's First-Tier Suburbs.* Washington, D.C.: Urban Land Institute, 2003.

Jackson, K. T. *Crabgrass Frontier: The Suburbanization of the United States.* Oxford: Oxford Univ. Press, 1985.

Jargowsky, P. A. "Stunning Progress, Hidden Problems: The Dramatic Decline of Concentrated Poverty in the 1990s." Living Cities Census Series. Center on Urban and Metropolitan Policy. Washington, D.C.: Brookings Institution Press, 2003.

Katz, B., and R. E. Lang, eds. *Redefining Urban and Suburban America: Evidence from Census 2000.* Washington, D.C.: Brookings Institution Press, 2003.

Lucy, W. H., and D. L. Phillips. *Confronting Suburban Decline: Strategic Planning for Metropolitan Renewal.* Washington, D.C.: Island Press, 2000.

Orfield, M. *American Metropolitics: The New Suburban Reality.* Washington, D.C.: Brookings Institution Press, 2002.

Palen, J. J. *The Suburbs.* New York: McGraw-Hill, 1995.

Schwartz, B., ed. *The Changing Face of the Suburbs.* Chicago: Univ. of Chicago Press, 1976.

8. Metropolitan Fragmentation: "Obsolescent Structure of Urban Government"

Fogelson, Robert. *The Fragmented Metropolis.* 1967. Reprint. Cambridge: Harvard Univ. Press, 1993.

Gordon, D. "Capitalist Development and the History of American Cities." In *Marxism and the Metropolis,* edited by W. K. Tabb and L. Sawyers. New York: Oxford Univ. Press, 1984.

Rusk, David. *Cities Without Suburbs.* 2d ed. Washington, D.C.: Woodrow Wilson Center Press, 1995.

———. *Inside Game Outside Game.* Washington, D.C.: Brookings Institution Press, 1999.

Teaford, J. C. *City and Suburb: The Political Fragmentation of Metropolitan America, 1850–1970.* Baltimore: Johns Hopkins Univ. Press, 1979.

Weiher, G. R. *The Fractured Metropolis: Political Fragmentation and Metropolitan Segregation.* Albany: SUNY Press, 1991.

9. Urban Economies: "All That Is Solid Melts into Air"

Bluestone, B. P., and B. Harrison. *The Deindustrialization of America.* New York: Basic Books, 1982.

Cohen, Lizabeth. *A Consumers' Republic: The Politics of Mass Consumption in Postwar America*. New York: Alfred A. Knopf, 2003.

Frank, R. H. *Luxury Fever*. New York: Free Press, 2000.

Kirby, A., ed. *The Pentagon and the Cities*. Newbury Park, Calif.: Sage, 1992.

Markusen, A. R. *The Rise of the Gunbelt: The Military Remapping of Industrial America*. New York: Oxford Univ. Press, 1991.

Piven, F. F., and R. A. Cloward. *The Breaking of the American Social Compact*. New York: New Press, 1997.

Sassen, S. "Economic Restructuring and the American City." *Annual Review of Sociology* 16 (1990): 465–90.

Schor, Juliet. *The Overspent American*. New York: Basic Books, 1998.

———. *The Overworked American*. New York: Basic Books, 1991.

U.S. Department of Housing and Urban Development. *Now Is the Time: Places Left Behind in the New Economy*. Washington, D.C.: U.S. Department of Housing and Urban Development, 1999.

———. *The State of the Cities, 2000: Megaforces Shaping the Future of the Nation's Cities*. Washington, D.C.: U.S. Department of Housing and Urban Development, 2000.

10. Race and Ethnicity: "E Pluribus Unum"

Berry, K. *Geographical Identities of Ethnic America: Race, Space, and Place*. Reno: Univ. of Nevada Press, 2002.

Betancur, J. J., and D. C. Gills, eds. *The Collaborative City: Opportunities and Struggles for Blacks and Latinos in U.S. Cities*. New York: Garland Publications, 2000.

Clark, W. A. V. *Immigrants and the American Dream: Remaking the Middle Class*. New York: Guildford, 2003.

Frazier, J. W., F. M. Margai, and E. Tettey-Fio. *Race and Place: Equity Issues in Urban America*. Boulder: Westview Press, 2003.

Gooding-Williams, R., ed. *Reading Rodney King/Reading Urban Uprising*. New York: Routledge, 1994.

Hacker, A. *Two Nations*. New York: Scribner's, 1992.

Klarman, M. J. *From Jim Crow to Civil Rights: The Supreme Court and the Struggle for Racial Equality*. New York: Oxford Univ. Press, 2004.

Laguerre, M. S. *The Global Ethnopolis: Chinatown, Japantown, and Manilatown in American Society*. New York: St. Martin's Press, 2000.

Lehmann, N. *The Promised Land: The Great Black Migration and How It Changed America*. New York: Alfred A. Knopf, 1991.

Lopez-Garza, M., and D. R. Diaz, eds. *Asian and Latin Immigrants in a Restructuring Economy: The Metamorphosis of Southern California*. Stanford: Stanford Univ. Press, 2001.

Massey, D., and N. A. Denton. *American Apartheid: Segregation and the Making of the Underclass*. Cambridge: Harvard Univ. Press, 1993.

Myrdal, G. *An American Dilemma: The Negro Problem and Modern Democracy*. New York: Harper, 1944.

National Advisory Commission. *Report on Civil Disorders*. Washington, D.C.: U.S. Government Printing Office, 1968.

Rodriguez, R. *Brown: The Last Discovery of America*. New York: Viking, 2002.

Saito, L. T. *Race and Politics: Asian Americans, Latinos, and Whites in a Los Angeles Suburb*. Urbana: Univ. of Illinois Press, 1998.

Shipler, D. K. *A Country of Strangers: Blacks and Whites in America*. New York: Alfred A. Knopf, 1997.

West, C. *Race Matters*. Boston: Beacon, 1993.

Wynter, L. E. *America Skin: Pop Culture, Big Business, and the End of White America*. New York: Crown, 2002.

Zhao, J. Li. *Strangers in the City: The Atlanta Chinese, Their Communities, and Stories of Their Lives*. New York: Routledge, 2002.

11. Housing and the City: "Shaky Palaces"

Alejandrino, S. V. *Gentrification in San Francisco's Mission District*. San Francisco: Mission Economic Development Association, 2000.

Radford, G. *Modern Housing for America: Policy Struggles in the New Deal Era*. Chicago: Univ. of Chicago Press, 1996.

Smith, N. *The New Urban Frontier: Gentrification and the Revanchist City*. London: Routledge, 1996.

Yinger, J. *Closed Doors, Opportunities Lost: The Continuing Costs of Housing Discrimination*. New York: Russell Sage Foundation, 1996.

12. Politics and the City: "Informal Arrangements . . . Formal Workings"

Gottdiener, M. *The Decline of Urban Politics*. Newbury Park, Calif.: Sage, 1987.

Hunter, Floyd. *Community Power Structure*. Chapel Hill: Univ. of North Carolina Press, 1953.

Jonas, A., and D. Wilson, eds. *The Urban Growth Machine*. Albany: SUNY Press, 1999.

Judd, D. R., and P. Kantor, eds. *The Politics of Urban America*. New York: Longman, 2001.

Judd, D. R., and T. Swanstrom. *City Politics: The Political Economy of Urban America*. New York: Longman, 2005.

———. *City Politics: Private Power and Public Policy*. New York: Pearson, 2004.

Logan, John, and Harvey Molotch. *Urban Fortunes: The Political Economy of Place.* Berkeley and Los Angeles: Univ. of California Press, 1987.

Stephens, G. R., and Wikstrom, N. *Metropolitan Government.* New York: Oxford Univ. Press, 2000.

Stone, Clarence. *Regime Politics: Governing Atlanta, 1946–1988.* Lawrence: Univ. Press of Kansas, 1989.

Teaford, J. C. *Post-Suburbia: Government and Politics in the Edge Cities.* Baltimore: Johns Hopkins Univ. Press, 1997.

13. Reimagining the City: "Place Wars"

Bailey, J. T. *Marketing Cities in the 1980s and Beyond.* N.p.: American Economic Development Council, 1989.

Gold, J. R., and S. V. Ward, eds. *Place Promotion: The Use of Publicity and Marketing to Sell Cities and Regions.* Chichester, England: Wiley, 1994.

Hall, T., and P. Hubbard, eds. *The Entrepreneurial City.* Chichester, England: Wiley, 1998.

Jonas, A., and D. Wilson, eds. *The Urban Growth Machine.* Albany: SUNY Press, 1999.

14. Civic Engagement in the City: "Civic Spirit"

Bookchin, M. *The Rise of Urbanization and the Decline of Citizenship.* San Francisco: Sierra Club Books, 1987.

Kaufman, J. *For the Common Good? American Civic Life and the Golden Age of Fraternity.* Oxford: Oxford Univ. Press, 2002.

Putnam, Robert D. *Bowling Alone: The Collapse and Revival of American Community.* New York: Simon and Schuster, 2000.

Putnam, Robert D., and L. Feldstein. *Better Together: Restoring the American Community.* New York: Simon and Schuster, 2003.

Schudson, M. *The Good Citizen: A History of American Civic Life.* Cambridge: Harvard Univ. Press, 1999.

Skopcol, T. *Diminished Democracy: From Membership to Management in American Civic Life.* Norman: Univ. of Oklahoma Press, 2003.

15. Emerging Trends

Bartlett, D. L., and J. B. Steele. *America: What Went Wrong?* Kansas City, [Mo.]: Andrews and McMeel, 1992.

Bluestone, B., and M. H. Stevenson. *The Boston Renaissance: Race, Space, and Economic Change in an American City.* New York: Russell Sage Foundation, 2000.

Bobo, L. D., M. L. Oliver, J. H. Johnson Jr., and A. Valenzuela Jr., eds. *Prismatic Metropolis: Inequality in Los Angeles.* New York: Russell Sage Foundation, 2000.

Brooks, David. *BOBOS in Paradise: The New Upper Class and How They Got There.* New York: Simon and Schuster, 2000.

Florida, Richard. *The Rise of the Creative Class.* New York: Basic Books, 2002.

Goldsmith, W. W., and E. J. Blakely. *Separate Societies: Poverty, Inequality in U.S. Cities.* Philadelphia: Temple Univ. Press, 1992.

Newman, Katherine S. *Falling from Grace: The Experience of Downward Mobility in the American Middle-Class.* New York: Free Press, 1988.

Phillips, Kevin. *Boiling Point: Democrats, Republicans, and the Decline of Middle-Class Prosperity.* New York: Random House, 1993.

———. *The Politics of Rich and Poor.* New York: Basic Books, 1990.

Remmick, D., ed. *The New Gilded Age.* New York: Random House, 2000.

Sjoquist, D. L., ed. *The Atlanta Paradox.* New York: Russell Sage Foundation, 2000.

Taylor, P. J. *World City Network.* London: Routledge, 2004.

Warren, E., and A. W. Tyagi. *The Two Income Trap: Why Middle-Class Mothers and Fathers Are Going Broke.* New York: Basic Books, 2003.

Works Cited

Bailey, J. T. *Marketing Cities in the 1980s and Beyond.* American Economic Development Council, 1989.

Baldassare, M. *Trouble in Paradise: The Suburban Transformation of America.* New York: Columbia Univ. Press, 1986.

Bauer, Catherine. "The Dreary Deadlock of Public Housing." *Architectural Forum* May (1957): 140–42, 219–21.

———. "House and Cities." In *Art in America in Modern Times,* edited by Holger Cahill and Alfred Barr Jr. New York: Reynal and Hitchcock, 1934.

Beatley, Timothy, and Kristy Manning. *The Ecology of Place.* Washington, D.C.: Island Press, 1997.

Beauregard, Robert A. *Voices of Decline: The Postwar Fate of U.S. Cities.* 2d ed. Malden, Mass.: Blackwell, 2003.

Berger, B. M. *Working Class Suburb: A Study of Auto Workers in Suburbia;* Berkeley and Los Angeles: Univ. of California Press, 1968.

Berman, Marshall. *All That Is Solid Melts into Air: The Experience of Modernity.* New York: Simon and Schuster, 1982.

Bernstein, Aarin. "Is America Becoming More of a Class Society?" *Business Week,* Feb. 25, 1996, 86–91.

Berube, Alan, and Thacher Tiffany. *The Shape of the Curve: Household Income Distributions in US Cities, 1979–1999.* Washington, D.C.: Brookings Institution Press, 2004.

Brooks, David. *BOBOS in Paradise: The New Upper Class and How They Got There.* New York: Simon and Schuster, 2000.

Calthorpe, Peter. *The Next American Metropolis: Ecology, Community, and the American Dream.* New York: Princeton Architectural Press, 1993.

Camarota, S. A. *Economy Slowed but Immigration Didn't*. Washington, D.C.: Center for Immigration Studies, 2004.

Caro, Robert A. *The Power Broker: Robert Moses and the Fall of New York*. New York: Vintage Books, 1975.

Cohen, Lizabeth. *A Consumers' Republic: The Politics of Mass Consumption in Postwar America*. New York: Alfred A. Knopf, 2003.

Crenson, M. *The Unpolitics of Air Pollution*. Baltimore: Johns Hopkins Univ. Press, 1971.

Dahl, Robert. *Who Governs? Democracy and Power in an American City*. New Haven: Yale Univ. Press, 1961.

Deparle, Jason. *American Dream*. New York: Viking, 2004.

Dobriner, W. M. *Class in Suburbia*. Englewood Cliffs, N.J.: Prentice-Hall, 1963.

Edel, Matthew, Elliott D. Scalar, and Daniel Luria. *Shaky Palaces: Homeownership and Social Mobility in Boston's Suburbanization*. New York: Columbia Univ. Press, 1984.

Ehrenreich, Barbara. *Nickel and Dimed: Or (Not) Getting by in America*. New York: Metropolitan, 2001.

Fasenfest, David, Jason Booza, and Kurt Metzger. *Living Together: A New Look at Racial and Ethnic Integration in Metropolitan Neighborhoods, 1990–2000*. Washington, D.C.: Brookings Institution Press, 2004.

Fisher, Philip. *Still the New World: American Literature in a Culture of Creative Destruction*. Cambridge: Harvard Univ. Press, 1999.

Florida, Richard. *The Rise of the Creative Class*. New York: Basic Books, 2002.

Fogelson, Robert M. *Downtown: Its Rise and Fall*. New Haven: Yale Univ. Press, 2001.

———. *The Fragmented Metropolis*. 1967. Reprint. Cambridge: Harvard Univ. Press, 1993.

Ford, Larry R. "Lynch Revisited: New Urbanism and Theories of Good City Form." *Cities* 16 (1999): 257–77.

Frank, R. H. *Luxury Fever*. New York: Free Press, 2000.

Frantz, Douglas, and Catherine Collins. *Celebration USA*. New York: Henry Holt, 1999.

Frey, W. H. "Melting Pot Suburbs: A Study of Suburban Diversity." In *Redefining Urban and Suburban America: Evidence from Census 2000*, edited by B. Katz and R. E. Lang. Washington, D.C.: Brookings Institution Press, 2003.

———. *The New Great Migration*. Washington, D.C.: Brookings Institution Press, 2004.

Gainsborough, Juliet F. *Fenced Off: The Suburbanization of American Politics*. Washington, D.C.: Georgetown Univ. Press, 2001.

Gans, Herbert. *The Urban Villagers.* New York: Free Press, 1962.

Garreau, Joel. *Edge Cities: Life on the New Frontier.* New York: Doubleday, 1991.

Gladwell, Malcolm. "The Science of Shopping." *New Yorker,* Nov. 1996, 66–75.

Glazer, Nathan, and Daniel Patrick Moynihan. *Beyond the Melting Pot.* Cambridge: MIT Press, 1963.

Gordon, D. "Capitalist Development and the History of American Cities." In *Marxism and the Metropolis,* edited by W. K. Tabb and L. Sawyers. New York: Oxford Univ. Press, 1984.

Goss, John. "The 'Magic of the Mall': An Analysis of the Form, Function, and Meaning in the Contemporary Retail Built Environment." *Annals of Association of American Geographers* 83, no. 1 (1993): 18–47.

Gottdiener, Mark. *The Decline of Urban Politics.* Newbury Park, Calif.: Sage Publications, 1987.

Guest, A. M., and S. K. Wierzbicki. "Social Ties at the Neighborhood Level." *Urban Affairs Review* 35 (1999): 92–111.

Haider, D. "Place Wars: New Realities of the 1990s." *Economic Development Quarterly* 6 (1992): 127–34.

Harrington, Michael. *The Other America.* New York: Macmillan, 1962.

Hartman, Chester. "The Housing of Relocated Families." *Journal of the American Institute of Planners* 30 (1964): 266–86.

Hayes, E. *Power Structure and Urban Policy: Who Rules in Oakland?* New York: McGraw-Hill, 1972.

Hendrick, R. "Assessing and Measuring the Fiscal Health of Local Governments: Focus on Chicago Suburban Municipalities." *Urban Affairs Review* 40 (2004): 78–114.

Hillier, A. E. "Spatial Analysis of Historical Redlining: A Methodological Exploration." *Journal of Housing Research* 14, no. 1 (2003): 137–67.

Hoyt, Lorlane. "Business Improvement Districts: Untold Stories and Substantiated Impacts." Ph.D. diss., Univ. of Philadelphia, 2001.

Hudnut, W. H., III. *Halfway to Everywhere: A Portrait of America's First-Tier Suburbs.* Washington, D.C.: Urban Land Institute, 2003.

Hunter, Floyd. *Community Power Structure.* Chapel Hill: Univ. of North Carolina Press, 1953.

Jacobs, Jane. *The Death and Life of Great American Cities.* New York: Random House, 1961.

Joassart-Marcelli, P. M., J. A. Musso, and J. R. Wolch. "Fiscal Consequences of Concentrated Poverty in a Metropolitan Region." *Annals of Association of American Geographers* 95 (2005): 336–56.

Jonas, A., and D. Wilson, eds. *The Urban Growth Machine*. Albany: SUNY Press, 1999.

Katz, B., and R. E. Lang, eds. *Redefining Urban and Suburban America: Evidence from Census 2000*. Washington, D.C.: Brookings Institution Press, 2003.

Kozol, Jonathan. *Savage Inequalities: Children in America's Schools*. New York: Crown, 1991.

Krieger, Alex. "Whose Urbanism?" *Architecture* (Nov. 1998): 73–77.

Krumholz, Norman. "Cleveland." In *Rebuilding Urban Neighborhoods*, edited by W. Dennis Keating and Norman Krumholz. Thousand Oaks, Calif.: Sage, 1999.

Kunstler, James Howard. *The Geography of Nowhere*. New York: Touchstone, 1993.

Lipman, B. J. *Something's Gotta Give: Working Families and the Cost of Housing*. Washington, D.C.: Center for Housing Policy, 2005.

Logan, John, and Harvey Molotch. *Urban Fortunes: The Political Economy of Place*. Berkeley and Los Angeles: Univ. of California Press, 1987.

Lucy, W. H., and D. L. Phillips. *Confronting Suburban Decline: Strategic Planning for Metropolitan Renewal*. Washington, D.C.: Island Press, 2000.

Massey, D., and N. A. Denton. *American Apartheid*. Cambridge: Harvard Univ. Press, 1993.

Mitchell, Jerry. "Business Improvement Districts and the 'New' Revitalization of Downtown." *Economic Development Quarterly* 15, no. 2 (2001): 115–23.

Moe, Richard, and Carter Wilkie. *Changing Places: Rebuilding Community in the Age of Sprawl*. New York: Henry Holt, 1997.

Mohl, Raymond A. "Planned Destruction: The Interstates and Central City Housing." In *From Tenements to the Taylor Homes*, edited by J. F. Bauman, R. Biles, and K. M. Szylvian. University Park: Pennsylvania State Univ. Press, 2000.

Moynihan, Daniel Patrick. "Toward a National Urban Policy." *Public Interest* 17 (1969): 3–20.

Mumford, Lewis. *The City in History: Its Origins, Its Transformations, and Its Prospects*. New York: Harcourt Brace, 1961.

Munnell, A. H., G. M. B. Tootell, L. E. Brown, and J. McEneaney. "Mortgage Lending in Boston: Interpreting the HMDA Data." *American Economic Review* 86 (Mar. 1996): 25–53.

National Commission on Civic Renewal. *A Nation of Spectators*. College Park: Univ. of Maryland, 1998.

Neill, W. "Lipstick on the Gorilla: The Failure of Image-Led Planning in Coleman Young's Detroit." *International Journal of Urban and Regional Research* 19, no. 4 (1995): 639–53.

Newman, Katherine S. *Falling from Grace: The Experience of Downward Mobility in the American Middle-Class*. New York: Free Press, 1988.

Packard, Vance. *A Nation of Strangers*. New York: McKay, 1972.

Palen, J. J. *The Suburbs*. New York: McGraw-Hill, 1995.

Persky, J., and H. Kurban. "Do Federal Funds Better Support Cities or Suburbs?" Discussion Paper of the Brookings Institution Center on Urban and Metropolitan Policy, 2001.

Phillips, Kevin. *The Politics of Rich and Poor*. New York: Basic Books, 1990.

Piven, F. F., and R. A. Cloward. *The Breaking of the American Social Compact*. New York: New Press, 1997.

Putnam, Robert D. *Bowling Alone: The Collapse and Revival of American Community*. New York: Simon and Schuster, 2000.

Rainwater, Lee. *Behind Ghetto Walls*. Chicago: Aldine, 1970.

Ross, Andrew. *The Celebration Chronicles*. New York: Ballantine, 1999.

Rusk, David. *Cities Without Suburbs*. 2d ed. Washington, D.C.: Woodrow Wilson Center Press, 1995.

———. *Inside Game Outside Game*. Washington D.C.: Brookings Institution Press, 1999.

Sandel, M. J. *Democracy's Discontent*. Cambridge: Harvard Univ. Press, Belknap Press, 1996.

Sarzynski, L., and R. Hanson. "All Centers Are Not Equal: An Exploration of the Polycentric Metropolis." Paper presented to the Urban Affairs Association Annual Meeting, Salt Lake City, Apr. 14, 2005.

Schor, Juliet. *The Overspent American*. New York: Basic Books, 1998.

———. *The Overworked American*. New York: Basic Books, 1991.

Schudson, M. *The Good Citizen: A History of American Civic Life*. New York: Free Press, 1998.

Scott, Janny, and David Leonhardt. *Class Matters*. New York: Times Books, 2005.

Shapiro, Michel M. *The Hidden Cost of Being African American*. New York: Oxford Univ. Press, 2004.

Shipler, David. *The Working Poor: Invisible in America*. New York: Alfred A. Knopf, 2004.

Short, J. R., and Y. Kim. *Globalization and the City*. Harlow, England: Addison Wesley Longman, 1999.

———. "Urban Crises/Urban Representations: Selling the City in Difficult Times." In *The Entrepreneurial City*, edited by T. Hall and P. Hubbard. Chichester, England: Wiley, 1998.

Soja, E. *Postmetropolis*. Malden, Mass.: Blackwell, 2000.

Stegman, M., R. Quericia, and G. W. McCarthy. *Housing America's Working Families.* Washington, D.C.: Center for Housing Policy, 2000.

Stone, Clarence. *Regime Politics: Governing Atlanta, 1946–1988.* Lawrence: Univ. Press of Kansas, 1989.

Sugrue, Thomas J. *The Origins of the Urban Crisis.* Princeton: Princeton Univ. Press, 1996.

Swanstrom, T., C. Casey, R. Flack, and P. Drier. *Pulling Apart: Economic Segregation among Suburbs and Central Cities in Major Metropolitan Areas.* Washington, D.C.: Brookings Institution Press, 2004.

Tabb, William K. "Privatization and Urban Issues." *Monthly Review* 52, no. 9 (2001): 33–40.

Talen, Emily. "Sense of Community and Neighborhood Form: An Assessment of the Social Doctrine of New Urbanism." *Urban Studies* 36, no. 8 (1999): 1361–79.

Taylor, P. J. *World City Network.* London: Routledge, 2004.

Townsend, Anthony. "The Internet and the Rise of the New Network Cities, 1969–1999." *Environment and Planning B: Planning and Design* 28 (2001): 39–58.

Turner, M. A., and F. Skidmore, eds. *Mortgage Lending Discrimination: A Review of Existing Evidence.* Washington, D.C.: Urban Institute, 1999.

Veblen, Thorstein. *The Theory of the Leisure Class.* New York: Macmillan, 1899.

Venturi, Robert, D. S. Brown, and S. Izenour. *Learning from Las Vegas.* Cambridge: MIT Press, 1972.

von Hoffman, Alexander. "Why They Built Pruitt-Igoe." In *From Tenements to the Taylor Homes,* edited by J. F. Bauman, R. Biles, and K. M. Szylvian. University Park: Pennsylvania State Univ. Press, 2000.

Walton, Sam, with John Huey. *Sam Walton: Made in America.* New York: Doubleday, 1992.

Weikart, Lynne. "Follow the Money: Mayoral Choice and Expenditure Policy." *American Review of Public Administration* 35 (2003): 209–32.

Whyte, William H. *The Organization Man.* Garden City, N.Y.: Doubleday, 1956.

Wilson, William Julius. *The Truly Disadvantaged.* Chicago: Univ. of Chicago Press, 1987.

———. *When Work Disappears: The World of the New Urban Poor.* New York: Alfred A. Knopf, 1996.

Wong, K. K., and P. E. Peterson. "Urban Response to Federal Program Flexibility: Politics of Community Block Grants." *Urban Affairs Quarterly* 21, no. 3 (1986): 293–309.

Index

Italic page number denotes illustrative and tabular material.